AMERICAN THEMES

AMERICAN THEMES

BY

D. W. BROGAN

HAMISH HAMILTON
LONDON

First published 1948

PRINTED IN GREAT BRITAIN BY
MORRISON AND GIBB LTD., LONDON AND EDINBURGH

To

GEOFFREY ELEY

CONTENTS

PREFACE

AMERICAN THEMES is a selection from a great mass of periodical writing on America done by me in the past sixteen years. In choosing pieces to be reprinted I have avoided all direct political reporting and commentary. The texts have been printed as they originally appeared, although this involves the reprinting of some judgments which I now think erroneous and some pieces showing a low degree of prophetic power. Despite the obvious drawbacks to this system, it has seemed to me wiser to do this than to open to myself the dangerous temptations of hindsight. I have made, however, two or three exceptions to this rule. I have corrected a few misprints ("Miranda" for "Mirand," for example). I have, in two cases, deleted sentences, one as unintelligible, the other as unnecessarily rude. I have altered an imaginary name which some readers found, in its original form, to be indelicate, and I have put two new paragraphs into the first piece, to make the narrative intelligible. I have to thank the *Times Literary Supplement*, the *Manchester Guardian*, the *Glasgow Herald*, the *Evening Standard*, the *Spectator*, the *Fortnightly*, the *Oxford Magazine*, the *Leader*, the *New York Times*, the Baltimore *Sun*, *Harper's Magazine*, for permission to reprint contributions, and the British Broadcasting Corporation for permission to print the text of the news commentary I made on the death of President Roosevelt. All the pieces have been printed in chronological order except the last.

D. W. BROGAN

Cambridge, 5th October 1947

AMERICAN THEMES

I

THE ADAMS FAMILY

(1931)

JOHN RANDOLPH of Roanoke was proud of his birth to a degree remarkable even in a Virginian of the first families, and he was bitter in his hates. It was natural, then, that he should rank high among the numerous affronts put upon him by fate that disastrous day when his brother, in his presence, was whipped away from the carriage of Vice-President Adams, struck, as the Vice-President's great-grandson put it, by "the servant of a Yankee schoolmaster." It was an affront even greater than that put upon Proust's Saint-Simon by the coachman of Prince Murat; but Randolph might have been consoled had he realized that plebeian John Adams was the founder of a family destined to adorn the State in five generations and to win a rank in America above even the Randolphs or not below that of the Byrds.[1]

Four generations of Somersetshire emigrants had lived in obscurity in Massachusetts, rising at highest to the minor office of minister in a New Hampshire village, when some sudden variation threw up in John Adams a new species, marked by talents and idiosyncrasies that his descendants preserved. His parents destined him for the Church, and so he went to that nursery of learned clerics, Harvard College, where his lowly social status was almost compensated for by his academic achievements. He spent the usual preliminary time as a schoolmaster and made the momentous decision not to enter the Church. He turned to the law and entered

[1] *The Adams Family.* By James Truslow Adams. (Oxford: University Press. London: Milford. 18s. net.)
  Letters of Henry Adams, 1858–1891. Edited by Worthington Chauncey Ford. (Constable. 21s. net.)

history. John's talents and industry would have carried him far in any case in a revolutionary age when caste barriers were breaking down, but he had the aid of a good marriage. Abigail Smith was socially above her husband; she was a granddaughter of Colonel John Quincy, who had been Speaker and Councillor, and she was a woman of extraordinary talent, wisdom and courage, fittest of wives for one of the most difficult of husbands. His marriage in 1764 seemed to set John safe in the ways that lead to safe eminence when events broke in on his hopes and set him on the way to greatness. The Stamp Act came in 1765 and the boycott of the courts and a cessation of legal practice that produced in John Adams a fit of that thick, querulous, Adams gloom that a not too patient world has heard so much of. Despite his fears for his livelihood Adams, as was inevitable, was on the side of the "Whigs"; he had no attachment to England, his superiors in rank were, as a class, "Tories." He was young, and he was full of public spirit, and for him his country was the assailed colony of the Massachusetts Bay. The Boston Tea Party came; the tea was thrown into the harbour and the fat into the fire; the American Revolution had begun.

To the new Continental Congress went John Adams, leaving his native colony for the first time, beginning that wandering of the family that has taken its members all over the world, to see, to judge and, so often, to condemn. Presently he was back in Philadelphia at the second Congress, a body rent by dissension, for blood had been shed at Lexington before Congress opened and the party of compromise was fighting a losing battle. That party had in John Dickinson, the once famous "Pennsylvania Farmer," a noted leader whom Adams, all impatience for the inevitable breach with Britain, in speech opposed and in writing referred to opprobriously as one who had "given a silly cast to all our doings." There was no Jowettian stabbing with an icicle about John Adams or about any of his descendants; their hates and contempts were hot, and when the letter fell into British hands and was published Adams had made a powerful enemy. But Adams performed a service to the Revolutionary cause that eclipsed his rudeness to Mr. Dickinson—a service he came to repent, but which it is almost impossible to over-estimate. On his own initiative he proposed Colonel Washington, of Virginia, as commander-in-chief of the rebel army, then besieging His Majesty's troops in Boston. Adams not only gave the infant army Washington; he founded the American Navy. This service has not been forgotten; there has always been a U.S.S. John Adams in the United States Navy, and the fame of the family has thus been carried to the ends of the earth, as Henry Adams found a century later in the South Seas. It is fitting that the present head of the family should be Secretary of the Navy in the Cabinet of President Hoover.

The stars in their courses were fighting for Adams's ideas; the fiction of subjects awaiting redress while replacing royal authority, expelling royal officials and attacking royal troops could not be long maintained; the compromises of John Dickinson had to give way to the root and branch ideas of John Adams. In the actual writing of the Declaration of Independence, Adams played merely the reviser's part; and it was well, for he was a fluent but not a striking writer. That masterpiece of elegant propaganda was the work of Mr. Jefferson. The great Virginian, like Cromwell and Napoleon, was no master in debate, and so has been slighted by Parliament-ridden English historians; it was to the vigorous and pugnacious advocacy of John Adams that the task of pushing the Declaration through Congress was entrusted. These were the chief of his activities in Congress, but few among many, for he was indefatigable, chairman of twenty-five committees and serving on many others. He had even, for a time, thought of entering the Army. Wearied, by the autumn of 1777 Adams had resolved to retire from public life, when duty called him to that field which his descendants were abundantly to cultivate. Congress sent him on a mission to Europe.

Congress was already amply represented in France; the Court of the Most Christian King was besieged by a triple-headed mission—Benjamin Franklin, Arthur Lee and Silas Deane. Adams was to replace Deane. The difficult negotiation that was to lead to the French alliance and the salvation of the weakling Republic was approaching its crisis, and to that negotiation Franklin was indispensable, though Adams was loth to admit it. The private and public morals of Franklin were distasteful to him; it was not for nothing that Franklin, a Bostonian by birth, had abandoned his native city to such upright immigrants as Adams. The French, as was to be expected, did not see things through Bostonian eyes; to them the amiable weaknesses of the Sage were an added ornament to his eminence as a philosopher and statesman. Adams was forced to recognize that whatever could be done with France could be done by Franklin alone; so he, in true Adams fashion, recommended his own recall and returned to America. He was in time to take some part in framing the new Constitution of Massachusetts, but by the end of 1779 was on the high seas again, on his way to France, for he had been appointed a member of the American commission to negotiate peace. Paris was little more to his taste on his second visit. He paid not very hearty compliments to the beauty of its buildings and the excellence of its cooking and to the other adornments of life, but "I cannot help suspecting that the more elegance, the less virtue, in all times and countries." He had abundant opportunities to digest these reflections, for he had fallen foul of the French Foreign Minister, Vergennes. He had shown a praiseworthy reluctance to be a mere lackey to the Minister, and had, characteristically, gone on to advise and admonish at great length till at last he was overwhelmingly snubbed. M. de Vergennes would, he was told, in the future confine himself to dealing with the accredited representative of the United States, the supple and tactful Franklin. The blow was crushing and public; Adams was furious and especially angry at Franklin for deserving so much less well and getting on so much better. The fundamental injustice of the wicked world was beginning to appear. Adams was still too sensible to sulk, that weakness came later; and he proceeded to serve his country most effectually in Holland by getting the United States recognized by the Dutch republic, by floating a loan, and by giving his son, John Quincy, a chance of pursuing his studies at Leyden.

The time for making peace had come, so obviously that

it was apparent to George III; and Adams was able not only to play a great part, but to serve his country and to score over Franklin and Vergennes. He and Jay made what was, in effect, a separate peace with England, forcing Franklin to acquiesce and Vergennes to swallow the affront. It was a bold and highly successful manœuvre about the morality of which there is perhaps more to be said than Mr. J. T. Adams allows. The immense revolutionary gamble in which Adams had played so great a part had come off, and its success was in large part his. As a father of Independence he ranks after Washington—and Franklin.

There was abundant work still to be done, and the family reunion so long desired took place in Auteuil, not Boston. There was soon a separation, for the boy, John Quincy, was showing himself a true Adams. His father had been appointed first American Minister "to the Court of St. James's," as his countrymen always put it, and had offered the post of secretary to his son. John Quincy had already tasted the delights of great events; he spoke French, German and Dutch, he was a respectable classical scholar; but he refused to go to England, and returning to America went to school for a few months and entered Harvard, graduating at the age of twenty in the class of 1787. John Quincy was wise; it was time to be back in America. His father had little to show for his years in England. He had his famous dramatic interview with George III.; but the rebel Republic could hardly be loved and, in the collapse of the Confederation, was too feeble to be feared. Futile negotiations, gallant attempts to keep up the prestige of a dissolving Government, were hardly enough to make exile worth while. It was natural to resign, and in 1788 Adams returned to a new land. The new Constitution had been ratified and John Adams was the first Vice-President. It was an inevitable choice. Massachusetts and Virginia had been the backbone of the Revolution, and since the first place must go to General Washington, the second was due to Adams; but what was an unsullied honour to Washington was turned into something very like a rebuff to Adams. Colonel Alexander Hamilton attempted one of those tricks of political sleight of hand for which he had so much more taste than talent. To avoid any rivalry with Washington, or so he averred, Hamilton arranged with his friends that the second votes should be scattered; thus, while Washington received all the electoral votes cast, sixty-nine, Adams got only thirty-four. He was elected, but without even a clear majority of the Electoral College. The office so ambiguously attained was hardly worth having. No Vice-President since has been able to make much of his office, and Adams had nothing to do but preside over the infant Senate. While Washington, Hamilton and Jefferson were getting the new Government to work, Adams had not merely an unimportant office, but one that was for him dangerous. He had a philosophy of government that was republican but not democratic. Like many Americans, especially those who have been at the Court of St. James's, he had a high opinion of the place of titles and ceremonies in the government of the mob, and spent much time and temper in discussing questions of precedence and title—all in vain, for even the President of the United States has been that and nothing else since 1789.

Four years spent listening to the Senate not unnaturally tired Adams, but he was again a candidate in 1792 and was re-elected; this time he had formal opposition, but Clinton was beaten. For Adams the great personal question was the succession to Washington. Parties were already forming. Jefferson was obviously the candidate of the Left; on whom would the Federalists, the party of "the wise, the good and the rich," rely? Adams was the obvious answer, and, reluctantly, the Federalists nominated a joint ticket, Adams and Pinckney—while Hamilton's fine West Indian hand was at work attempting to manœuvre the election to Pinckney. Adams was elected President, but Jefferson was elected Vice-President, an ominous sign of the progress of democratic notions among the people whom the Federalists had so often saved from themselves. Party unity was the only salvation—and unity required the submission either of John Adams or of Alexander Hamilton. The outrages of the French Republic brought war near. Adams was zealous for the Navy he had founded; approved of the Alien and Sedition Acts that displayed the authoritarian zeal of the "révolutionnaires nantis";

but was sceptical of the value of the new Army—especially as the real commander of that force was to be Hamilton. Adams had taken over Washington's Cabinet and was rewarded by treachery unequalled except in his son's case. The Cabinet looked to Hamilton for orders and gave him all the information he needed. Hamilton wanted a war with France. At the head of the Army who could say what he would do? He may have hoped to emulate his *protégé* Miranda or his rival Aaron Burr, but John Adams turned at last. He defied his Cabinet and did what the circumstances and the country demanded— he reopened negotiations with France and found the First Consul easier to deal with than the corrupt Directory. It was the bold and wise and patriotic course and the act on which John Adams in his old age most prided himself; but it ruined his political career.

John Quincy Adams, as was natural with such an ancestry and early training, was profoundly interested in public affairs. He began practice as a lawyer; but though he would hardly have regarded law as harshly as did his grandson, Brooks, his heart was not in the courts. He wrote a reply to Paine's *Rights of Man* under the name of "Publicola," which was much admired by those of a conservative turn of mind and was so mature as to be attributed, in both America and Europe, to his father. With his experience and linguistic training John Quincy Adams was admirably qualified for diplomatic work; he became American Minister to Holland and had to negotiate with Lord Grenville in London. Meantime his father had become President, and both father and son showed some uneasiness at any appearance of nepotism. Washington had a high opinion of young John Quincy, who in turn, despite his father's dislike of the hero, had a high opinion of Washington. The ex-President urged the merits of the son on the father; John Quincy was appointed Minister to Portugal, then to Prussia, and in the winter of 1797 he set out with his wife for Berlin. He had just married Louisa Johnson, of London and Maryland. "She was charming, like a Romney portrait, but among her many charms that of being a New England woman was not one." So wrote her grandson Henry a century later, and it is hinted by Mr. J. T. Adams that, though John

2

Quincy was a loyal and loving husband, there were some
aspects of him in which he was more Abigail's son that
Louisa's husband.

When the new American minister arrived at the gates of
Berlin, he was held up by a Prussian officer who had never
heard of the United States. It was not an auspicious beginning
and a more promising field was apparently opened by his
election to the Senate from Massachusetts. But no Adams was
a good politician in the party sense. The increasing bigotry
of the Federalist party alienated him. He refused to join in
the die-hard opposition to the Louisiana purchase and, graver
sin still, supported the policy of Jefferson and Madison in
their dealings with England. He was no blind believer in it,
but his patriotic pride was outraged by the attack of H.M.S.
Leopard on U.S.S. *Chesapeake*—and still more by the tepidity,
to put it no lower, of Federalist patriotism. The party leaders
had their way; he was denied re-election and resigned and
the Adams family had a new feud on its hands, a feud of
which the publication of the *Documents Relating to New
England Federalism* by his grandson, Henry Adams, was a
later stage.

The mission proved unimportant; better opportunities
were at hand when in 1809 he was offered and accepted the
Russian mission by President Madison. In Petersburg he
was a spectator rather than an actor. He was poor among the
rich, but was well treated by the Emperor and had the oppor-
tunity of watching the climax of the great drama. He had seen
the flames of burning Charlestown in 1775, he was now to
hear the news of Borodino and of the retreat. Meantime his
own country had been pushed into war by the West and
Alexander was anxious to make peace. The mediation came
to nothing, but at last Gothenburg was fixed on as the meeting
place of the peace delegations. Adams went as far as Stockholm
to learn that Ghent had been substituted. All the autumn of
1814 was spent in negotiation. The American delegation was
strong. There were Bayard and Russell, then the real chiefs,
Gallatin, the Swiss aristocrat who had become the Pennsylvania
demagogue, Henry Clay, who was the chief author of the
war, and Adams making peace with England as his father

had done before him. The Peace of Ghent was an odd affair. It ignored the ostensible causes of the war and the apparent superiority of British arms. The British delegates were natur- ally inferior to the American; they were merely the best that could be spared from Vienna. Brooks Adams was to compare the delegation "sent to Ghent by Mr. Madison . . . and the present American delegations at Paris (1919) and they stand in pretty much the same position in which General Washing- ton's Cabinet stood to the Cabinet of Jackson. It is a subject for meditation." Whatever may have been the strength of the delegation of 1919, the Peace of Ghent was a triumph for the chief American delegate and it was fitting that Adams should be sent as Minister to England. His legation was not very pleasant. America was no more loved, if more feared, than it had been in 1785; as Mr. J. T. Adams points out, it was always when relations were most strained that an Adams was sent to London. Again, the Minister's sons were with him, and Charles Francis Adams learned to know English nature at school at Ealing. The boys were forced to fight their corner. The burning of Washington had been the most famous British exploit on land, and when peace had been already concluded Louisiana creoles and Tennessee back- woodsmen under that frontier hero, Andrew Jackson, had mowed down Pakenham's Peninsular veterans. Young John Adams was asked if he had ever been in Washington. "No, but I have been in New Orleans." Neither he nor his brother, Charles Francis, had any premonition of the part to be played in their father's life by their hero, General Jackson.

On April 16, 1817, Mr. Adams received a letter from the new President, James Monroe, announcing his appoint- ment as Secretary of State. A famous collaboration was to begin and John Quincy was to return to America for good. President Monroe is now allowed more credit for his Message than used to be the case, but Adams was an admirable colleague and servant, whether he was dealing with the ideology of his old acquaintance, Alexander I., or the designs of George Canning. John Quincy Adams was probably the greatest Secretary of State the United States has ever had, but his secretaryship was marked by an achievement that he and his family prized more than the cession of Florida, the "Report" on weights and measures. This was the fulfilment of a duty laid on him by Congress, laid on him lightly enough, but undertaken with the utmost seriousness by Adams. He laboured with the slightest equipment of apparatus and books, through the heat of a Washington summer, to produce a history of the subject that would fill a gap. He did so, and the "Report" is not merely a masterly summary of the history of a difficult subject, but an astonishing performance for a statesman whose only academic post had been a Chair of Rhetoric at Harvard. Yet, while negotiating and researching, Adams had to think continually of his future. Since 1801 the Secretary of State had been the heir-apparent to the President. Adams was consumed with ambition and saw with growing apprehension the rise of formidable rivals—Crawford, of Georgia, Henry Clay and General Jackson. The election was indecisive; Clay was eliminated, Crawford a hopeless third and dying; the conflict was between Jackson and his former protector, Adams. The decision lay with Clay, for he could throw his supporters either to Adams or Jackson. It was natural that Clay should favour Adams; they had not been close friends and they had been rivals, but there was every reason why the civilian of experience, the sharer in Clay's nationalistic views, should be preferable to a soldier whose views, so far as they were known, were distasteful, and whose capacity for civil rule was unknown. Moreover, Clay was Jackson's rival for the control of the new frontier states. "Harry of the West" had no object in putting his opponent from a neighbouring state into the White House.

Jackson's managers had no equals in political craft and they made an asset of a liability; they spread the story of a corrupt bargain between Clay and Adams; Adams was to be President and Clay Secretary of State. What was the natural and open action of Clay and Adams was stamped with infamy as the corrupt defiance of popular choice. Adams was elected; he naturally made Clay his chief Minister and all the obloquy manufactured with such skill in the camp of Jackson was poured out on Adams. Almost the only untarnished blessing the election brought him was the pride it gave his father. At the next election, in 1828, he was cruelly disillusioned. His defeat by Jackson was bitter. So far one President alone had been refused re-election, John Adams; now came the turn of his son. Emulating his father, Adams refused to meet his successor on Inauguration Day, a childish act in which he had no imitators; Johnson met Grant and Wilson, Harding.

The succession was now taken up by Charles Francis Adams. He was, in a quieter way, as much of a "come-outer" as his father and grandfather. He left the Democrats and then the Whigs on the slavery question, and ran as the "Free Soil" candidate for Vice-President on the ticket with that old enemy of his father, Martin Van Buren. There were not many immediate prospects for a politician of this stamp, and he was given plenty of time to edit the *Works* of John Adams. But as the crisis grew more and more acute, he entered Congress for the district which his father had represented in the House of Representatives when, the "old man eloquent," putting aside the pride of an ex-President, had accepted the invitation of his Quincy neighbours to represent them in Washington.

The storm cloud of the Civil War was blowing up, as John Quincy had foreseen. When Lincoln was elected there was a possibility that Charles Francis would be in his Cabinet, representing New England, but nothing came of it; and it was with some difficulty that Seward got Lincoln to appoint Adams Minister to England. The great moment in the life of the third Adams was at hand. His departure for England was delayed for the marriage of the eldest son, John Quincy II., and when Adams presented his credentials to Lord Russell the British Government had already recognized the belligerent rights of the Confederacy. To the heated American imaginations of the time the recognition was a deliberate affront and evidence of bad faith; but to-day it is hard to contest its legitimacy or to disagree with Mr. J. T. Adams in his judgment that Adams's delay was a blessing in disguise, as it presented the American Minister with a *fait accompli* and saved him the necessity of contesting the inevitable. Yet it set the note, and for four anxious years Adams had the impression of being in the enemy's country. He was not, but his was a post of which the potentialities for good or evil were great. The main hope of the Confederacy was foreign recognition. London, indeed, between 1861 and 1863 was the real battle line. English recognition would have saved the South as French recognition had saved the United States in the revolution. Adams was in the position of Lord Stormont, and Mason, the Southern agent, as Henry Adams saw, might have been a new Franklin with society at his feet. But the roles were reversed: Mason was incompetent and Adams a diplomat of the highest class. There was, of course, a still more important difference between the Paris of 1777 and the London of 1861; Palmerston and Russell were not Vergennes. They were old men, and Russell was hardly a strong one. He had to contend with the exuberance of Gladstone and an occasional return to his early bad manner on the part of the Prime Minister. But Palmerston was no longer the man of 1830 or 1851. He could endure a snub without claiming tit-for-tat and he never took a more severe one than from Minister Adams over the Butler controversy. More formidable than the English Ministers was the folly of Seward before Lincoln tamed him and the excessive zeal of Wilkes that led to the affair of the *Trent*. The high-water mark of the Minister's diplomacy was his handling of the affair of the Confederate cruisers, culminating in the famous message to Lord Russell—"It would be superfluous in me to point out to your lordship that this is war." It matters little that Russell had already decided to hold the rams; the long duel was over and Adams had not only kept England neutral but had kept the record clean for the " Alabama " claims. It was a tremendous achievement; the filling of the Legation in London was more important than the choice of a commander for the army of the Potomac and Seward's chief claim to gratitude is that he forced Lincoln to appoint Adams.

The Minister's third son was in London with him, according to the family tradition, and it is an example of the superiority of literary fame that Henry Adams is better known on this side of the Atlantic than any other of the clan. What Henry thought of his education we all know, and the letters for which we are indebted to Mr. Ford show us a young man differing less than most young men from his later years.

Henry Adams was a good letter writer and these letters are a valuable supplement to the *Education*, but they lack the persuasive power of that work of art. His nominal profession of law had little attraction for Henry's brother, Charles Francis II., and he attacked the great problem of the railroads while Henry began a career in that other great power, the Press. The first result was the assault on what Charles Francis called the " Scarlet Woman of Wall Street," the Erie Railroad. Henry attacked with an article on the " Gold Conspiracy," and the two penniless young men thus assailed the power of Jay Gould and Jim Fisk, the power that ruled the New York Bench and Bar and stretched its tentacles into the White House. It was, with one possible exception, the most degraded age of American politics, and the spectacle of the Republican Party that had saved the nation eating it (to borrow a phrase from a disillusioned Italian patriot) had already driven the eldest son, John Quincy II., into the Democratic Party. He was immensely popular, the only member of the family to be a "good mixer," but he never held office.

As readers of the *Education* will remember, Henry found journalism no means to power; the editorship of the *North American Review* was the only office that resulted and Henry was turned by President Eliot to the field that was to be his life work. Teaching medieval history at Harvard, he was the greatest force in reforming historical training in America. His great *History of the United States* was a seminal work; it delivered American historiography from the spirit of Bancroft and on it his fame as an historian will rest. Of the writing of his books the *Letters* give many pictures, they are entertaining and instructive peeps into an historian's workshop. The two remaining brothers had very different careers. Charles Francis II., by sheer energy, broke into the railway system, and became a distinguished public servant, head of a great meat-packing company and head of the Union Pacific system till ejected by Jay Gould—who had not forgotten the " Erie War " of twenty years before. Charles Francis was the first member of the family to accumulate great wealth, but he was no mere money-grubber. He turned to history and found his service with the Fifth Massachusetts Cavalry an equivalent for the

Hampshire Grenadiers. He was a military historian of great learning and courage, competent to correct Parkman, to expose the blunders of Washington (Old John must have smiled), and to praise, with especial right, the greatness of Lee. In the youngest son, Brooks, the independence of the family was near eccentricity. Yet Brooks was the author of *The Emancipation of Massachusetts*, a work assailing the clerical interpretation of New England history, blazing a trail since followed by better equipped explorers, notably the author of the *Adams Family*. He was a quasi-Marxian and laid sacrilegious hands on that law which he, like five others of the family, had followed as a science, if not as a profession. His acute, critical and occasionally fantastic mind was taken a little too much for granted in the complacent America of to-day; but when he died in 1927 and when the old house at Quincy was at last abandoned by the family, the American world should have felt that an age in the life of the nation had at last found symbolic end.

II

THE CONDOTTIERE[1]

(1931)

IT rhymes with "throne," the American public was told over the radio recently, and thus a problem of a kind common in America was settled. No longer would the sophisticated sneer at the simple-minded who had not taken a course in key words. In America, as the election of 1928 shows, the pronunciation of "radio" can become a political issue of the first water, and the man who knows that the *h* in *hors d'œuvres* is silent, is always made sales manager over the hick from Keokuk who has not learned French in six lessons. That the pronunciation of his name should have become a national issue is only one tribute among many to the position won by the simple Italian gunman who, by ability and attention to business, has gone so far as to become what an English wit called "the nineteenth amendment." If, for technical reasons, it is necessary to amend the jest, Scarface Al is certainly the greatest of those numerous riders to the Eighteenth Amendment who have so attracted attention to the world's centre of moral legislation.

There were gangs before Prohibition, there will be gangs after them. The spirit that made Dodge City and Abilene so lively, in the great days of the "cow country," is not dead, and it is worth remembering that there are many Americans alive who have seen the national Robin Hood, Jesse James, and are proud of it. What Prohibition did was to open a market for illegal gain far surpassing the dreams of the old-timers who hardly rose above seizing a Wells-Fargo coach in Deadwood or doing a roaring business with games of chance in

---

[1] *Al Capone: The Biography of a Self-Made Man.* By Fred D. Pasley. (Faber & Faber. 7s. 6d. net.)

Poker Flat. Millions of Americans were and are willing to pay large sums for liquor, willing to connive at lawlessness, corruption and their consequences in breeding anarchical habits of mind, as a protest against the rule of the Methodist Board of Temperance, Prohibition and Public Morals—and as a means of assuaging a thirst that shows no signs of diminishing. Where Mr. Capone comes in is where any American captain of industry comes in. He is a trust-builder. The Capone beer trust is "a combination in restraint of trade" like the Standard Oil Company and, like that famous corporation, is not so unpopular with its customers as with its rivals.

If Mr. Capone had held his hand, someone would have tried to corner the Chicago liquor market instead, just as if Bonaparte had not made the 18th Brumaire, Augereau or Moreau would have. Mr. Capone had to control the supply, the distribution, the organization of the sales force of liquor in Chicago, and he was forced to war on his rivals to keep his system going, just as the exigencies of the Continental system forced the Spanish and Russian wars on Napoleon. Mr. Capone had hitherto shown more moderation than his distinguished fellow-countryman; his attempts at truces have been incessant, less mere obvious gaps in war than were the Peace of Amiens or Tilsit, but always the ambitions of his rivals or the treachery of his allies and servants has forced war on him. A true Polonian, Mr. Capone is wary of entering on a quarrel, but, once he is in, his opponents have much reason (and little time) to beware of him.

He has, of course, great advantages. A minor Alcibiades suggested the occupation and political control of the town of Cicero, from which the gang raids Chicago as Brasidas did Attica—though with more support or tolerance from the authorities of Cook County than the Spartan got from Athens. Then his understanding of his Sicilian hoplites is of the greatest possible service. His Nordic rivals may be daring— they are (or, in most cases, were): but there is more in war than courage, as even the astonishing Pole, Hymie Weiss, discovered. Armoured cars, armour waistcoats, and constant guarding have all made the simple "bumpings off" of the early period difficult, if not impossible; hence the importance

of the "torpedo," the killer who can "jolly his victim along"
till the bump-off is due. The removal of Dion O'Banion was
a fine if simple example of torpedo work, but the *chef d'œuvre*
was the "chopping up" of the seven unresisting members of
the Moran gang on St. Valentine's day. It was a coup that
would win from a modern Machiavelli the delighted approval
that was given to the "torpedoing" of the Orsini at Sinigaglia
by that kindred spirit, Cæsar Borgia. George "Bugs" Moran,
by a lucky chance, escaped, and when he saw the job he broke
the gangster's code by murmuring, "Only the Capone gang kill
like that." It was a pardonable slip; no breach of professional
confidence was intended; it was the admiration wrung from
the reluctant lips of a competent craftsman by supreme artistry.
Mr. Moran had his own great qualities, but one is reminded
of the writing by Brahms of a few bars of the "Blue Danube"
in an album with the inscription "Not, alas, by Brahms!"

In many ways, Mr. Capone recalls that great figure of
fiction, Professor Moriarty. It will be remembered that this
master mind was in the habit of demonstrating mathematical
problems on a blackboard, miles away from the spot where
his satellites were pulling off a job. Just so, Mr. Capone is
likely to be chatting amiably to the District Attorney of
Miami at the moment when a rash pretender is running into
a machine-gun barrage in the "Loop." It is also worth noting
that the device whereby Moriarty's lieutenant, Colonel Moran,
proposed to remove Holmes, has become a classic method in
Chicago. When used by Mr. Capone it works admirably;
when pursued by his rivals, the vigil is apt to be interrupted
by the arrival of the local Gregsons and Lestrades.

Much of Mr. Capone's success is undoubtedly due to the
excellence of his intelligence department and of his diplomacy.
His relations with the ruling powers of the state, country and
city seem to be satisfactory; certainly no other "hook-up" has
been so helpful to its owner. It is unnecessary to add that none
of Mr. Capone's employees have any reason to fear more than
temporary detentions by the police. One is reminded by Mr.
Pasley's account of the zeal shown by certain judges for the
gangsters' liberty of Judge Barnard, of New York, in the great
days of Jim Fisk and Jay Gould. Some of my readers will

appreciate the allusion when I suggest that Mr. Capone's legal, political and business "hook-up" might be found as far-reaching as that of the Erie Ring of 1870. Owing to the tiresome law of libel in this country I can do no more than refer readers to Mr. Pasley's veracious pages.

When an important business man took Mr. Capone into partnership as the only effective insurance against "Racketeering," there was an outcry, but in fact nothing could be more natural. It is not much more helpful to appeal to the public authorities in Chicago than it was to appeal to the Carolingian kings in the tenth century. Such a "Commendation" as we have described was an incident of the new feudalism. It remains to be seen who will be the Hugh Capet of Chicago.

Mr. Pasley has much knowledge but little power of planning, so that his book is fascinating but at the same time irritating reading. The map that serves as an end paper is a confusing but helpful afterthought. Those who know Chicago will be able to place the Lake and the other main topographical marks, but a stranger will be puzzled. Lastly, Mr. Pasley keeps closely to his theme; though candidly mentioning some of the most sacred names of Big Business, he draws no conclusions as to the causes of the anarchy that Mr. Capone is slowly mastering. For light on that interesting question resort may be had to Mr. Dreiser's *Titan*. Frank Cowperwood explains much of Al Capone, as is natural in men having such friends and tools in common as Bath-house John and Hinky Dink.

There are, of course, other sides to Mr. Capone than business. He is a lavish gambler and generous to all good causes. A family man, he finds the restraints imposed on him by the risks of his business an impediment to that domestic life, which like so many Latins, he prizes as one of earth's greatest goods. According to Mr. Pasley he is (unlike Tony Perelli) loyal to his assistants, never "putting them on the spot," though quick to repress any indiscipline. He is lavish in his floral tributes to dead competitors as well as dead allies, and his annual flower bill is immense. It is no wonder that Angelo, in Mr. Edgar Wallace's masterpiece, thinks "it would pay us to grow our own flowers." A fondness for music has not seriously impaired a native capacity for treasons, stratagems and spoils, but it is annoying to have to go to the Opera attended by eighteen guardsmen. Altogether, like many other successful men, Mr. Capone is inclined to wonder "Is it worth it?" He talks wistfully of the old days before he became Chicago's most famous citizen, when he was a simple private tough in New York, but he does not tell us where he got the scar, or rather, many refuse to believe him. Did he get it (as he asserts) in France or in the course of his profession? It is a point that could be settled, and ought to be, for the sake of American scholarship.

III

THE DILEMMA OF THE AMERICAN RICH

(1934)

IT is a hundred years since Alexis de Tocqueville came on pilgrimage to the United States to observe the workings of that political system which, for good or ill, he deemed to be the destiny of the Western world. Nearly a century later another Frenchman came on a similar errand, but this time his eyes were set on economic, not on political activities, on Detroit, not on Washington, and M. Siegfried offered the Western world the choice between Ford and Gandhi. It is only a few years since that choice was offered and, in those few years how great a change! To a foreigner who, like the writer of these notes, left the United States in the days of Calvin Coolidge (gloriously reigning) and returned to find Franklin D. Roosevelt boldly ruling, the shock can be compared to the first emergence from an air-conditioned car into a railroad station in a heat wave. This is, if not a new world, a new climate! Gone are the days when the Ford assembly-line was what the visitor really came to see. In that distant age the United States was the hope of the capitalist world. Thecrists might sneer, economists prophesy doom, moralists lament the dangers of luxury, and the natural "knocker" point out such blots on the sun of prosperity as a West Virginia coal field or a New England mill town enjoying their own private depressions; the boosters had it. If this was not the best of all possible systems, it was on the way to becoming the best—and it had no competitors in the brilliance of its achievements or of its prospects. The United States was:

> An emporium then,
> Of golden expectations and receiving
> Freights every day from a new world of hope.

The "golden expectations" were more material than those which delighted Wordsworth in the revolutionary Paris of his

hope and love. "Liberty, Equality, Fraternity" sound better
than "a car in every garage (or even than two cars in every
garage), for every family," but to a world bled almost to death
for fine phrases, there seemed something reasonable and
practicable in the promise of American life. The machine was
to deliver mankind: seeking first technical efficiency and
business success, all things would be added to the fortunate
citizens of the United States. They could buy from Europe
books and pictures, artists and musicians, scholars and
sophists. Here was the new Rome with all the plunder of the
world pouring in on it. Those days are, for the moment, gone.
It is not my intention to dwell on the inconvenient results of
the change for Europe, especially for parasitic Europe, on the
now empty fashionable restaurants and hotels where once
Americans thronged to see the élite of a decadent continent
do their stuff; on the sad fate of popular authors who have
now to rely on the cold appreciation of their countrymen,
instead of on the generosity of an American public ready to
take European geese for swans. Far more important and far
more striking is the change within America, the crisis of faith
that has come upon a nation optimistic beyond the dreams of
Candide and on a class in that nation that has not, for two
generations, had to give an account of its faith or its works to
itself or to the rest of the American people. For what it is
worth, I give my impression of this crisis of faith, of this
sudden doubt of the American business man, doubt in his
own future and in the future of the system to which he gave
such a full measure of devotion. Some American business men
are beginning to ask themselves the question, "Can the good
old days ever return; are we attributing to politics, to the
President, to inflation or fears of inflation, to labour troubles,
difficulties that are really inherent in the situation? Have we
overplayed our hand so badly that no one, not even our old
reliable partner, the Republican party, can take us out? Is it a
case of paradise lost, not merely of paradise mislaid?"

That such doubts can find lodging in the minds of men
who are still on the winning side in the economic game, men
whose financial position has suffered only to the extent that
they cannot now keep their yachts in commission or, lower

down in the social ladder, have to ask their wives to be content with a Buick instead of a second Lincoln, is ominous indeed; for ruling classes that have lost faith in themselves seldom stay ruling classes long. It is true that the loss of faith is not of the kind that weakened the dominant classes in France and Russia before the revolutions in those countries. A French *émigré* noted that Coblenz in 1793 was full of noble refugees who a few years before had quarrelled with their notaries over the insistence of the men of law on describing their employers in deeds as "high and mighty lords." All the revolutionary parties in imperial Russia had friends of great position and wealth; even the Bolsheviks had an "angel." The American business man, so far as I have been able to judge, is not having his morale weakened by any sentimental or intellectual sympathy with his enemies and critics. He is still convinced that he more than earns his keep in the economy of society, that his opinion on matters of state or of general economic policy is, if not the only, by far the most important opinion for any rational government to listen to. He believes, as firmly as did Mr. Coolidge, that the business of the United States is business, consequently that any government that goes against the mass of business opinion is sinning against the light. But he does not believe any longer, or, at least, he does not believe it with the simple animal faith of a few years back, that business leadership is sure to be on and up. That the country will be ruined if it does not follow "business" leadership is still an axiom, but he fears that leadership may be forced to change its old marching orders, to order a retreat, instead of that headlong pursuit of happiness in terms of wealth and production which has been the battle doctrine of the high command for two generations. American business men, in numbers big enough to be significant, are beginning to sell America short.

"There are ten million superfluous people in this country who will never earn their keep. The only thing to do is to put them on subsistence farms, take them out of our calculations altogether, and get the rest of the country that is really fit to keep itself in an ordinary way on its feet. Relief is a mistake, for there will never be a place for these people, working in industry. The machine has superseded them and will supersede more of them." "This city has stopped growing, it will never get any bigger, the best we can hope to do is to slow down its decay, and we can't do that if labour troubles keep on recurring. We find it hard enough to keep afloat as it is." "This land should never have been occupied, it will have to go back to prairie, the people on it will have to go back to the East or to the towns." "What's the use of talking of international trade? It's going to shrink and we won't get a share of what's left anyway." These opinions are samples of what I heard from men in many lines of business and in many parts of the country (I did not visit the Far West and the South). A Rip Van Winkle, going back to Russia or Turkey after twenty years' sleep and talking of the Tzar or the Padishah, of the Bible or the Koran, would hardly be more surprised than I was. I remembered the scorn with which my diffident suggestions that the boom might not last for ever, that the "secret of high wages" was a good deal of a secret still, that perhaps all the business in South America and China would not fall to energetic drummers from Scranton, Pa., and Dayton, Ohio, had been greeted in the past. The sceptre of Western culture had definitely passed across the Atlantic, to a civilization that realized that business was business and that was unweakened by scepticism, undrained by war, unstrained by class conflict. For the moment that faith is weakened, if not gone; that Paradise is behind, not before, and in the way of any hopeful returning exile stands the archangel with the flaming sword of the underconsumption theory and the shield of technological unemployment. Technocracy may have been slain but its ghost still walks.

The reluctant acceptance of a national necessity for cutting losses, not for a year or two, but as far ahead as man can usefully calculate, has its comic side, for it is a revenge of theory on practical men, on the men who kept "both feet on the ground," who had no use for abstruse speculations, who kept economists as Roman senators kept Greek metaphysicians, because it was the respectable thing to do. Now when theory might do something to allay private fears and support public claims, the business man is unconscious of the aid it might

3

give him and keeps together in his mind two incompatible beliefs: that American industry has passed its peak, and that in the struggle for the lessened assets of the national estate the American people can be induced to let the business man, his lawyers, his managers, his bankers, his brokers have not merely as big a share relatively as they had before, but a bigger share. For if there is going to be less to divide, only by increasing his share can the business man hope to continue to live in the style to which he has been accustomed—and to which he still feels himself morally entitled.

II

The question of underconsumption, of technological un-employment, of the menace of the machine cannot be dicusssed here and could not be discussed competently by me even if this were the place for it. But there are two points about it which the men of eminence who shared their doubts with me seemed to ignore. First of all, the necessary failure of modern industry to provide means whereby the consumer could buy the product of the machines is not a self-evident truth. It is doubted by many economists and by economists who approach the question from very different angles. Even very radical economists, men who harbour the most subversive views, men whose attitude to life and society almost justifies the direst fears of the Daughters of the American Revolution, are not neces-sarily believers in the existence of this dilemma. There is a theoretical case against all these fears, a case which, given the willingness of the human mind to believe in good news, would certainly convince many of the alarmed business men, if they heard of it—and *if they realized the implications of their position*. For, if the best that business, as a system of society, can offer the American people is a deliberate limitation of the powers of production, the exclusion of millions from a price economy to get production down to the assumed maximum level of consumption, the American people will not long endure business leadership. If business begins to hint that a part of the Garden of Eden will have to be railed off, that the whole complicated price structure can be kept going only by an ascetic refusal to use production to the full range of its possibilities, business has proclaimed its own abdication. For American business is not loved for itself, nor for the men who lead it; it is respected because the American people still see in it the promise of a "more abundant life," and by more abundant life they mean more of this world's goods. Any candidate or party which promises two cars in every garage and can make itself believed will win triumphantly; for I see no signs that this pessimism has gone very deep or that the resignation of business to less will have any result other than the rapid growth of a determination to try some system, *any* system, which promises advance. The alternative system may only promise paradise at the risk of falling off a precipice; but the American spirit is still youthful enough to prefer a leap in the dark to a slow and ignominious retreat down hill.

Put this way, the answer may seem easy enough; few would-be leaders of the people, politically or economically, would dare to announce openly their doubts or fears. How can they hope to conceal them, how can they hope to be obeyed blindly, since few among them can hope that they will find many followers to stand in this new Thermopylæ with their eyes open while the Leonidases of the present ruling class return to Sparta to explain away the sad necessities of economic strategy? The clue is in the words "ruling class"; a ruling class, however, great its scepticism, seldom or never carries it to the ultimate point of doubting its own place in the scheme of things. It may put away formal honours in a fit of good taste, it may develop radical views; but there is the underlying assumption that the class, or the individual, will not really lose anything substantial. The young duke in Disraeli's *Lothair* was a dreadful radical. Nothing in church or state was free from his iconoclastic zeal—except dukes. "Dukes," he said, "are a necessity." American business has its full complement of dukes.

The rosy illusions which make this world tolerable deserve kindly handling, since we all live by them; but one of the commonest is so easily seen through (in the forms that it takes in our neighbour's view of life) that we can bear to look at it with a fair degree of candour. We all know the teacher, in

school or college, who makes a fool of himself by an exaggerated sympathy with the young, who seeks to conceal the fact
that he is older and wiser and more learned than his young
charges (sometimes he *is* more learned), who wants to be liked
for himself, not respected for his office. This type of pedagogue
is not more widespread than those who are his opposites in
other professions, the pretty girl who wants to be admired
"for herself," the athlete who fondly believes his popularity
will survive his legs, the class which believes that its power
and prestige will survive the function or attributes which won
the power and prestige.

The sad fate of King Louis XVI. is a case very much in
point. He was the heir of a tradition, of a function, of psycho-
logical assets, all tied up together, none of which could survive
the other. His family had been the historical vehicle of the
growth of France in external and internal unity; the Capetians
had been the more or less conscious allies of the French
bourgeoisie in the liquidation of the feudal system. As long
as they continued to fulfil that function or, at least, did not
obviously neglect or refuse to fulfil it, the unbreakable loyalty
of the French people to the House of France remained un-
broken. To separate France from the dynasty, to conceive
France as existing without the dynasty, was an effort of the
imagination beyond the vast majority of Frenchmen even after
the fall of the Bastille. It was, of course, quite beyond the
imagination of the dynasty itself. Yet the impossible was
achieved in a few years; for the King and his brothers and
their hangers-on convinced that part of the French people
which mattered that the dynasty was falling down on the job,
that the traditional function of the dynasty could no longer be
fulfilled by it—and, before that new conviction, the great
tradition of a thousand years, a tradition far more deeply
rooted, far less conscious than is any American tradition of
loyalty to "business," withered away. In four years the French
monarchy was dead and, though restored in the flesh, could
never be restored in the spirit, not by the arms of Europe or
the pen of Joseph de Maistre or of Charles Maurras. The
parallel, I hope, is not very obscure. It is dangerously easy for
the American business magnate to repose confidently on the

traditional hostility of the American people to "socialism" and "radicalism," to be sure that the United States will never follow the lead of politicians and, still less, of professors, against the will of its natural leaders, the rich. It is easy to be confident that the habit of command will tell, that the long tradition of success that inspired so many business victories both directly and under the political aspect of the system, through the Republican party, will not long be broken. The leaders of American business have, like Browning's cardinal, seen four and twenty leaders of revolt—and the "New Deal" is merely the twenty-fifth rebellion of momentarily enraged sheep. The rules of the game make victory certain—in the not very long run. The magnates may be right, but what are the rules?

The first and almost the last rule is that the rulers must deliver the goods, that they must share some of the winnings of the game with their clients, with the great mass of the American people, and that these winnings must be absolutely more than any rival system can plausibly promise. I have used the words "clients" advisedly, for the rulers of America have not the advantage of some of their European brethren, the advantage of a patina of age. After two or three generations in Europe the reverential mind of some of its peoples, of the English for instance, forgets the origin of wealth and admires it with a naïve disinterestedness for its own sake. The Russells, for instance, laid the basis of their fortunes by speculations in real estate, like the Astors; but in a time not much longer than the century that has elapsed since the founding of the Astor fortune they had merged themselves in the high and mystic fraternity of the English rich who had forgotten how they made their money—and, more wonderful still, had managed to share their amnesia with the mass of the population. The Russells had tenants, men who were grateful to be allowed to live on the Russell lands, men who rejoiced, as befitted the kindly commons, in the glories of Woburn Abbey and Bedford House.

The American rich have not been so lucky. The American does not admire wealth as *such* as does his more simple-minded English brother; the long-lived sense of grievance that the Astor money now comes from mere landowning, not from business activity, is proof enough of that. What the American admires in wealth is achievement, success in a game in which all are playing and whose rules are reasonably fair. He gets hurt if the prize is awarded to someone who has been too obviously lucky in the "seeding," who has been passed into the final round, or if the rules have been too obviously doctored from the start; but he resents the first more than the second, the easy triumphs of hereditary wealth, rather than the occasional hit below the belt of the self-made man. The admirers of the American rich have been not tenants, but clients, economic dependents who are not disposed to go farther in the way of devotion or loyalty than the economic bond suggests is advisable. It is the absence of the tenant attitude of mind that makes the country life of the American rich so empty of the solid spiritual satisfactions which their English brethren enjoy to the full. A successful English furniture dealer can buy more loyalty (with the estate) than could the whole House of Morgan, in their own country, at least.

III

It might well seem to the casual observer of the public prints that there *is* something more reverent in the attitude of the average American to the American rich than this. Advertisers certainly think so, or else why spend so much money selling their products with the aid of more or less fashionable names? Does not the presumed willingness of the public to smoke Sorghum cigarettes because Mrs. Lowell van Flagg (who drinks her rum neat and never kicks her friends) finds that they take the taste of hashish out of her mouth, show a true appreciation of aristocracy? Do not those car advertisements, apparently the achievement of an out-of-work court flatterer, testify to a deeply rooted aristocratic tradition? You know the kind of thing. The unnamed most ravishing debutante of Des Moines is advised to unbend so far as to ride in a car costing less than its weight in gold. The best rider to hounds in Hennepin County is requested to put what Shakespeare, in a slightly different context, called his "imperial seat" into something cheaper than a Rolls Royce. But even these simple appeals to snobbery have to sell the idea with an art beyond that of the simple English "By Appointment to His Majesty, the King of Barataria."

In the main, the American rich are for use, not ornament, and if the selling talk is overdone it may induce in the mob a bad attack of that dire disease, called by the famous social pathologist, Dr. Frank Sullivan, "the tripes." It may even induce it in the extreme form of "the gags" (*nausea pudica*). The public *is* interested in the marriages of the rich; they are dramatic, especially when the course of true love runs roughly, with accompanying public tantrums. It is also interested in the love life of film stars, of gangsters, and of wives (or hubands) who bump each other off, rather than offend convention by a divorce. It has not, I think, the simple reverence of the English mob which murmurs an ecstatic "coo" as the horselike daughter of a duke moves off to matrimony with an even more equine bridegroom.

Mark Twain noted the difference when he told his story of his tactless surprise at the willingness of some English friends to stand in the rain to see a minor princess whom they had seen before. Anxious to let them down easily, he made the handsome concession of saying he wouldn't stand in the rain to see General Grant, for a second time. The shocked horror with which his English friends received his comparison of General Grant with the Princess Hedwige of Hohenstiel-Schwangau, seventh cousin, thrice removed of the Good Queen, taught him a lesson. But how many Americans are not of Mark Twain's opinion? How many would dare admit to the simple superstitious snobbery of many English people? How many Americans would wait to see the King of Italy rather than Mussolini? John Jacob Astor rather than Max Baer or Albert Einstein? People have talked as if young Mr. Astor's marriage were an event in American history. It is a natural mistake, but a mistake nevertheless. A Rockefeller marriage, a Ford marriage, a Morgan marriage might well be; for the Standard Oil Company, the Ford Motor Company, and the House of Morgan have been (and still are) great forces in the advance of American life. The controllers of these fortunes are very powerful as well as very rich; great destinies are bound up with their activities. The Astor family is very rich, but it cannot make New York City grow or decline. They have not even the importance that comes to the English branch from owning *The Times* and *The Observer*.

Americans admire their rich for the energies that made them rich. They may admire them for their splendour or extravagance—and, I think, they do admire them for it more than they resent it. The poor, whatever may be the case of the middle-classes, may envy and resent riches, but they do not feel especially aggrieved that its owners have the time of their lives with it. Splendour is the only popular justification of a great fortune. But the great claim of the American rich to admiration, to trust, to obedience is their economic success in getting rich, in keeping rich, in getting richer. Their fellow-countrymen are clients, not feudal followers. The Roman dictator Sulla put horns of plenty on his coins to show he was favoured of the gods and Rome through him. The American people are like Sulla's clients and soldiers: they do not resent the good fortune of their betters as long as they share it.

This client attitude is no doubt distressful to the would-be squires, but it has been a safety-valve of the utmost importance in the last few years; for it has meant that the American people have been astonishingly tolerant of the sins of commission and of omission of their betters. They were all in the game together, and as long as the game was being played in the same spirit by all parties the disasters were suffered in common. The corresponding English (or British) classes would have been far more loyal and blindly admiring as long as the money lasted, but would have been ready to transfer their allegiance at the drop of the market. If, however, they themselves had been involved directly in the disasters that befell their betters their resentment would have been deep and long-lived. In my native city of Glasgow the older generation still refer to the "year the City Bank failed" (1878) as a grand climacteric of their lives; even people who did not lose directly are still bitter vicariously and think occasionally of the fraudulent directors doing time on the bleak breakwater of Peterhead with a satisfaction that is barely Christian. If that attitude is rare in America it is not merely because there are more recent bank failures to exhaust the store of gall that makes oppression bitter; it is because the American is singularly tolerant of losses endured in the course of *economic advance*.

When one considers the events of the last five years, and the revelations of the "goings-on" of the years before that, the lack of resentment which the visitor encounters is staggering. To contemplate in Cleveland the magnificent ruins of the Van Sweringen enterprises and to reflect on the losses that went to erect the buildings surpassing the marble and the gilded monuments of princes, and then to discover how little the collapse has affected the position of the too enterprising brothers, is to be enlightened on the American temper, a temper which the American rich seem in grave danger of misunderstanding. The Van Sweringens, no doubt, displayed an excessively broad and flexible outlook in their dealings with the Union Trust Company, but they were *builders*. Their buildings may not only be losses to themselves, but a cause of losses to others; but the buildings are there. They believed in the future of Cleveland, and for that much shall be forgiven them. A Cleveland woman who knew her own mind very decidedly, who had an acute memory of the troubles brought on her by the bank closing, of her inability to buy coal in semi-arctic weather, for instance, was still angry but her resentment was not directed against the Van Sweringens; it was directed against another Cleveland magnate who plundered the bank without any worthwhile results in the way of steel and marble, and against mortgage-holders who were still insisting on their 6 per cent. after the dollar had been devalued!

It is obvious that the point of view here displayed does not commend itself for clarity to the academic economist, but it is very widespread. In Minneapolis the Foshay tower, a fairly tall but not otherwise impressive building, still proudly bears the name of its sponsor, although he has been for some years in a federal prison. There is no widespread feeling that any grave injustice was done, but there are sober citizens who regret that the arrest was not put off until after the last corner of the building was completed! In his own slightly irregular way, Mr. Foshay was a builder; he *did* something.

IV

Now important sections of the American rich, contemplating, with what seems to me excessively great apprehension, both the New Deal and its possible consequences, are in danger of misunderstanding the temper of the average American. I do not believe that he is as yet in the least revolutionary. If he does not shrink from some of the practical aspects of "Socialism," he shrinks from the name; he still associates it with famine and the nationalization of women. Strikers may, consciously or unconsciously, follow socialist or communist leaders, but they are very far from accepting the ideas which these leaders represent. The idea of a conscious rebuilding of society on a basis of common ownership is still un-American.

The alarms of the business men seem absurd to an outside spectator who has had some slight acquaintance with a really disgruntled and sceptical proletariat. Whatever ravages communism may have made among the Irvings of New York City, it has left the Elmers of the Middle West quite untouched, as untouched as Rousseau's political doctrines left the petty bourgeois of the provincial towns and the peasants in the France of 1789. But as there was more to Rousseau than the *Social Contract*, so there is more to Bolshevism than the dreary polemics of the *New Masses* or the *Daily Worker*. The eyes of the world, once turned to the Detroit assembly-line, are now turned to Moscow or Stalingrad. There, more and more simple souls are beginning to believe, the machine gets its chance, unhampered by the financial bonds that tie it down in capitalist countries. "We have got to get away from what Veblen called the 'vendibility standard,'" said the Middle-Western engineer to me, discussing an obviously "uneconomic proposition." Veblen may be merely the Marx of the tender-minded, but such ideas are dangerous—yet they are widespread. "Of course there is plenty of work to do, but the big men in the profession are timid, they hate all new ideas," so

said the New York engineer. "The only building is government building, museums of all the styles," said the architect,
"and private building is no better—look at Harvard, look at
the banks: new ideas are barred." "You ask why big business
is so sore at the New Deal," said the advertising man. "Because
business is full of stuffed shirts at fifty thousand dollars a year
that *any* shake-up will shake out. They're hoping to keep
their jobs by sulking."

If I were a rich American, I should fear the annoyance of
the technicians more than anything else; for their consciousness of social bonds with the owning class is the most formidable obstacle both to revolution and to a socialist remaking of
society—as the Russians have discovered. Yet men who should
know better are beginning to talk and think in a way that will
put before the technicians the dilemma of loyalty to their caste
and loyalty to their craft. Let them once suspect that what
stands between them and the free and fruitful exercise of their
profession is the American business man, and the struggle may
become an earthquake. If the American business man got the
loyalty of his employees it was because they were thought to
be engaged in a common enterprise, the production of tangible
wealth. That wealth is tangible goods, obviously "useful
goods," is still the simple faith of most Americans, and the
business man, the rich business man, is not dialectician enough
to infect the public mind with Austrian subtleties about value
being a state of mind. An eminent, and far from obscurantist
corporation lawyer told me that he had been shocked to see in
a state, supposedly suffering from severe agricultural depression, so many gas stations, hot-dog stands, movie houses, all
"producing nothing." The theory of value involved struck me
as naïve, although it is shared by millions lower down the
economic ladder; but if it was once brought home to them
that they *had* to do without gas stations, they would hardly be
likely to respect the necessary existence of corporation lawyers!
For dukes, despite the simple belief of Disraeli's hero, are no
more a necessity than earls.

If I were a wealthy American (to return to this fantastic
rhetorical device), I should be shy of the "Liberty League,"
not because it attacks the President or the New Deal, not

because there is not a reaction under way, but because, as the President pointed out with his usual political acuteness, "Wall Street greeted it as an answer to prayer." It is not merely because it is a "rich man's lobby"—to quote the private remark of an eminent Republican who refused to join—but because it might be represented as the lobby of one type of rich man. The emphasis on "property" conceived of as static, as an asset to be held on to at all costs, is not an American idea. The fate of the slave-holders and the brewers suggests how lightly Americans treat vested property rights which seem out of date. Citizens of New York might remember what happened to the just and legal rights of the patroons when the people decided that quit rents were a handicap to development. The corporation lawyers in the Liberty League, no matter how honourable and how eminent, should be kept in the background. Let Al Smith denounce the Administration not as an enemy of property, but as an obstacle to more and bigger Empire State Buildings. Let Mr. Irénée du Pont forget the bondholders, even the insurance policy holders, and promise more Duco and more Chevrolets. The American people may not be angry with Mr. Mitchell, but they have not forgotten him. They have not forgotten a system which demolished property rights with a speed and efficiency beyond the dreams of Dr. Wirth. The engraver who was induced by a high-pressure salesman to exchange his Liberty Loan for National City Bank stock is very forgiving about it, but he is unlikely, I think, to lose much sleep over the dangers to savings and investment involved in the government's monetary policy. It is too late to lament this philosophical attitude, for had the American temper been less tolerant of unsuccessful experiment, some of the eminent bewailers of the approaching doom of all things would have learned that it is possible to throw more than ticker-tape out of Wall Street windows. Let them think of the bullet marks on the Place de la Concorde and reflect that if the Parisians did that for the trifling Stavisky affair, what would they have done for—but fill in any name that occurs to you!

The answer to this dilemma may be non-existent. A good Marxian must believe that capitalism in its later stages has to

strangle production and that, sooner or later, the new methods
of production will overthrow a society which tries to limit them
on behalf of an outmoded property system. If that be so, we
need not worry; history will have its way. But rich Americans
are not Marxians; they are merely complacent leaders who
believe that they can lead the people back as they have led
them forward. The American people will become ungrateful
for the blessings that have flown from the American variety
of "private enterprise" just as soon as the flow begins visibly
to diminish. The answer, if there is an answer, lies in Detroit
not in New York. Justly or unjustly, Wall Street is now
detested to a degree which is only faintly appreciated east of
the Hudson River. It is detested not merely by radicals, by
farmers, by small business men, but by big business, by its
satellite Wall Streets west of the Alleghenies. Any crusade
back to normalcy which seems to come from lower Manhattan
is doomed; any crusade that seems chiefly designed to protect
that type of property which economists call "titles to money"
is doomed.

The answer, if there is an answer, is in the Ford exhibit at
the Chicago World's Fair, in the legend running round the
walls, assuring the American people that the machine and the
abundance flowing from it are not enemies but friends. The
average American believes this anyway, but he is glad to be
told it by the only rich man whose position in the heart of the
people is unshaken. The new Ford is worth a hundred appeals
to the Constitution and the spirit of Alexander Hamilton as a
talking point for capitalism. The World's Fair has another
lesson, for in the Science Building, beside the ingenious illus-
tration of the fourth dimension, is an equally ingenious series
of refutations of perpetual-motion machines. More people look
at the latter exhibit, and not all of them, I am pretty sure, are
convinced that they can't do better! That is the American spirit
and on that the American rich should work. There is more life
in capitalism, especially in America, than most of my radical
friends believe; but it is life on condition that the job of
delivering the goods goes on and that the system does not become, or even appear to be, an obstacle to production. It will
be fatal to go on believing in an abstract American devotion

to "property rights," to "rugged individualism," and the rest. The instinct that kept the Republican party from recognizing Russia—absurd on the surface—was perhaps based on a deep instinct that evil communications might corrupt American manners, that the Bolshevik and the American had too much in common to meet without mixing. If the American rich continue to trust in a habit of command, they may forget how awkward a habit of command becomes when the rank and file have lost the habit of obeying. The American rank and file may lose that habit, and the American ruling class, confident in the fidelity of its followers, may, like an Irish landlord confident in the loyalty of his tenantry, be awakened too late. The Irish landlord was sometimes aroused from his pleasant meditations by a dose of buckshot; the American equivalent may not be dynamite, it may simply be a turn over to the machine, with probably too hasty a dismissal of the economic functions of the price system, even when worked from Wall Street. In any case, the time for decision may be quite short and the failure to decide as fatal as an error in decision. All ruling systems make one last and, seemingly, avoidable error—and then all their good intentions and great achievements go for nothing.

IV

MR. DOOLEY

(1936)

FINLEY PETER DUNNE is dead, a distinguished American journalist, closely associated with important journalistic developments in America, notably with the great firm of Colliers, but with Finley Peter Dunne has died a far more famous and important figure, "Mr. Dooley."

It is nearly forty years since the American and then the whole English-speaking world began to ask "What does Mr. Dooley say?" and in the abounding and confident days of the turn of the century the sage of the "Archey Road" was not only a source of amusement but of enlightenment for his own countrymen and for other people too.

He began, like many great men, in a modest way. F. P. Dunne, a writer on a Chicago paper, had been struck with the sagacity and wit of an obscure saloon-keeper, and with that figure as a basis built up the myth of Martin Dooley, of his patient auditor Hennessy, of the erudite Hogan, of the German rival Schwartzmeister, and the rest of the dramatis personæ.

It was the time of the Spanish-American War, the most comic military enterprise of modern times, of the great Fitzsimmons and Corbett fight, of the first real fame of Theodore Roosevelt (or Teddy Rosenfelt, as he was called in the Archey Road), and of Admiral Dewey, promoted to the rank of "Cousin George." What began as a local joke became, in a few months, a nation-wide institution, to the delight of all except the original of the hero, who was not sure that he was being laughed with and not at.

No American journalist since Artemus Ward had rivalled "Mr. Dooley," and until the rise of Will Rogers no one has rivalled him since. The comparison with Artemus Ward was often made, and it was fair enough, though "the Showman"

47

had a more elaborate background than had the saloon-keeper. But it would be easy to find in Ward dicta that (*mutatis mutandis*) might have been uttered over the bar in the Archey Road.

The comparison with Will Rogers was made even oftener, but was not nearly so appropriate. Will Rogers was a character, a humorist of a mild kind, but his importance was in his representative character; what Will Rogers said the "plain people" were thinking, and so Mr. Coolidge wanted to know what Will Rogers thought. But Mr. Dooley did not say what the plain people thought; he was a wit rather than a humorist, and he was fundamentally far more irreverent than Will Rogers.

It was the intelligentsia who laughed when Mr. Dooley said that Roosevelt's account of the Spanish War ought to have been called "Alone in Cubia," the plain people took the colonel at his own valuation. The description of pragmatism which rejoiced many philosophers, that a lie wasn't a lie if it worked, was not the view of the man in the street. Such jests were more than "wise-cracks"; they were not very obvious truths given the necessary condiment of Attic salt, even if expressed in a barbarian dialect.

"Mr. Dooley" followed the old American comic convention of bad spelling and exaggerated dialect, but at his best he owed nothing to his Irish-American jargon. The famous exposition of the basis of the power of the Supreme Court that "No matter whether the constitution follows the flag or not, the supreem coort follows th' iliction returns" is improved in force by having its jargon removed. Neither Mr. Beard nor Mr. Boudin could express the modern point of view of judicial review better than Mr. Dooley, and Mr. Justice Holmes was not a greater master of language.

Mr. Dooley was not at bottom a humorist, or rather, his real talents were not those of a humorist. Many of his essays to-day suffer by an elaborate building-up of a rather simple situation, as well as from a lavishness of local and temporal reference that makes annotation necessary.

Not every reader knows who was the great "Carter Haitch," Mayor of Chicago in the good old days. Indeed, that Chicago is remote enough. Promiscuous shooting was then the prerogative of Kentucky and the Far West, and rows in the Archey Road were not settled by sub-machine guns or by pineapples; indeed, the term as applied to fruit was little known in that street, and as applied to hand grenades not at all.

The Chicago of Dion O'Banion and Al Capone and Studs Lonergan was present in embryo, but when the monstrous growth was visible to all the world "Mr. Dooley" had little to say. During the war and again during Prohibition he wrote a little, but his hand had lost its cunning and his tongue its edge. The petty corruptions of politics that had been exposed with kindly irony (and far more profound understanding than more pompous experts could command) were both out of place in the city in which the gangs from Cicero worked their will, when the old Archey Road saloon was merely a selling agency for the "Big Shot," and where the old moral standards on all sides were shaken.

Was not the Cardinal Archbishop a German? Were not the once dominant Irish struggling desperately to hold their own in a new city full of Negroes and Italians?

And the outside world was no more attractive. It was as a satirist of war and warlike glories that Mr. Dooley had first won fame, but who could joke in face of the European butchery? It is as a monument and a study of American life, of politics and social ideas of the turn of the century, that Mr. Dooley will be preserved.

But fragments of his wisdom are already entered into proverb and some are of present utility. There are many assailants of the present President in the name of Thomas Jefferson, who would be better for pondering the rebuke to "ancestor worship" administered over thirty years ago to their predecessors. And even the soldiers he mocked have had something to learn, for, if the Spanish-American War started Mr. Dooley on his career, the Boer War spread his fame further. "On'y armies fight in th' open. Nations fights behind threes and rocks." That maxim was recently printed at the head of British operations orders; it might be pondered in Rome. Now its author, long silent, is gone to join his compeers, La

4

Rochefoucauld and Addison. The plump figure of "Mr Dooley" will no doubt occupy a lowly enough place in the heaven that shelters these greater masters, but it will be a real place from which time will not wholly eject him.

V

THE AMERICAN CONSTITUTION[1]

(1937)

IN the Library of Congress in Washington there is a shrine before which there is usually a group of Americans reverently gazing at two pieces of parchment. And the enshrining of these pieces of parchment and the reverence of the spectators are fully justified; for the United States in theory (and largely in fact) is what the draftsmen of the Declaration of Independence and, still more, the draftsmen of the Constitution have made it. The Declaration is merely the most famous and most admirably written of many declarations of rights, of some of which it is the child and of many of which it is the parent. But the Constitution of the United States is unique in the world. None of the obvious parallels, the Twelve Tables or Magna Carta, really fits; for, sacred and important as they may be, they were written in States already comparatively old, States which existed before the great codes and which would have continued to exist had they never been issued. But it is to the Constitution that the Government of the most powerful State in the world owes its birth, its powers, and its character; and it is fitting that the hundred and fiftieth anniversary of the publication of the instrument should be celebrated by the nation whose character and destiny have been so profoundly affected by those few thousand words.

"We the people of the United States, in order to form a more perfect union, establish justice, insure domestic tranquillity, provide for the common defence, promote the general welfare, and secure the blessings of liberty to ourselves and

---

[1] *Constitutional History of the United States.* By A. C. McLaughlin. Appleton-Century. 1935. 21s.

Histoire Constitutionelle de l'Union Américaine. 4 Volumes. Par Jacques Lambert. Paris: Recueil Sirey. 1934–37.

our posterity, do ordain and establish this Constitution for the United States of America." That is the preamble of the instrument: a preamble whose every phrase has engendered controversy, from the ambiguity of "We the people," which raised a question only settled by a great war, to the meaning of "the general welfare," round which, at the present moment, rages a bitter controversy. But the clue to the character of the Constitution as its makers saw it is in the phrase "in order to form a more perfect union"; for in 1787 there was in existence an American union. The revolted colonies had, in the course of the struggle with England, framed for themselves a federal Constitution, the "Articles of Confederation." In the generation that followed the Civil War it was almost treason to suggest that the old Constitution was really in many ways like the new and that, if it had ended in discredit, that was due as much to bad luck as bad draftsmanship. But to-day the death of the old Constitution and the birth of the new are a legitimate subject for historical inquiry and criticism.

The main results of that spirit of inquiry are hardly questioned now. The new Constitution drafted at Philadelphia in 1787 was not made in response to any urgent demand of the "People of the United States," even if we assume (and that would be rash) that there was any "People of the United States" in existence in that year. The new Constitution was designed to remedy certain defects in the old, defects which bore mainly and heavily on the present and future interests of a powerful and intelligent but small group. The "Articles" provided a Government which worked inefficiently because the main problems then facing the Federal Government were financial and, unable to tax directly, Congress had to demand quotas from the States which, since it had no coercive powers, took more and more the character of appeals for voluntary subscriptions. The men and interests behind the movement to alter this state of affairs were largely men to whom the United States owed money.

But not only was the Federal Government bankrupt; it was weak in organization; it could not make its own authority, or the authority of the States, respected. And it must always be remembered that the American Revolution had been a real revolution, not the polite if prolonged tea-party that one incident and the propagandist talents of Whig orators in England have made it seem. Above all, there had been great transfers of property; and the rising men of affairs to whom such transfers had been made were as anxious as their spiritual kin in sixteenth-century England or in nineteenth-century France to have an end of questioning of their right to hold what they had won. But the average American was not quite ready to consider such questions closed; and within the States, by open rebellion and by the use of the legislative sovereignty of the States, property rights were frequently assailed. The American plebeians (to use an analogy familiar to the age) were increasingly ready to secede, and it was evident that no number of mere fables would bring them back. So the gentlemen who made the Constitution forbade States to make "any thing but gold and silver coin a tender in payment of debts . . . or [a] law impairing the obligations of contracts." In their deep regard for the rights of the lenders of money, as in so many other matters, the "Founding Fathers" acted in the high Roman fashion.

That the new Constitution was designed, not by a group of selfless patriots deeply concerned with the deplorable state of the union, but by a group of men whose shrewd worldly wisdom was equal to their patriotism, is now generally admitted. And certainly the main author of the Constitution, the ingenious and learned Mr. Madison, had too clear a grasp of the economic basis of contemporary American society to be shocked by the discoveries of Mr. Beard. But it should also be remembered that because the Founding Fathers were pursuing a class and, in some cases, a private interest, it does not follow that they were not both sincerely and effectively seeking the general welfare too. The framers of the Constitution deserved well of the Republic, for they gave to a group of small and not very friendly commonwealths the means of growing into a great nation.

In the past hundred and fifty years the Constitution of the United States has changed less than any institution save the Papacy. When the first President, General Washington, took the oath of office in Wall Street, the States-General was

assembling at Versailles. There was a Holy Roman Emperor
and a Venetian Republic; the Emperor of China was just
beginning to be bothered with the absurd exigencies of the
Western barbarians, and the Shogunate seemed secure both
from the Mikado and from intrusive Christians. Since 1789
even States that have not known formal revolution have
changed profoundly. Not the whole twenty-one amendments
have changed the Constitution of the United States as the
Reform Bill, the Parliament Act and the Statute of Westminster have altered the British Constitution. Personalities
apart, President Washington could take the place of President
Roosevelt with less bewilderment than King George III. could
take the place of King George VI.

But the Constitution has not survived by remaining un-
changeable. The parchment has been a *peau de chagrin*,
expanding instead of contracting. The general lines of that
growth have, indeed, been laid down; there are limits that no
emergency can abolish. But the brevity of the Constitution (it
can be read in a few minutes), some fortunate ambiguity and
the great practical wisdom of its framers have enabled the
nation that has grown up under it to live and thrive; in a
century that has seen the ruin of so many of the great works of
time, the American Constitution has earned its place among
the venerable political relics of an age not rich in them.

Some of the ambiguities and omissions to which so much
of the success of the Constitution is due were deliberate. It
was necessary that a good deal should be done in a corner.
It was necessary, too, that the authors of the Constitution
should accept, at once, ten amendments designed to protect
the more democratic conquests of the Revolution, the "Bill of
Rights." It was necessary that the doctrine of "judicial review"
held by most of the framers, the doctrine that it was for the
Courts to decide all debatable questions of constitutionality,
should not be stated expressly. And it was not stated in its
classical form, until in 1804, in the great case of *Marbury v.
Madison*, Chief Justice Marshall, bidding defiance to the
odious theories of his detested kinsman, President Jefferson,
claimed for the Supreme Court the power of determining the
validity of Federal as well as State legislation. This weapon

was not used in the first years of the Union; the great Chief
Justice was merely adding to the weapons of his successors;
but thanks to Marshall the Supreme Court grew rapidly to a
height of importance that has little textual justification in the
Constitution. And so it has followed that what battles and
edicts and statutes are to other countries, cases are to America,
McCulloch v. Maryland, Paul v. Virginia, the *Dartmouth
College Case, Dred Scott v. Sanford, Hepburn v. Griswold,
Adkins v. The Children's Hospital,* these are names to stir to
applause or fury; and the Court, like the Constitution, has
shown its unique power of adaptation, for it soars (as it has
done this year) above the petty consistency of *stare decisis.* It
was noted as a sign of the superiority of the position of Louis
XIV. to that of Napoleon I. that the King could admit on his
death-bed that he had been grievously wrong. So it is with the
Supreme Court.

But not all developments of the Constitution were the
work of the Court. It was President Jefferson, hostile as he
was to all exaggerated claims of any Government, who bought
Louisiana from the First Consul without any constitutional
authority. And this doubling of the territory of the federation
made possible the creation of States which owed everything
to the Union. The original thirteen States and even their own
children, Kentucky, Vermont and the rest, might justifiably
regard themselves as the creators and superiors of the Union;
but how could the States formed out of what had been in less
than four years the territory of Spain and then of France and
then of the United States, be anything but children of a
political body on its way to being a nation? And it was another
radical President, Andrew Jackson, who showed to the
Supreme Court and to Congress what immense powers lay
latent in the one officer of the Union elected by the whole
people. In the first seventy years of its life the Constitution
had met most emergencies admirably, and had acquired in
the eyes of Americans that sacred character which it has never
since lost.

But there is a limit to what legal and political ingenuity
can do, and it should be remembered that one fundamental
ambiguity, the exact nature of the relationship between State

and Union, led to the greatest civil war of modern times. That war marked a failure, not only by occurring, but by the damage it did to the theory of a Government drawing its very existence and all its powers from a written instrument. Under cover of an undefined "war power" unmentioned in the text, President Lincoln took revolutionary steps, like the abolition of slavery and the suspending of the guarantees of public liberties, and, in the Gettysburg address, gave perfect literary form to a theory of the nature of the Constitution as the child of a pre-existent nation that would have startled Washington as much as Jefferson. It was made obvious after military success had been obtained, that the Civil War was no mere affirmation of the constitutional *status quo ante bellum*. The defeated South naturally, though, as M. Jacques Lambert points out, with little consistency, took this line. The one fundamental question involved, the right of secession, was settled and settled against the Southern thesis; the South accepted the verdict of arms, but otherwise the Constitution was as it had been left in 1861. But Grant and Sherman and Sheridan had done more than reverse *Dred Scott v. Sanford* and refute the doctrines of Calhoun on the battlefield. A new federal system very different from the old had been created in those four years in which the Federal Government had raised millions of men and thousands of millions of dollars and had spent hundreds of thousands of lives. The illusion of the South was not confined to the South; it was an illusion shared by President Johnson, and it can be seen perplexing that shrewd Connecticut Yankee, Gideon Welles, the Secretary of the Navy, all through the troubled years of the Johnson administration; for Welles never seems to have understood that his admirals, Farragut, Dupont, Porter, had, like the generals, made a new Constitution for America.

The new power might possibly have been wielded with moderation and with a more decent regard for form had Lincoln lived; but, with his assassination, the Executive Government passed into the honest hands of Vice-President Johnson, hands which could not hold what an accident had given, and from them it passed to Congress, to zealots and to practical politicians. The Radicals knew that the Civil War

had been a revolution and a revolution that could not, and
should not, end with a mere restoration of the old Government. So Congress governed the defeated South by the sword;
so it imposed on the conquered the three Amendments (XIII.,
XIV., XV.) that, like the War guilt clauses of the Treaty of
Versailles, forced them not merely to admit defeat but to
admit error. The Supreme Court, pushed on one side during
the war, was if not intimidated at least shackled during "Reconstruction." And to complete the breach with the old
traditions and the old limitations, the last stronghold of the
separation of powers was attacked: the President was im-
peached with a disregard for legal plausibility and decency
that had no precedent. But here the Constitution, twisted and
maimed as it was, showed that it was not without power. For
the impeachment failed; and failed because enough Senators
were found whose consciences were bound by the obvious
intent of the instrument and also by the salutary detail that to
impeach the President required a two-thirds majority, and, in
the very height of the revolutionary fever, no way could be
found round this paper barrier. The Presidency was saved
from sinking to the level of the Presidency of the French
Republic; the successors of Andrew Johnson were to be kept
far above the position of the successors of MacMahon.

But the formally registered constitutional results of the
Civil War were not confined to ratification of the victories of
Grant. For, in the fourteenth amendment, accepted if not
exclusively proposed in the presumed interests of the freedmen
and of the party which had freed them, there was inserted a
clause that was to facilitate the most remarkable transformation
of the modern Constitution. "No State shall deprive any
person of life, liberty, or property without due process of law."
"*Without due process of law*"; this most fecund of all the
ambiguous phrases of the Constitution was already imbedded
in the instrument in the fifth amendment, as a natural sequel
to the Fourth Article of the "Bill of Rights" with its inter-
diction of unreasonable searches and seizures and other
instruments of the tyranny of George III., against which Otis
had argued and under which the martyred Wilkes had suffered.

The fifth amendment thus limited the administrative

discretion of the Federal Government, and it was not until the
very eve of the Civil War that Chief Justice Taney had begun
to suggest that "due process" meant more than procedural
regularity. The fourteenth amendment extended this prohibition to the States obviously, as the context and the history of
its adoption shows, to protect the Negro. But, as some foresaw,
it could be used to defend legal "persons," the great new cor-
porations, against the States. Gone were the days when a great
conservative lawyer like Rufus Choate could talk contemptuously about the glittering generalities of the Declaration of
Independence. Such glittering generalities were an essential
part of the equipment of another great lawyer, Joseph Choate,
defending the same type of interests that had been dear to
Rufus. It took twenty years or so for the Court to accustom
itself to the role of a censor of the moral and economic merits
of State and Federal legislation, a censorship based mainly on
the new interpretation given to "due process." But by the end
of the last century both the Courts and the profession were
fully reconciled to their new role. The Supreme Court was no
longer an ordinary if very important tribunal construing a
legal text and deciding comparatively simple questions of
ultra vires.

Faced with the results of the industrialization of the United
States, the national and the state governments were, during all
the past generation, attempting to regulate the social effects of
the economic revolution. To the uncertainty and unwisdom of
these statutes the Supreme Court decided to put limits; and
those limits were necessarily determined by the philosophical
and economic doctrines to which the individual Judges
adhered. For if "due process" was a term of art, its history
in early American and in English law gave little comfort to
the new doctrines of the Court; if it was not merely a term of
art, then the Judges were exercising a function which, however
useful and however admirably fulfilled, was not merely judicial.
It was this point of view that Justice Oliver Wendell Holmes,
while still a very junior member of the Court, expressed in his
famous dissent in the case of *Lochner v. New York*. Whether
night work in bakeries should be prohibited or not was, he
believed, a question for the Legislature of New York; no

number of legal veils could conceal the fact that the majority of Judges in this case found that the statute was invalid because they did not think that was the kind of statute that a Legislature should pass. The fourteenth amendment, it was suggested by Mr. Holmes, did not enact "Mr. Herbert Spencer's *Social Statics*." But no dissent could turn the tide. In a few years' time, Mr. Brandeis appearing before the Court he was later to adorn, defended a piece of social legislation by a mass of physiological and economic evidence. He thus, on the one hand, made it easier for the Court to decide on the reasonableness of the legislation, but, on the other, as Professor Corwin has pointed out, he surrendered the position that the Court was a judge of powers, not of policy. And before the Supreme Court there came to be argued in increasing numbers cases that were more like proposals or evidence before a Royal Commission than cases argued before any English Court.

One consequence of this great change was, formally at least, deplored by the profession. Ever since Marshall's time, places on the Court had been among the most important parts of presidential patronage. The differences in constitutional interpretation were not of a kind to range all the legal science on one side, and, as a technical lawyer, there is no evidence that Spencer Roane would have been a worse Chief Justice than Marshall, had death or impeachment delivered Jefferson of that troublesome clerk. But, in the early days at least, the changing of the temper of the Court by new nominations did not always give satisfactory results. Joseph Story became from a good Jeffersonian a bigoted Marshallian. And the same result has been noted since. A French critic has suggested that, as in the case of the candidate for a bishopric in Anatole France's novel, the actual induction changes the attitude of the Judges to the nominating power, as the amethyst ring did that of the Abbé Guiterel or (in that case with some warning) that of ex-Chancellor Becket. But more potent and respectable is the influence of *esprit de corps* and of professional training. For, to apply to the Supreme Court the judgment of Robert de Jouvenel on the Chamber of Deputies, there is often more in common between two Judges, one of whom is a radical, than between two radicals, one of whom is a judge. But however that may be, no President who has reason to expect that his policy or that of his party may be subjected to judicial review of the modern political type, can be blamed if he seeks to make sure that his nominee (if otherwise by character and learning suitable to the high office) should think more or less as he does concerning the Republic. This, it is true, throws the composition of the Court into politics and makes necessarily public comments on the merits of Judges which, in England, are confined to the loyal discretion of the profession. But this cannot be helped; and, until a Justice of the Supreme Court is of no more importance than a judicial member of the House of Lords, nominees will have to run the gauntlet of inquisition.

Of the current controversies this is no place to speak; and a more fitting conclusion is an appeal for a more serious study of this great political document in the country in which the Constitution (as far as it has a European pedigree) has its ancestral home. And by a serious study is meant the kind of accurate and respectful knowledge that thousands have of the elements of the Roman and Athenian constitutions. Aristotle, one may be sure, would have found this barbarian document as interesting as the constitution of Carthage. And in its own text, so elegantly draughted, in the literature that it has inspired, in the *Federalist*, in the judgments (and dissents) of the great judges, in the constitutional writings of Calhoun or Jefferson or John Adams, there is a wealth of good writing as well as of deep wisdom. The practical importance of the subject for anyone who wishes to understand the modern world need not be emphasized. But there is another side. Is it too much to hope that the study of this great political achievement may be more widely recognized as a legitimate part of a liberal education: not, as at present is too often the case, as the sign of an eccentric taste which is, at best, harmless?

VI

INVITATION TO THE VOYAGE

(1937)

"How did you cross?" asked a colleague. "I went out by the *Queen Mary* and came back by the *Normandie*," I replied and was gratified to see what I took for awe registered. But the impression of opulence was immediately shattered when I added that I had gone third-class both ways and a change of countenance (which I surmised was admiration for such hardihood) replaced the deference due to wealth. It was not my first trip to America "third" and it will not be my last, yet the revelation that it is possible to go to America in the third-class and survive (with no visible marks of hardship) startles almost everyone I meet.

That this belief should be widespread is unfortunate, for it diminishes the number of persons of modest means who are willing to risk going to America and also of course it diminishes the potentially much larger number of Americans who think seriously of coming to England. Economically, socially and politically it is desirable that these numbers should be increased, and one way to increase them is to suggest that going third-class to or from America is not equivalent to enduring the hardships of a slave on the Middle Passage or, indeed, any serious hardships at all. It involves no more than a certain sense of proportion and a willingness to abate a little those high and worthy principles of social exclusiveness that are the backbone of English life. The bone, bent a little for less than a week, springs back into position within a few hours of landing, except in those deplorable cases where the bone is not really there at all.

The objections to going third when the alternative is not to go at all, or to cut down time in America or other expenditure that one would like to make, arise from vague memories of the old emigrant traffic, of hundreds of passengers of all nationalities being packed like herrings *en route* for Ellis Island. To-day, a bad thing for the world but a bad thing with its bright side, there is no emigrant traffic to America. From the point of view of the third-class passenger of the modern type this is an advantage in all respects but one. The old emigrants may not have been given luxuries, but they were given space and if you travel on a pre-War vessel you benefit by the abundant deck-space provided for the old masses and now available for the much smaller as well as more select body of modern third-class passengers. To one who remembers the old *Mauretania* or even the *Aquitania*, the deck-space available in third on the *Queen Mary* or the *Normandie* is meagre and it is far more meagre, in usability if not in mere space, on the British than on the French ship. The third-class deck-space on the *Queen Mary* gives the impression of being an afterthought and, for those who like sitting in deck chairs and in general leading a "healthy ship life," the *Normandie* offers better facilities. But the true third-class passenger is the one who wants to get to America or Europe as quickly and as cheaply as possible. Without taking such drastic steps to discover this truth he agrees with Mr. Astaire that "the Pacific isn't terrific and the Atlantic isn't what it's cracked up to be." If you don't think this, go and cruise in warmer waters at less expense.

On every other point the comparison is vastly in favour of the new third-class. The accommodation is at least as good as that of second twelve years ago and much better than that of tourist in its early days. There is hot and cold water in every cabin; there is good ventilation on the *Queen Mary* (and better on the *Normandie*) and there are adequate public rooms. It is, perhaps, characteristic of something or other that the chairs in the public rooms of the *Queen Mary* are much more comfortable than those of the *Normandie*, while the beds on the *Normandie* invite slumber more easily than those of the *Queen Mary*.

In feeding, the contrast is still more striking. On the *Queen Mary* one is offered, indeed pressed, to consume vast quantities of food of which the raw materials have been abundant and good. Every kind of meat is there and it is perhaps being hypercritical to complain that they all taste much alike. One has no desire to encourage foreigners in their deplorable illusions, but I have not met an American who has tried both, who has not preferred the food of the *Normandie*. There one is invited to take a *table d'hôte* meal (there are *à la carte* facilities for such as want them) but the meal, less lengthy and less elaborate than that on the British ship, is more appetizing. It is more of a composition. Then the presence of unlimited quantities of white and red wine, not very good but decidedly drinkable and *free*, no doubt gives some persons a higher opinion of French Line cooking than it may deserve. On older Cunard ships wine used to be served in jugs, but the *Queen Mary* is not so generous. This is a mistake.

Energetic persons cannot walk round the ship or swim in third, but they can play deck games to their hearts' content and the more idle have really well-chosen little libraries on both ships; they have too, the bar and the movies. In the matter of films the improvement, even over the last two years, has been startling. I have seen films at sea that may have been made on board during charades or in film studios which are to real film studios what trade-gin factories are to the distilleries of Grantown. To-day one can see the pick of current films (whatever that may be) and there was a certain amusement in seeing *Lloyds of London* on the *Normandie*, for that film ends with Trafalgar. But the French Line is very far from being chauvinist. On a very elaborate menu-card was the picture of the *Soleil Royal* which, the legend informed us, fought at La Hogue under Tourville. Will the Cunard reciprocate by giving a picture of some British ship which fought at Beachy Head under Torrington?

The real fear of many otherwise hardy souls which keeps them out of third and so out of America, is the danger of evil communications corrupting excessively good manners. There is such a danger; if your social position weighs heavily on your mind you will be more at home at home. That little group which dressed for dinner every evening on the *Queen Mary* last September, kept itself to itself so rigidly that it cannot have heard the comments it provoked by its upholding the standards of decency, but it may well have suspected a slight note of irreverence. But one passenger, at least, was completely converted on that Sunday night when (as is eminently proper) they appeared in day clothes (subfusc of course). The "Pukkas" (for so some ill-conditioned young men had christened them) had won.

On the whole, it is better not to dress for dinner or to frown too severely at the ill-conduct of one's fellow-passengers. If one is on a British ship it is in order to hint, quite soon, that one is travelling this way for all sorts of reasons except financial. On a French ship such a confession would be not merely unnecessary but scandalous. The English bar is a cheerier spot than the French bar, but there is more sociability on the *Normandie*. When the film was late, for example, the audience encouraged song and were rewarded by praise of Sorrento from a cheerful young man who was obviously ready to amuse us till the film arrived. He didn't get the chance to exhaust his repertoire as the show began just after he had promised "Sole Mio," but his exhibition of simple pleasure in his voice would have been decidedly out of place on a British ship, except of course in a bath room or on such formal occasions as those on which Mr. Peasemarsh renders the "Bandolero."

Of course, one may have passengers as neighbours who do more than drop aitches. It was not unreasonable for a friend of mine to ask for a change of cabin since his Greek neighbour went to bed in his boots. And it is usually easy, except at the busiest times of the year, to effect exchanges or to get suitable company at the little tables in the dining-room.

If you are fond of sailing as such, there is no point in going on the North Atlantic where you get, in every class, less miles of salt water for your money than on any other route. If you cannot bear the thought of being immersed even for five days in an inferior social atmosphere, don't go third. But if your motive is to see as much of America as you can in as short a time as you can, save time and money by going third if the alternative is not to go at all. As for the company, it is hard, after a day or two, to discover who is looking down on whom.

VII

TOM PAINE; CITIZEN OF THE WORLD

(1937)

It is two hundred years since Paine was born at Thetford, and the world (so far as it remembers him) deprives him of the dignity of his full name. "Tom Paine," the "filthy little atheist" of Theodore Roosevelt's characteristically vehement denunciation, was taller than Roosevelt, not filthy and not an atheist. He was a man who played a really important part in the making of the United States; who was deeply involved in the French Revolution; and who was long, for English-speaking freethinkers, a lesser Voltaire. A formal education stopped at thirteen, service on privateers, two brief marriages, ended in the first case by the speedy death and in the other by the speedy separation of the wife, two dismissals from the Excise, once for neglect of duty, once for excessive activity as a "lobbyist" for the underpaid revenue officers, the undignified trade of a stay-maker (worse than Place's leather breeches), bankruptcy and ill-paid schoolmastering, a taste for mathematics and mechanics, these were not much to give a man of nearly forty confidence in his ability to deal with life.

Yet it was such a man that came to Philadelphia in 1774. Paine had Quaker connections, but he was not a Quaker, and his introductions to the Quaker capital came from the sceptical Franklin. Fate had, in fact, projected him on to the stage where he was at last to find a part to suit him. For the American Revolution was beginning; Paine discovered or revealed his talent as a writer; and, when war came at last, it was the obscure editor of the *Pennsylvania Magazine* who furnished the most popular arguments for that independence of the mother country which the revolutionary party, in most cases

5

sincerely enough, shrank from, even when in arms against the King. In *Common Sense* the case for independence was put clearly and unsentimentally, and as soon as its author's name was known, Thomas Paine was famous.

It is one of the problems of Paine's life and temper that a man with so remarkable a talent for controversy should have written nothing (except the excisemen's petition) until he was nearly forty. No doubt there was a less obvious market for the talents of a poor and poorly educated man in England than in America; but the England of the early years of George III. was avid of controversy and Paine's talents might have made of him at least a formidable hack. But Paine lacked the necessary compliance of a hack and he had to wait for an occasion that moved him. That occasion was provided by the American Revolution, and though Paine affected to deplore that he had hardly got to America before his adopted country was swept into war and revolution, in fact, the times (to amend Paine's famous phrase) tried his soul and mind and showed that they were eminently fitted for political and social controversy.

The reader who goes to *Common Sense* or *The Crisis* to-day, knowing that, after all, the United States did proclaim and then maintain their independence, will naturally find them not dull indeed, but not very stirring, for their merits are not of the kind that endure the criticism of time very well. It is possible to read and enjoy Swift or Paul Louis Courier without caring much or anything for the fortunes of the Tory Party or for the politics of the French Restoration, but in Paine's polemical writings the argument dominates the presentation. Yet the effect of *Common Sense* in preparing the rebellious but still formally loyal colonists for the assertion of their independence was, by common testimony, immense. The effect of the first *Crisis* in restoring the morale of the army and of the civilian population during the disastrous autumn of 1776 was even greater. Paine's vanity was comic in its simplicity and magnitude, and he came easily to think that there was nothing to choose between the service rendered by the sword of General Washington and the pen of Mr. Paine. But, vanity apart, Paine's services were great, as Washington was eager to testify. His tracts were designed to bring about immediate action of a practical kind, to restore the confidence of the inhabitants of Philadelphia, to get recruits for the army, to explain away the fall of Charleston. That they cannot compare in permanent interest with the "Declaration of Independence" or the "Federalist" is not merely due to Paine's inferiority to Jefferson or Madison as a writer of State papers or as a political theorist, but to the limitations of the work Paine set himself to do.

One limitation Paine seems to have suspected little. He was too much a citizen of the world to be a mere American. No one, indeed, could emphasize more vigorously the superiority of American institutions to those of Europe. "Freedom hath been hunted round the globe," he said in *Common Sense*, and America had heard his plea to "receive the fugitive, and prepare in time an asylum for mankind." The future of America was far more important than that of England, not merely because of her "vast extension," which made it ridiculous for her "to be cast like a pearl before swine, at the feet of a European island," but because once the victory was gained it was "in our power to make a world happy—to teach mankind the art of being so." This conviction of the American mission was not confined to Paine; but the native American, even a very optimistic native American like Jefferson, thought that it was one thing to teach and another to learn, that the happiness of America was not due to mere institutions, though these were important, but to the special virtues and opportunities of the American people. To Jefferson the road to American felicity was long and arduous, not to be traversed in a generation by any European people. To Paine, the American Revolution had demonstrated in practice the curative power of a simple political panacea which, once taken even by old and long abused nations, would restore the bloom and happiness of youth. It was an illusion that was to lead Paine into strange places.

The services of the pamphleteer had been rewarded by the post of Secretary to the Foreign Affairs Committee of Congress, but Paine was not made to be a clerk, even a confidential and important clerk. As Professor Brinton suggests, Paine had the true revolutionist's nose for corruption and he involved himself in the bitter controversy over the honesty of Silas Deane, Franklin's predecessor at Paris. Whether Deane was honest or not mattered little; but by insisting that he was not, Paine involved much greater interests, for it was essential to Paine's case that the Government of Louis XVI. had aided the colonists long before it allied itself with them, an awkward truth denied with all diplomatic solemnity by the French Minister and by Congress. Paine, who had as little respect for the canons of diplomatic art as he had regard for his own interests, refused to be put off or later bought off, and he lost his job. Though he afterwards accompanied the younger Laurens on a mission to France. Paine's official career in American affairs was over. His rewards, grants from Congress and Pennsylvania and a farm from New York were less than he might have expected and less than he might have got had he not alienated powerful Virginian interests by his characteristic attack on the land claims of that State. Paine was an ardent advocate of American union, but though the selfish folly of Rhode Island and other opponents of the common good was to be deplored and attacked, Europe called to him. His return was very different from his departure; he was famous; he was, for the moment and by his standards, rich. He made the acquaintance of the great Whigs; of Loménie de Brienne; he attacked the foreign policy of Pitt and he planned and saw built his iron bridge. His technical and mathematical interests revived, and, though he found plenty to criticize in contemporary England, it was something more important than Mr. Pitt's armaments that called him back to politics.

The French Revolution appealed deeply to him as it was bound to do. The American example was now being imitated and Paine had the interest of the missionary in the success of the imitation. It was his duty to see that the French went the right way, and that meant, at any rate after the flight to Varennes, that France must become a republic. To Paine the question of the monarchy, like all other questions, was simple. Whatever was to be said for keeping an hereditary chief of the State when the revolution began, there was nothing to be said for running after the King and bringing him back to the throne he had abandoned. Paine was astonished that all did not see this truth. The immense excitement caused in Paris by the flight of the King irritated Paine. What a vicious institution monarchy must be when it put it in the power of one dull man to cause such a commotion in a great nation! Paine had not the slightest comprehension of what a great event the flight to Varennes really was, what it meant to Frenchmen that there should have come this open breach between the head of the House of France and his people. The King's attempt to escape ruined "the great work of time," but to Paine time was not important; you set up and took down Governments like so many iron bridges; some bridges and Governments were well designed, some ill. Instead of being alarmed and wounded by the King's action, Frenchmen should rejoice that the way was clear to get rid of an intellectually indefensible institution and thus save a great deal of money. No king, no civil list; that in itself was enough to justify the republic!

It is this completely unhistorical character of Paine's mind that made him so formidable an opponent of Burke. As they seldom talked about the same things, Paine was able to score off Burke or off the weakest side of Burke, his excessive reverence for the great. To-day the *Rights of Man* may seem poor enough stuff to set beside the *Reflections*. We can understand Burke's horror at Paine's assumption that France could safely be remade overnight. In his dedication to Lafayette of the second part of the *Rights of Man*, Paine does admit, indeed, that there may be a difference of opinion between men of good will upon the speed with which the reconstruction of a State can be carried out. For what Lafayette supposed "accomplishable in fourteen or fifteen years I may believe more practicable in a much shorter period. Mankind, as it appears to me, are always ripe enough to understand their true interest, provided it be presented clearly to their understanding."

There were certain self-evident political truths which it was the interest of rulers to keep from their dupes, but which, when once made evident by a competent writer or speaker, carried their own conviction and almost their own execution. To doubt this was to despise the natural dignity of man. But Burke did doubt it; such doubts were the basis of his system

and of the British Constitution—that obvious fraud on the
poor taxpayer, which excited so much foolish admiration. "I
become irritated at the attempt to govern mankind by force
and fraud, as if they were all knaves and fools, and can scarcely
avoid disgust at those who are thus imposed on." Paine was
to find that most of his countrymen were in this disgusting
class, but, for the moment in England, the great debate across
the Channel seemed to be reduced to debate between Mr.
Burke and Mr. Paine. The upper classes might agree with
King George III. on the great merits of Mr. Burke's book;
the dissidents among them might rely on the capable Scot's,
Mr. Mackintosh's, *Vindiciae Gallicae*, but the man in the
street, when he was not ready to join a Church and State mob,
was only too liable to be impressed by the clarity and simplicity
of Paine.

As has been suggested, Burke had a vulnerable side that
Paine saw and assailed. It was not only that in his lamentations
over the Queen he forgot the dying bird, but his reverence for
the revolution of 1688 led him into phrases and arguments
which gave Paine a chance to treat Burke as Locke did Filmer.
The position of an institution whose historical origin is recent
and known is made difficult when its defender uses words that
might be in place in a Japanese treatise asserting the preroga-
tives of the Mikado to be intangible because of his descent
from the Sun Goddess. One other aspect of Burke's case was
then far more vulnerable than now, for Paine was able to outbid
the quondam economical reformer by his attack on the cost of
monarchy. That type of argument was dear to Paine; he used
it to justify the American Revolution, to justify the French
Revolution, to bring about an English revolution. And it was
then an argument of some force, for not only was the cost of
the monarchy very perceptible in the small Budget of those
days, but democracy could then plausibly be represented as
being in general theory and in American practice the cheapest
of all forms of government.

For the main theme of Burke's argument, Paine had no
ear. Burke doubted all the things that Paine affirmed to be
obvious to all not bribed to be blind. Paine could only assume
that Burke was bribed, and appeal to the vast majority of the

English people who had no interest in identifying their corrupt profits with those of King George III. Paine had no doubt that, in a fair field, his writings would convert the British people to revolution as he believed *Common Sense* had converted the American people. But he was deprived of the fair field. Already such typical representatives of the old sceptical ruling class as Lord Orford in England and Mr. Gibbon at Lausanne were alarmed. Soon English peasants would be astonished by the sight of the coroneted coaches of formerly indifferent noblemen drawn up before long-neglected churches. Paine was right, as Pitt is said to have told his niece, but his propaganda (the word was then lacking) had to be stopped. Paine had plenty of courage, but by the autumn of 1792 the duty of a practising revolutionary was not to be content with deserving success; he must command it. So Paine got off to France before the warrant, to take one of the seats to which he had been elected in the Convention.

In the American Revolution Paine had been an actor; in the French he was a patient. It was inevitable that this should be so. Paine's strength was his pen, but he could not write or speak French, and France had her own supply of capable doctrinaires. Paine had failed to see that the American Revolution was peculiarly American; he failed to see that the French Revolution was peculiarly French. Sir William Howe, occupying Philadelphia, had not seriously impeded the progress of the United States to independence, but a Duke of Brunswick in Paris would be another matter. The winning party in the Convention realized this. But Paine, though he had served for a time under Washington, had nothing of the military spirit in him. With the proclamation of the Republic France had done half her task; there remained only to write a sound constitution and, if the war went on, to free Germany and the other oppressed nations to make all Europe as happy as America. These ideas were not Paine's alone, but at a moment when the fate of France was at stake even the most sympathetic foreigner was out of the main current of things. The manifestoes of Citizen Paine that were read at the tribune were listened to respectfully, but where they differed from the apparent needs of the time their author was ignored and forgiven as an impracticable Quaker. Paine's claims to be a Quaker were imperfect, but they were good enough for a country that had made Franklin one. To his religious beliefs was attributed his opposition to the King's execution, though his political argument was not at all mere sentiment. Paine was no man of blood, and, in any case, his lack of understanding of the place of the French monarchy in the minds of Frenchmen made him unable to understand the apparent necessity of a bloody breach with the past that made the execution of the King so important a gesture. Paine could see that Louis XVI. was a rather stupid man, more sinned against than sinning. What he could not see was the centuries old union of the French people and that stupid man's office. He had had no difficulty in renouncing George III., why should such a fuss be made of a man of much the same type?

It was with ironical satisfaction that the class that in England had feared Paine, that had seen him everywhere plotting (even plotting in French, an implausible story that led Addington to waste some public money), learned that he had only escaped prison in England to earn it in France. Paine's imprisonment, which he resented so much and whose continuance he attributed to his American enemies, was natural enough. The legal grounds were based on a law for confinement of aliens, and though Paine was legally either an American or French citizen (or both) he was an Englishman and a friend of the Girondins, a nuisance. His escape from death was less due to a happy accident than to the indifference of those in authority to his fate—so long as he was out of the way. But this was not how Paine saw it. The humiliation of his imprisonment had to be blamed on wicked individuals and, above all, on the American Minister, Gouverneur Morris. Paine was not the type of man that the aristocratic, not to say snobbish, Morris liked. Moreover, in the party conflict that was raging in America, Paine's *Rights of Man* had been a battle-flag. Published under the patronage of Jefferson as an antidote to Federalist heresies, it had been replied to by Federalist pens, notably by that of *Publicola*, believed then to be Vice-President John Adams, but really his son, John Quincy Adams. In

England the tract had been welcomed as a refutation of those "who, with Mr. Paine and others, think Revolutions easily effected." In America the days were past when such defenders of the rights to rule of the good, the wise and the rich as Hamilton or Dwight could talk loosely of the "rights of man." That title had become almost the exclusive property of the party whose head was Jefferson and whose most famous pen was Paine's. So it was not unnatural that Morris did not see Paine's case in Paine's own light. By becoming a member of the Convention Paine had accepted the risks of the trade, and he was lucky that they involved in his case merely not too rigorous confinement in the Luxembourg. There were some who thought that President Washington did not do all that might have been expected for his close friend Lafayette, so it was natural that the same belief should have been held by Paine and by Paine's friends in his own case. The revolution of Thermidor, though it did not lead to the immediate release of Paine, saved him from any danger of death that he may have run; and when the more sympathetic Monroe replaced Morris as American Minister, Paine was released and nursed back to health in the Legation.

Paine took his seat in the Convention again and remained a member till the life of the assembly ended. But the Convention that created the Directory was even less Paine's spiritual home than the Convention of 1793. The great days of the gospel of the rights of man and the citizen were over. Paine's anger (for he was not really disillusioned) expended itself in a violent attack on Washington. The republican hero to whom had been dedicated the first part of the *Rights of Man* was now a monster as mischievous as George III. Attacks on Washington were common enough in the bitter party conflict that then raged in America, but the attack by Paine was different from attacks by the *Aurora*; the denunciation of the father of the United States by so prominent an accoucheur was momentous. But if his attack on Washington made Paine many enemies, they were nothing as compared with those made by the book which he had written in captivity, the *Age of Reason*.

For one common reader who remembers Paine as a political pamphleteer there are ten who remember him as the

"infidel" or the "atheist," and it was not only his enemies in
the religious controversy who echoed Wilberforce's "God
defend us from such poison." Good Whigs like Erskine
denounced the book with persuasive vehemence; members of
the ruling class with very much the same opinions approved
the prosecution of the printer. There was no nostalgia for a
less critical past in Paine; he was no Renan or Arnold. The
defenders of the established order of iniquity used the established religion as a bulwark. (Paine himself had used the Bible
with its gloomy picture of Jewish monarchy as a weapon in his
political campaigns.) He had now decided that the Bible was
an imposture, like the British Constitution, and he proposed to
tell the world what he had discovered. As a Biblical critic in
the modern sense Paine was negligible. Even a rather friendly
American biographer ranks him below Bishop Colenso as an
assailant of scriptural inspiration. Leslie Stephen describes
Paine's work in his table of contents under the head "ignorance
and impudence." Much of what Paine wrote was common form
to the eighteenth-century deists who were more learned, as
well as more polite assailants of revealed religion than Paine.
But these critics had not written for or been read by the
multitude. Paine aimed at the same audience that he had aimed
at before, the intelligent Radical workman and tradesman. He
hit his mark.

Until he was replaced by the Darwinians, Paine was the
chief weapon of the Messieurs Homais of the English-
speaking world. There was much in the *Age of Reason* to offend
the pious; its manner was often flippant, and Paine, who had
no reverence himself, had, in political or religious polemic, no
tenderness for it in others. There were plenty of holes in
Paine's rather Manichean deism, but the *Age of Reason* was
admirably designed for the classes which were most wed to
Biblical literalism. In England the book had its martyrs; in
America its author was attacked by all the enemies of Jefferson
as indicative of the religious as well as political perils to be
expected from his rule. When Paine at last returned to America,
President Jefferson went out of his way to receive him at the
White House, and the conviction of the Federalist Party that
Paine and Jefferson were united in a conspiracy against religion

and laws was confirmed. Even the President's own party was not quite happy at his patronage of the infidel. The great days of American deism in high places were over; and though, as Henry Adams pointed out, it was absurd to think of the lay and clerical leaders of New England as obscurantist Calvinists, they did not want their nascent unitarianism preached in every village store by the local rebel—and that was what Paine did want.

The last years of Paine's life in America were not very happy. Though most of the stories told about him were the work of professional slanderers like Cheetham, well trained in the shady politics of New York, Paine probably drank as much as was good for him. He had always managed his own finances carelessly and he thought the Federal Government ungrateful in not easing his position. But services nearly thirty years old were as ill-remembered by a republic as by a prince. Paine's relations with his friend, Madame de Bonneville, who had followed him from Paris, were not scandalous as his religious and secular enemies asserted, but the cost of keeping her and her family told on his purse. When Paine died in 1809 he had outlived his age, and most of his fame. His notoriety was a poor substitute. Cobbett, who had violently assailed him but who owed to Paine his vision of the folly of Pitt's financial policy, made expiation (dramatic or ridiculous according to taste) by bringing Paine's bones back to England, where they were long lost and never completedly recovered.

Of Paine's positive achievements little remains but a few striking phrases—and his share in the making of the United States, which, though real, was far less important than Paine believed. *The Rights of Man* and the *Age of Reason* affected many men, chief of them perhaps was Abraham Lincoln, but they did not destroy either monarchy or belief in the inspired nature of the Bible. At no time has Paine's simple belief in the power of reason, in the simplicity of the problems of social life, in the readiness of man to follow his obvious advantage seemed more baseless than it does to-day. Yet the hope that was destroyed in the French Revolution, the hope in an easy and bloodless ending of many of the miseries of life, was a hope, foolish perhaps, but not ignoble. Burke was far more right than Paine, since most men ask more of life than the simple material and spiritual environment that satisfied Paine. That it did not satisfy others, Paine would have asserted was due to their folly, for he never suffered the last pang of the defeated revolutionary, the feeling of having been wholly self-deceived and wrong.

VIII

OUR UNCLE'S TONGUE [1]

(1937)

THERE was a day when the efforts of Mr. Mencken to assert the independent status of his mother tongue, its intrinsic value and its historical importance were taken as yet another sign of the fundamental corruption of mind of the Bad Boy of Baltimore. The embattled pedagogues, the harassed Anglomaniacs, all the forces of Ku Klux Kriticism resisted but in vain; and the sign of their defeat is a fourth edition of *The American Language* nearly twice as long as the third and more than twice as useful. We are all, necessarily if regrettably, interested in the nature of the linguistic domination of the modern world by American, so that if only in self-defence or for self-education we must be willing to sit at the feet of the master and of his disciples. And, if *The American Language* is not so directly useful to us as is Mr. Horwill's admirable *Modern American Usage*, it is quite as educational and entertaining. With both books mastered, we may begin to hope to understand the talkies, the most popular novels and the better musical comedies, the wise-cracks of Mr. William Powell, the lyrics of Mr. Cole Porter, the belles-lettres of *The New Yorker*, the historical narratives of *Time*. It is the duty, then, of a journal published in a university city to call attention to the appearance of a work combining the useful and the sweet in so appetizing a mixture. It is, however, impossible to avoid fears that even the most serious Oxford attention to the most widespread tongue in the world may be misunderstood. For Mr. Mencken, if mellowed a little by time, still

---

[1] *The American Language: An Enquiry into the Development of English in the United States.* By H. L. Mencken. Fourth Edition, corrected, enlarged, and rewritten. Pp. xl+769. (Knopf. $5.)

regards the island where the mother tongue of American is spoken with suspicion. If Oxford gave Mark Twain a degree in 1907 it was only to help along "the graceful liquidation of the Venezuelan unpleasantness of 1895." The true attitude of "Britishers" (as Mr. Mencken styles us) is still that of Dean Alford who, in 1863, accounted for the wickedness of American assaults on the tongue of Tennyson and Tupper by stressing the general wickedness of people who at the moment were engaged in "reckless and fruitless maintenance of the most cruel and unprincipled war in the history of the world." But Dean Alford who, we are told (with a rather distressing looseness of language), "brought out a monumental edition of the New Testament in Greek" was only an exaggerated specimen of a common type.

It would be idle to deny that the type is common. While Mr. Agate is in New York putting the Americans in their place, his role as dramatic critic of the (London) *Sunday Times* (June 6, 1937) is being played by Mr. Alan Dent, who shows his command of American folk-poetry by referring in a knowing way to the "popular American rhyme" which runs: "Mother, may I go to bathe?" "Yes, my darling daughter. Hang your clothes on a hickory bush, but don't go near the water." The sight of a hickory bush would be a pleasant novelty to the botanist, but more revealing is the fact that Mr. Dent doesn't think it important that his version (unlike the original) barely scans or rhymes. Substitute "limb" for "bush," and a serious improvement is attained, but why bother? So is the American tongue treated in the English press! Of course, *if* we decided to study American seriously, we could do better, but despite the protests, in prose from Mr. Mencken and in poetry from Mr. Nash, we are more likely to be capable of producing perfect versions in the ancient tongues than in the greatest of modern languages. But (I am told), although the Japanese have been writing classical Chinese verse for fifteen hundred years, no Chinese critic has ever admitted any of their versions to the canon, which shows that Japanese teaching of Chinese must be on the level of our teaching of American, not on the level of our teaching of Latin or Greek. It would be absurd to pretend that we are likely to do anything about it, so with a mild protest that, feeble as our Oxford slang may be, we no more call St. John's "Jaggers" (p. 569) than Americans talk of the "Yale Tiger," it is better to plead guilty to all Mr. Mencken's charges. American is a more living language than English and it is destined to a greater future; to doubt this is to be pedantic or chauvinist or both.

The future of American is bound up with the economic and political facts of the case. Even if we assume that all persons in Great Britain speak "English," there are three times as many people who speak American. And that is not all; the simple souls who ask in Parliament and in the press for deliverance from American speech on the screen ignore the fact that it is not only to Americans like Mr. Cain, author of *The Postman* (not the *Letter-Carrier*) *Always Rings Twice*, that Oxford English has "a mauve, Episcopalian ring" (p. 323). American speech may be unpleasant, but it is on top. Even if British movies were a lot better than they are, no mere accent would tip the balance in their favour. *Hae tibi sunt artes*, the American Dent may well sing.

The plasticity of American is, of course, a great asset. That plasticity it owes to climate, to social conditions, to educational limitations, to many forces operating little, if at all, with us. Especially is this flexibility to be seen in the verb-coining that goes on incessantly. In the last *New Yorker* to reach this neck of the woods (May 22, 1937) I find "a department store has been propositioned by a gentleman," *i.e.*, a proposal has been made to a big shop. In *Gone with the Wind* I read: "If only she had gone home at the beginning of the siege, when everyone else was refugeeing" (p. 346). The verb "to promote" may acquire the factotumious character of "get" and "fix." Thus Mr. Damon Runyon's hero tries to "promote" Miss Billy Perry. A Meriden (Conn.) silver-catalogue talks of "crafted silver ware." *Liberty* writes (September 26, 1936) of the "modest stone-and-brick house," in which the Duchess of Windsor "adolesced," and one Congressman is described in the *Congressional Directory* as having "interned"—but in a hospital, not a prison camp. Many of these verbs die; many of them deserve death; but some live; and English is full of useful importations that first saw the

light when an ingenious or harassed American took a noun
and put wheels under it.

English attention is more often directed to American
nouns, and it is against these that defenders of the faith
thunder. Thus Mr. Chesterton attacked such importations as
"boulevard" and ended with the great protest (unheard by
Mr. Gordon Selfridge):

> Ere every shop shall be a store
> And every trade a Trust. . . .

But nouns come in for a shorter or longer time because they
are useful; they do not alter the structure of the language.
Indeed, one may, at mad moments, regret that we borrow so
timidly. We don't really need "pantatorium" (where pants
[*Anglicé* trousers] are pressed) or "walkathons" (walking dance
competitions), but there are many American words that we
could use. But it is so hard to use them correctly! Even Mr.
Mencken falls more than once when it comes to giving the
English equivalent of American terms. The list of words
differing in English and American is not as exact as it should
be. The English for "bathing suit" is not "swim suit" in
speech, whatever it may be in advertiser's prose, and if that is
to be the canon I have found "swimsuit" in the *Boston Herald*
(September 16, 1936). A number of differences are differences
between English and Scotch as well as between English and
American. Others are differences arising from the fact that the
things described are not identical. It is not enough to say that
the English for "letter-box" is "pillar-box." We have both
words since we have both things, while Americans have only
one. The same criticism might be made of Mr. Mencken's
reiterated preference for "office-holder" over "public-servant"
as being "more honest, more picturesque, more thoroughly
Anglo-Saxon than public-servant" (p. 96). Begging the
question whether "public-servant" is ever used in England,
the argument falls to the ground for another reason. The term
"office-holder" is vivid and accurate because it is truly descrip-
tive. An American official may well be described as an "office-
holder" because he has had to grab the office and has to hold
it against competition. In sport we talk of "title-holder" for

this reason. American politics are a sport; English administration is not. The same title will not fit the careers of Mr.
Raymond Moley and of Sir Robert Vansittart, not because
English is inferior to American, but because the State Department is not very like the Foreign Office. There are other
translations that might be questioned, though on less fundamental grounds, "stores," "drawers," "syrup," "accumulator,"
"pool-room," "low gear," "rubberneck wagon," are all given
English translations that are less than perfect while "caroussel"
is not "runabout" (a type of motor car), but "merry-go-round,"
and as such it is rightly translated in the *Manchester Guardian's*
account of the Derby "By an American Visitor" (June 3,
1937).

One interesting theme, excellently if briefly discussed by
Mr. Mencken, is the difference in taboos between the two
countries. As he notes, American taboos are still more rigid in
journalism and (I think) in speech than are English. But it
might be noted that, in fiction at least, the reverse is now true.
Mr. Cole Porter has told us that:

> Good authors, too, who once knew better words
> Now only use four letter words,

but anything goes only in America, and I understand that the
works of Mr. James Farrell, for instance, have to be expurgated
for the English market. The taboos are not merely sexual. They
are social, parts of the general climbing process. Thus we have
"mortician" (once defined by a wit as "the man who buries a
realtor"). But romance can bring back old and once dis-
credited names and Greenwich Village recently boasted an
"Olde Pawnshoppe." I have failed, however, to find Madison
Avenue's famed "Olde Radio Shoppe." Mr. Mencken points
out that many slang terms in popular use are joys in widest
commonalty spread just because their true character is not
generally understood. This phenomenon, as Dr. Sigmund
Spaeth has pointed out in *The Facts of Life in Popular Song*,
accounts for the latitude accorded to some lyricists by public
opinion. And it is worth noting that the most famous of all
stories about the Yale Prom, has been told at an Oxford high
table without any understanding of its real point—which was

6

just as well. But the two branches of the "English-speaking race" usually have their taboos in common. If Mrs. Trollope tells us of Americans who were shocked by the very title of "The Rape of the Lock," was not Mr. Wordsworth, the poet and moralist, equally shocked by the first line of the "Grecian Urn?" And if Philadelphia toned down a patriotic film "To Hell with the Kaiser" to "To H——"; the song "Get Thee behind me Satan" in *Follow the Fleet* was sung with the last word reduced to a blurred noise in England. There was a case for omitting it, but a more English compromise was reached, probably by the same master-mind that altered the title of *Strange Interlude* to *Strange Interval*.

A rich field for social research is opened by the study of American names, personal, Christian (or "given") and place names. The last class is being studied in London at the moment and data is regularly provided by the *New Yorker*. The name composed of two others, Mexicali, Suellen (and presumably the "Zasu" of Miss Pitts) is always worth investigating. Mr. Mencken notes that few Americans survive the name Claude (the only male descendant of one of the most robust American politicians bears this name), but why should Clarence be so common? We know that Clarence Day, junior, objected to it, but many Americans seem to flourish under the burden. "Alf is also uncommon in the United States." No doubt it is, but it was not merely borne but borne proudly by an American whose name appeared several times in the American press last year, Mr. Landon, of Independence, Kansas. Why should Elmer be so prevalent in America (we have one in Oxford), and has the name "Homer" ever had the run for its money it has in the present Senate and Cabinet? There are many other themes that might be developed and the *genius loci* might lead one on to pick holes in some of the most interesting parts of this book (for example the brief and misleading account of the intellectual origins of Jeffersonian Democracy, or the still imperfect account of British university ranks and titles. And surely, "Waldo" is a name like "Calvin" or "Luther," and needs no "Waldow" to explain it?)

But to do this would be to run the risk of classing oneself with the reviewers of American books for the Literary Supplement of the (London) *Times*, a body of men for whom Mr. Mencken appears to have a strong dislike. But one would rather end on a note of interrogation, before thanking Mr. Mencken for this learned and entertaining book. Did Alfred E. Smith, LL.D., really talk of "alphabetical soup" when he was assailing the New Deal and the Brain Trusters? If he did, it is no wonder that so few went walking with him? Only the belief that he said "alphabet soup," combined with the knowledge that he is not in New York, prevents one putting in a trunk call (long distance) to the Empire State Building and, borrowing a phrase from the anguished baseball fan, pleading: "Say it ain't true, Al, say it ain't true."

IX

AMERICA'S ARISTOCRACY [1]

(1937)

O N his epoch-making visit to the United States in 1860, the future Edward VII. caused shocked consternation in Philadelphia by asking "What is a Biddle?" and the error of the Prince of Wales has had innumerable parallels in the reactions of other Europeans to the mystery of American "Society." Novelists have put rich American families into quite impossible sections of American cities, and have shown a deplorable inability to distinguish between a descendant of a Signer of the Declaration of Independence (or of an early stockholder in the New York Central) on the one hand and some upstart multi-millionaire automobile or air-conditioning magnate on the other. With a generous hospitality, exclusive European society has welcomed Americans who were not received by the best circles in New York, not to speak of those higher spheres, Boston, Philadelphia and Charleston. Across the ocean *tous les chats sont gris* or, perhaps it would be more exact to say, *toutes les chattes sont dorées*. As for the European rank and file, they know well from the movies what American aristocrats are like. If elderly, they have lots of white hair and a frozen manner; if middle-aged, they are stuffy; if they are young males, they are clubmen who marry the poor but lovely girl; if girls, they are tamed by some honest fellow-countryman, Clark Gable for preference.

Mr. Wecter has made such ignorance unnecessary and indefensible. Here we have classifications of families, of fraternities, of country clubs, all with a wealth of detail and a candour that not *Burke*, not *Debrett*, not the *Almanach de Gotha*

[1] *The Saga of American Society: A Record of Social Aspiration*, 1607–1937. By Dixon Wecter. (Scribner. 18s.)

dare equal. And both the historical and contemporary low-down on the high life of the United States is given. Such a book could be useful and yet silly; amusing and yet contempt-ible. But Mr. Wecter is too careful a scholar, has too much humour and too serious and respectable an interest in his subject, to fall into the many traps laid before the would-be historian of this long ascent of the ladder of aristocracy. He is fully aware of the devastating researches of Professor Werten-baker into the origins of the "F.F.V.'s" (the First Families of Virginia); and, though he takes a kinder view of the claims of Massachusetts families to the dignity of coat armour than does the current head of the greatest of Massachusetts dynasties, he realizes that in New England, as in Virginia, it was extremely rare for anyone of really impressive rank to settle, and still rarer for him to stay.

· But it is with the acquisition of great wealth in the nine-teenth century that there comes the real chance for the chronicler who is a serious historian and yet is not too hostile to the idea of hereditary aristocracy. Mr. Wecter takes that chance; here we have the rise of the Astors to a dominating position in New York society, a position based not merely on great wealth, but on suitable marriages to women with respectable pedigrees and vigour enough to impose their own view of their own importance on the highly self-conscious society of New York millionaires. We have the highly comic story of Ward McAllister, the brummagem Beau Nash who invented the "Four Hundred"; the history of the successful arrival of the Vanderbilts and the repulse of the Goulds. We have, too, the story of the international marriage market. To the swapping of millions for coronets Mr. Wecter is almost as hostile as was Charles Dana Gibson in his early crusading days, so hostile, indeed, that he is a little indiscriminate in his way of lumping together mercenary and often short-lived marriages with others that seem to have been quite normal. After all, people do travel a good deal, and a peer might want to marry an American woman for honourable reasons.

Wisely, however, Mr. Wecter does not confine himself to New York, and we learn a great deal about the social barriers of other cities. Chicago, if we can believe what we read here, seems to have been less successful than other metropolises in building really exclusive pens. Perhaps there is something in that brisk air that makes it hard to keep out the newcomers? But what has happened in Chicago is happening everywhere.

The best days of the old closed circles are over. Fundamentally, social power in most American societies was based on wealth, not on wealth alone it is true, but on wealth as a *sine qua non*. But some of the wealthiest American families, like the Rockefellers and now the Fords, have almost ignored "Society." The newest millionaires may still move to Newport as of old, but there is no one person or group that can admit them within all pales. Then, as Mr. Wecter points out, the competition of the movies is strong. The romances that tear the heartstrings of the great American public are those of the stars, not the marriage of an heiress with the tenth transmitter of an overdraft. Mr. Wecter does, indeed, suggest that some of the society names are still better drawing cards than those provided by Hollywood for its darlings, but the instances given are not very convincing. The people he lists had other claims on the public attention than their exclusiveness; usually their endearing habit of washing their dirty linen in public with the effect on the "folks that ride in jitneys" that Mr. Cole Porter has dwelt on. But in most cases who would hesitate to choose between waiting to see the marriage of Mr. Bronson Stuveysant Saltontail and the marriage of Mr. Robert Taylor? No, as a distinguished Columbia professor made that disillusioned socialite, the Countess Almaviva, ask,

Dove sono i bei momenti?

when to be called on by Mrs. Astor was the summit of human felicity? And the *élite* realizes this, for the "endorsing" of cigarettes, face creams and, to the joy of the ribald, beds, has another side to it than that stressed by Mr. Wecter. It does not only make the aloof figures of the self-chosen less aloof, it reveals the fact that they want to "sell" themselves as well as the product. In the modern advertisement it is difficult to say who is endorsing what; the cigarette usually gets less space than the endorser who is anxious to tell the world that her friends like her, that she drinks her gin neat, is a convinced and expert toxophilite and has a book.

Mr. Wecter is convinced that a cultivated and public-spirited aristocracy is worth having, but he has no illusions about the proportion of the members of American society who qualify for either of the adjectives. There are many reasons why this is so; many reflecting merely the absence in America of a soil that grows Russells or Broglies easily. There is the lack of the deferential attitude for one thing. American fox-hunting may be a far better sport than English hunting; the foxes and hounds alike may be finer animals; but where is the loyal tenantry? Where the grumbling but really delighted farmers? The real trouble is that American society has never developed any indigenous standards of its own except in small areas. It has been parasitic on Europe, especially on England, for its ideas as well as for its butlers. In his introduction Mr. Wecter talks of Proust. But Proust's heroes have no qualms. Clovis may have been like an American parvenu when he accepted the insignia of a Roman Consul from the Byzantine equivalent of the Court of Saint James's, but by the time of Gilbert the Bad, the Guermantes family had acquired a sense of security that has been achieved by only a tiny handful of American families—and those not the leaders of society. America has been rich in Swanns, not to speak of Blochs, but she has been short of Charluses. So it is that in any faithful chronicle of American society, comedy must prevail.

X

THE AMERICAN MOVIES

(1938)

I HAVE been reading recently a popular daily that has been running a campaign in praise of British movies, a campaign which has been gratefully acknowledged by several leaders of that important industry and art. And the tearful gratitude of this campaign has recalled the battles that raged in Parliament and in the correspondence columns of *The Times* over the new Films Bill. In all the dust and noise of these combats it seemed to me (and to others as I have discovered) that one not unimportant group was being rather neglected, the group of people who go to the movies to be amused in the general sense of the term, not to have their ideals or brows lifted, or to help or hinder the great cultural campaigns that are being waged over all this unfortunate world. Members of Parliament talked with indignation and alarm of the dire influence of American films; not since 1066 or 1588 had English civilization been in greater danger and, with only a little touching up, one might have taken some parliamentary voices for those of Goebbels, Gayda and Goga. As a consumer, as a person who goes to the movies every two or three weeks, perhaps a little oftener, I suggest that a great deal of this indignation is mere xenophobia which we could recognize if the debates had taken place in the Skuptshina, and that a great deal of it is the good old protectionist indignation of the seller of a competitively inferior article against the wicked foreigner.

We are for ever being given reasons to account for the financial success of American films compared with those sad results that have made the journey from Wardour to Carey Street so often a short-distance event. There was the war which gave America such a start, an excuse that lasted until talkies came in. Since then we have been told of block-booking, of coercion of exhibitors, of the quota quickie. All of these causes may have helped Hollywood and hindered Elstree, but the great dominating fact that is conveniently ignored is that, class for class, the American picture is better; it is more entertaining, it is more intelligent, it is more varied, it is more courageous. For all these reasons, but above all for the first, the British consumer with a constancy that should delight Professors von Mises, Hayek and Robbins has, when given a chance, chosen to spend his sixpence or a shilling on poison from Hollywood instead of on the more wholesome and duller British product.

The superiority of American films will be denied not only by the trade, but also by the not uncommon type of English reformer of the cinema who has not seen a film since *Broadway Melody* (or, in some cases, since *Tillie's Punctured Romance*). It will be admitted by others but explained away. We shall be told that thanks to its greater resources Hollywood can outbid any British film company. So it can for such feats as the giving Miss Claudette Colbert in *Cleopatra* a barge twice as big as the *Queen Mary*. But surely the sets for Miss Colbert in *It Happened One Night* or in *She Married Her Boss* must have been well within the resources of the British industry? One of the most successful films of recent times was *The Thin Man*, yet, unless I am misinformed, it cost very little. It costs a lot now to star Mr. Powell and Miss Loy, so I don't ask the British industry to rival *Libelled Lady*, but where is our *Thin Man*? In this field of light comedy the successes of America have been many, have been profitable and have not been imitated here. They have not been imitated here because they require the assembling of a combination of writing, directing and acting talent that it is perhaps impossible to combine with writing letters to *The Times*.

Another type of American film that we cannot produce is the exposure of abuses, the film equivalent of the novels of Charles Reade, Charles Dickens and many other great and near great novelists. A country in which a play on Parnell is banned to save the feelings of the children of the men concerned is not likely to produce rivals to *Fury*, for instance, or to give us a film on the British prison system as seen by

Mr. Macartney, or on the Native slums of Johannesburg as a pendant to the speeches of General Smuts. But not only are serious social films of this kind out of the question; comedies with a satiric touch are impossible. Can we imagine a British film actor being allowed to parody the manner of Mr. Chamberlain as Mr. Eddy Cantor is allowed to parody the manner of Mr. Roosevelt in *Ali Baba Goes to Town?*

These limitations are not the fault of the film industry; they are limitations imposed by that good taste that has emasculated the Press and Stage of the country that produced Fielding, Hogarth and the early *Punch*. But if the British film industry cannot be blamed for this limitation, it can surely be blamed for its refusal (in its big commercial films) to picture ordinary British life at all. It should be remembered that the world of British films is as remote from the lives of the average filmgoer as anything that Hollywood can produce. The majority of filmgoers are people with less than £300 a year. How many of their problems get on to a British screen? When people of this economic class appear at all it is as comic or absurdly pathetic figures seen from *above*. In American films an out-of-work billiard-marker in a comedy or a thriller is seen from his own level. The American producer knows that a man with $25 a week is no funnier in himself than a man with $5,000,000 a year. In *On the Avenue* the Greek lunch-counter owner is no funnier than the multi-millionaire. The objective comic eye is rare in English films.

One result is bad casting of minor characters; another is a slowness in getting on with the story that is partly a bad inheritance from drawing-room comedy, partly a belief that any scene in which the stars are not acting is not worth taking a great deal of trouble over and partly an excessively low view of the quickness of the English spectator. I remember, with pleasure, the performances in *Boys Will be Boys* of Messrs. Hay, Harker and Dampier, but I can remember very little about the film as a whole. I cannot remember the name of a single performer in an American film of a roughly comparable type, *Rackety-Rax*, but I can remember the whole film very well. In the British film there is too much of what boxers call telegraphing your punches. Every joke is rubbed in after being well announced. The English spectator is not as quick in the uptake as the American, but largely owing to his training by the American films he is a good deal quicker than British producers believe.

I do not know what will result from the new Films Bill, in what way the British industry will be given the shot of aspirin that revives the flaccid aspidistra. The debates over the proposed tests of merit have not been encouraging. The proposed money-test ignores the fact that some of the most successful and, from most points of view, excellent films have been made cheaply, and some of the most awful flops have cost millions of pengos or francs or whatever currency the British industry uses. The suggested quality test is almost equally alarming. What kind of quality? That admirable but Trotskyite critic, "Huguette ex-Micro" (late of *Le Canard Enchaîné*) used to say that the first idea of a French film producer who wanted to do something for art was to film *Le Maître de Forges*. I am afraid that the idea of quality that will appeal to an official committee will be more "Deeds that Won the Empire," and some filmed novels with Galsworthy as our Georges Ohnet. If and when we have a committee, every member should have the qualification that is the main asset of Lord Tyrrell as the film censor, that of having been a frequent visitor to the movies before he had any official connection with them. There is this danger in neglecting the opinions of the *cochons de payants*, that by the time the British film industry and the uplifters have done their best, we may all be tempted to imitate the home life of a Hollywood star and instead of going to the pictures, curl up in front of the fire with a good book.

XI

THE CAMERA CANNOT LIE

(1938)

In the Bronx, in Massachusetts, in towns all over the Union, a recent number of *Life* has been suppressed because of its special supplement showing stills from a film *The Birth of a Baby*. The controversy over the film and over the reproduction in a magazine of these obstetrical pictures will rage for weeks or months, but while it rages the American public will continue to buy and look at and even read the new picture magazines which are the latest addition to the American scene.

It is nearly a generation since the first English picture paper was described as being designed for those who cannot read. How large is the class that cannot or will not read the career of *Life* and its imitators shows. There is *Life*, there is *Look*, there is *Click*, there is *Foto*, there is *Pic*, and there are many more. There are picture magazines of the new type devoted wholly to Hollywood, and the Oxford groups have imitated the secular Press and put *Rising Tide* on the market, imitating as far as their special camera angle will permit, the technique of the school. The most famous and most successful of these magazines is *Life*. What kind of public is won by them and how are they won?

It should be said at once that some of these journals are far from catering solely to the illiterate. *Life* runs, for example, series of reproductions of famous pictures in America and its readers can learn in a few lines of type and several pages of reproductions the main points of difference between Breughel and Rubens. One magazine explains a current historical problem like China in a number mainly devoted to that country. *Life*, in less detail, has just done the same for Mexico. None of the picture magazines try to compete, say, with the

Illustrated London News in showing the news of the week in pictures; the proportion of topicality is seldom more than 50 per cent. and in most cases not nearly that. America is very camera-conscious at the moment and all of these magazines cater to the amateur camera-fan or fiend. *Life*, has for instance, "Pictures to the Editor," as well as "Letters." Some magazines have trick photographs, distorted women and impossibly elongated horses. Others illustrate the tricks of film-camera manipulation.

But what the imitators of the pioneers illustrate more than anything else is crime and sex or combinations of the two. Even the leader, *Life*, has never been willing to hide the fact that women are bipeds and mammals. In once puritan America, theatrical nudity, vigorously sexual advertising and the acceptance of the "war between the sexes" as a contest in which almost anything goes, are a hardly noticed part of the American scene—as far as Americans are concerned, though to a European visitor who can remember the time (only a little over'ten years ago) when it was impossible to show a picture of a girl smoking, the breakdown of the old folkways is significant of the speed with which modern America is being changed. But the lesser breeds in the new picture magazines are catering to a naïve interest in sexuality that exists in all countries, but which is seldom given such abundant adolescent expression as it is in America. For there is no "sophistication" about these minor magazines. Even *Life* makes a good news story out of the fact that "the most famous legs in history lose their job"—and shows several pictures of these legs, which of course are Miss Dietrich's. One realizes the serious economic upset that would result if nudism became general—unless that bred an appetite for pictures of young women with their clothes on.

From nudity to "social problems" is a short step. American prison methods are often barbarous and an exposure of them has a certain social value. This presumably justifies elaborate pictures of tortures, of whipping posts, of all kinds of methods of carrying out the death sentence, culminating in pictures of a criminal being hanged in Kentucky and a close-up of a smiling man smoking a cigar just before he enters the Arizona gas chamber. The scrap of letterpress which accompanies this series hints that capital punishment is unnecessary, which may count to it for righteousness, and perhaps the argument is helped by photographs of mothers and wives whose sons and daughters and husbands have been sentenced to death. "The Innocent Must Suffer" runs the caption; whether the readers (or lookers) of this periodical are among them we can only guess.

But crime pays in another way, for we have in some of these magazines the most effective criticism of the modern detective story. In a page of photographs and two or three hundred words of type, a detective solves a crime mystery as efficiently as any of the great sleuths of modern literature. You are left to find out the solution by yourself, but if your patience fails you have only to turn a few pages and there it is all cleared up in a paragraph. No tiresome settings in English country houses or American luxury penthouses. No laborious building up of the "character" of the detective; no mechanical badinage or laborious erudition straight from the encyclopædia. Above all, no love interest or so little that only one shot or so is devoted to it. Here, it seems to me, the picture magazines (and other journals) have got something, as the Americans say.

But the picture magazines, the lesser ones at any rate, being less fitted economically and technically to supply equivalents of the more magnificent of *Life's* wares, have to find substitutes. There are pictures of the scenes of "Notorious American Murders" and pictures of a " Sex Store" in Kobe, Japan, which seems (from the picture) to be not unlike a common type of Charing Cross Road emporium, but which the horrified American public, unused to English candour, will take as a symbol of Japanese degradation. Another magazine which runs rather more letterpress than the average makes the romance of Marshal von Blomberg a diving-board from which it plunges into an account of mistresses and lovers who have altered history. Louis XIV. is reported as telling "Mademoiselle Louise de Queroualle 'Mark well the name of Buckingham.' " From that we move on to Mesdames de Pompadour and du Barry, thence to Lola Montez, who is credited with causing a war between Austria and Bavaria which, unless my memory fails me, has hitherto escaped the notice of historians.

The reader can learn how to dance the shag; and the young lady who goes out into café society is taught the necessary minimum of manners, as a secretary is instructed not to roll her stockings below her knees in the office. Lourdes and the American dust-bowl area, the love-life of a girl in Ur of the Chaldees, what becomes of old Follies girls, the economics of owning a racehorse and the technique of competent make-up: the camera tells all or quite enough. Then there are intelligence tests of the simple information type; a question about the density of population in New York is apparently made easier of solution by a picture of New York.

More original are moral and intellectual problems designed to test your courage, presence of mind, etc. What should a girl do if locked in a bathroom designed by an eccentric—a bathroom whose doors won't open for three hours after being locked. The water is turned on and after an hour it is up to the terrified girl's neck. How can she escape? The solution is given on page 66; with the water round her ears it occurred to her to open the bath drain. Surely no unkinder comment on the mental age of the "lookers" could have been conceived than this? But with wireless, the films and now the picture magazines, the necessity for learning to read has been reduced almost to vanishing point. And we may be sure that if the American field proves as fertile as at the moment it seems likely to be, imitations will spring up in England. There is only one barrier —price. The American public can and will pay fivepence or sevenpence-halfpenny for these camera triumphs. The same public here won't or can't go above twopence, so what we shall get, if no better in quality, will be less in quantity. That's always something.

XII

AMERICA AT OXFORD

(1938)

I N an article in the January number of *Scribner's*, the results
of the establishment of the Rhodes Scholarships is discussed
from the American point of view. The emphasis of the headlines, "The most amazing educational experiment of modern
times," is not reflected in a sober and sensible article, whose
author has probably heard of the bringing up together of the
child of a Yale professor and a chimpanzee, and so would
hardly claim pre-eminence for an experiment consisting of
introducing to Oxford a number of young men looking like
human beings and using the larger of the two children of the
tongue that Shakespeare spoke. That a useful and unsensa-
tional article should have been given headlines more worthy
of such sociological documents as "Latins are Lousy Lovers,"
or other communications of this type, does no real harm. It
reminds America that there are hundreds of returned fellow-
countrymen who have spent years in an atmosphere com-
memorated in the great lines of Lee Wilson Dodd,

> And dourly hourly showers
> Water old Oxford's towers.

And once reminded of this fact, the American public may be
provoked to ask whether the Rhodes Scholarships have fulfilled
the hopes and plans of the founder and, if they have not, whose
is the fault and also whether there are no compensations for
the disappointments of the early days. Mr. Mackaye tells the
readers of *Scribner's* that "it is an ancient and honourable
tradition of the American bar-room that its most decrepit and
repulsive drink cadger is a man of learning fallen upon evil
days. Usually the bar-tender confides, with a mixture of pride

and irritation, that Dr. Felling knows both Greek and Latin and was a Rhodes Scholar at Oxford." The temptation to test this story by accosting the sot and suddenly demanding his name and college would be great, and the test would probably be too much for the presence of mind of the modern Porson. However, as Mr. Mackaye, after what must have been laborious research, has failed to find a vile body to experiment on, the dream must be left a dream, like the comparable design harboured in some breasts to make a member of a famous Yale secret society leave (let us say Congregation) by murmuring the esoteric version of "scram." Whatever else the returned Rhodes Scholars may be, they do not seem to have become drunkards; indeed, as far as this person can judge, they are more likely now to be found in milk bars than in pubs. It follows, therefore, that they are not likely to be engaged by detective agencies of the type described by Mrs. Dashiell Hammett or Mr. Jonathan Latimer in their lively fiction, any more than they can expect to get jobs in the cast of *The Women*, but such barriers to fame and fortune are few. Why, then, asks the indignant critic, have so few Rhodes Scholars got far on the road to either, why have they avoided both the extremes of "Ten Nights in a Bar-room" and from "South Parks Road to White House?"

Of course fame and fortune are relative terms. No Rhodes Scholar is as famous as Messrs. Gable, Cooper or Taylor. No Rhodes Scholar is as rich as Mr. Ford. But many Rhodes Scholars are well known in their own communities, and some are known all over the United States. It was, perhaps, reaction from the speed with which college food was swallowed that led one former Rhodes Scholar to become a founding member of the "Three Hours for Lunch Club"—and that is not the only, or chief, claim of Mr. Christopher Morley to fame, even if the fact that he is the brother of two other Rhodes Scholars, both eminent in their own professions, is not counted in.

But the criticism of the American Rhodes Scholars is not based on a general standard of achievement that it would be rash to impose on any body of men, but of one particular shortcoming, their failure to become a ruling class in their own country, a kind of Platonic guardians accepted as rulers

7

and leaders when they returned to Magna Anglia from Athens on the Isis. Few or no American tyrants, such as Mr. Pendergast, of Kansas City, have invited the new Platos to give advice. Fewer still have been displaced by men taught to rule wisely by the sages and the spirit of this University. As has been pointed out before, the root cause lies in the misunderstanding of American society by Cecil Rhodes, who was, as Mr. Mackaye tells us, "a romantic." If he really wanted men of brains and brawn to rule the nations after an Oxford training, he ought to have made France one of the objects of his missionary activities, for in that country alone, at this moment, does political power oscillate between the local equivalent of Fellows of All Souls and Rugger Internationals.

That a great many persons who have been formally educated at Oxford are to be found in places of authority in this country proves more about the English social structure than it does about the merits of an Oxford education, and only a very naïve Rhodes Scholar would be surprised at the refusal of his congressional district to send him to Washington, as soon as he expressed a willingness to sacrifice himself on the altar of his country. One reads, therefore, with calm the statement that "No member of the Cabinet has ever been a Rhodes Scholar. No member of the Senate has ever been a Rhodes Scholar. One member of the House of Representatives—C. R. Clason of Massachusetts—is a Rhodes Scholar." The proportion of senators and congressmen who have received a higher education or been present in establishments where it was being dispensed is much larger than the naïve British critic thinks, but the scarcity of Rhodes Scholars in Congress is a minor puzzle easily explained by the locality rule and obvious financial and professional limitations. On the other hand, it *is* a little surprising that no Rhodes Scholar has entered the Cabinet. Eight of the ten members of the present Cabinet received a university education, and the proportions of self-and-college-made members has not been very different in the cabinets of this century. Indeed, one can look higher. Since the death of McKinley there have been seven Presidents of the United States, all of whom (except one) were college men. Since the retiral of Lord Salisbury there have been eight Prime Ministers, of whom two have not been subjected to a university training, and two entered the Universities. but did not graduate. Most Rhodes Scholars, it is pointed out, either become college teachers or lawyers, but in America both trades have led to high office. It was a short jump from Wilson's Presidency of Princeton to his Presidency of the United States, and if it is a little early to look for presidential material, one would not have been surprised to find a former Rhodes Scholar an ambassador, like Professor Dodd, or a Supreme Court justice, like that great academic lawyer, Mr. Stone.

However we may account for the limitations of past Rhodes Scholars (that is if we admit that there is, in their achievement, anything to explain or explain away), there remains the question of the present Rhodes Scholars. Does Oxford do much for them or they much for Oxford? Mr. Mackaye stresses, and rightly, the results of the changes in the method of selection. No longer recruited by single states, there has been provided a wider field of choice, or, as some of the critics of the new order put it, the big colleges have had their natural advantages increased. However that may be, the Rhodes Scholars are now more frequently to be found in the first class than in the past and, if what the Schools test is worth anything, that is an improvement. Whether it follows so automatically that what we gain in the study we lose in the field is a subject worth investigation by the devotees of gymnastic. Yet one might demur to some of Mr. Mackaye's examples of the intellectual evils of recruiting from single states. Nevada, to refer to one of his examples, has produced a very distinguished historian and as for Arizona, it is not necessary to go as far as Yale to find an exception to the assumed rule that brains follow the population density.

Of more immediate local interest are various illusions that may be fostered in the mind of the intending Rhodes Scholar by various details of the article. It may matter little that he thinks that compulsory Greek was only abolished to make things easy for him, instead of tolerable for a much larger body. The lavishly Gothic character of the illustrations may prepare a disappointment for the young man from Yale or Princeton who is used to a really Gothic atmosphere and who will be surprised (and perhaps pained) when he finds how post-medi-eval is the general appearance of central Oxford. A more serious shock (it is to be hoped) will be suffered by the American who comes up believing on Mr. Mackaye's authority that "there is no scholastic discipline whatever. He may attend lectures or absent himself as he pleases. He may spend his time in Oxford studying racing charts and boning up on the Henty books; no one will protest." The serious student of racing form will be better advised to go to Cambridge where the subject is earnestly and acutely studied, and Henty is probably now old enough to be B.Litt.-ed, but in any case it is to be hoped that the authorities in America make plain to candidates that whether they are studying ancient or modern classics, the Olympic Games or Goodwood, they will not be left alone to decide how and when they shall do their work. Oxford, con-ceived as an Abbey of Theleme ending in a ceremonial exit through gates guarded by the fiery swords of Final Schools, will be more of a painful surprise even than the real Princeton must be to a British visitor whose whole previous knowledge of that University has been got from *She Loves Me Not*.

But the average Rhodes Scholar, despite his comparative maturity, has one great quality often lacking in his comrade from Narkover; he has a clear grasp of the fact that the world doesn't owe him a living, and one of his greatest gifts to Oxford is the spirit of "root hog or die" to offset the "Dieu et mon droit" attitude of many natives, who strain all the literary art of their tutors when the fatal moment of testimonial writing comes. Not all Rhodes Scholars settle down and make them-selves welcome. The same was said in the eighteenth century of the first invading Scots. But few can doubt that the existence of the foundation is an advantage to the University. Whether there is a mutual exchange of benefits it is for Rhodes Scholars to say.

XIII

UNCLE SAM'S GUIDES [1]

(1938)

EVEN worse as a source of irritation for the traveller in America than the infamous badness of American picture postcards, has been the absence of useful guide-books. Baedeker is out of date, and, in any case, the methods suitable for Europe, the standards of interest, the canons of relevant information, were inapplicable. And the gap remained unfilled until the past year or so when it has been at last more than adequately repaired by the activities of the federal government. For we now have the beginnings of a series of State and local guides far more amusing and useful than any known to Europe, all as a by-product of federal relief.

Faced with the results of the breakdown of the American economic machine between 1929 and 1933, the Roosevelt administration, in addition to making many administrative mistakes which would never have occurred in a sound bureaucratic system like our own, showed a courage and originality which, like the mistakes, would have been totally out of place in Whitehall. Out-of-work actors were not offered jobs as navvies on the roads, but as actors. Painters were encouraged to paint in post-offices, which now have tolerable frescoes where we have air mail posters of a devastating competence. And most bold experiment of all, authors were enrolled by the "Federal Writers' Project"—and one result has been this series of guides.

The sub-title of the Massachusetts volume gives a clue to the special character of the these guides "to . . . places *and* people." For we are not fobbed off with a cursory account of

---

[1] *U.S. One: Maine to Florida.* (Modern Books.)—*Massachusetts: A Guide to its Places and People.* (Houghton Mifflin.)—*New Orleans City Guide.* (Houghton Mifflin.)

the historical background. We are given a long and lively essay on the forces that have made Massachusetts what it is—and the writers do not disguise the fact that what Massachusetts is, does not fill them with unmixed delight. There are skeletons in the Bay State cupboard and they are not left there. It is notable that there are four separate references to the most noisy of recent skeletons, the Sacco-Vanzetti case. "Here in 1920 occurred the hold-up and murder of a paymaster for which Sacco and Vanzetti were executed (*see* DEDHAM)." And under Dedham is an account of "the most notorious of all Dedham trials" ending with a quotation from Mr. Heywood Broun, "Though the tomb is sealed, the dry bones still rattle!" It is believed that the latest rattle has evoked protests from that vigilant defender of the commonwealth, Governor Hurley, and can we be surprised? How would Lord Craigavon like comments on the conduct of the trial of the assassins of Sir Henry Wilson—in a government-subsidized publication?

But the past of Massachusetts, or of the other States, roads and cities is full of other things than skeletons. There is, for example, abundant record of Yankee ingenuity. One is reminded of how many minor aids to life have come from the laziness of Yankees who wanted to make machines do the work of hands or in other ways make for more abundant life. Here we are told of the man who made the first paper-pattern and of the invention of the "Boston Rocker," in whose lap so many more gadgets have been thought out. There is the home of the American meat-chopper, no doubt an improvement on the European or Japanese model. And happiest thought of all, in North Weymouth is "the first *Drive-in Theatre* (cinema) in New England with terraced levels to allow an uninterrupted view of the screen without passengers leaving their cars." Besides these dodges, the information given in *U.S. One* that in Elizabeth one can see "the Standard Oil herd of goats" is less exciting, since the explanation is technical, the sort of thing a college-trained engineer works out, not the brain-wave of a bored farmer or over-worked craftsman. But why the goats? "They are used instead of mechanical lawnmowers because of the risk of sparks." What a pity Veblen is not alive to read this!

But America is a tradition-minded as well as a tradition-breaking country. It is astonishing how many haunted houses and spook-ridden roads there are to be listed. Why Mr. René Clair had to bring ghosts west is more of a mystery than ever.

Many of the historical achievements are, of course, deplorably old-fashioned. In bed after bed, George Washington, as well as lesser yet illustrious lights, slept. Fights with Indians, with French, with British, with Americans, are all listed. But not all the glories of the past are military. On Cape Cod there is the grave of Freeman Hatch with its epitaph: "In 1852 he became famous making the astonishing passage in the clipper ship *Northern Light* from Frisco to Boston in 76 days, 6 hours, an achievement won by no mortal before or since." And you are given your choice of several locales for the great moment when the Governor of North Carolina said to the Governor of South Carolina: "It's a damned long time between drinks."

Although amusements and food are not neglected in any of the guides (*U.S. One* gives a list of regional dishes covering the whole thousand mile route), it is naturally in New Orleans, that providential American Abbey of Theleme, that the lighter side of life is cultivated most. It is eminently in keeping with the *genius loci* that this official guide to New Orleans tells you how to get to the gambling resorts adding, "Although gambling is strictly speaking illegal, these places are usually open for business from dusk to dawn." There are even scholarly accounts of that once great New Orleans industry, the light ladies, familiar to students of literature and the movies. Indeed, this section might have had as a title "From Manon Lescaut to Mae West." The forces that forced Miss West to alter the title of a film which reminded the world of how recently New Orleans was the American Sodom and Gomorrah (a title more difficult to win in America than in rural England) are not likely to be pleased by this guide!

But if the flesh and the devil get their due, so do their enemies. From the austere Puritan meeting-houses of New England to the modified Voodoo of New Orleans is a long step. But even New England backslides from Yankee sobriety. It is in sober Maine, at Shiloh, that one finds the home of the "Holy Ghost and Us Society." When the promised advent was delayed, the new Elijah sailed to convert the heathen on his ship "the *Coronet* with a flowing beard, purple robe, sailor hat and Bible. Several voyages were made without noticeable results. . . . He subsequently dropped from sight." But the sect is not quite dead. In 1936, Shiloh was reopened, but the "small group of cultists does not welcome visitors," in which they are of the same mind as the Burgoyne Trail Association who opened the first nudist colony in Massachusetts. They believe that "physical and mental health, a relaxing of nervous tension, a normal attitude towards sex, and a spiritual re-creation are fostered by properly regulated nudism." It would be interesting to have the views of Gentleman Johnny on this theory. It might have suggested the subject of a new comedy to him, or made him regret that, when he was unsuccessfully blazing the trail in 1777, New England was still backward. But it is at the other end of the Atlantic seaboard that the richest variety of "cultism" can be found. Out of the rich crop that the mixed races and cultures of New Orleans produces, it is hard to make a choice, but there is much to be said for " Zatarain's Sanctuary of Christian Divine Healing." Mr. Zatarain is a retired business man who built this shrine in 1929, after the death of his wife. "Near the rear entrance is Elisha's Healing Well, decorated with numerous ornaments, illumin-ated by underwater electric lights, and containing 'holy gold-fish.' . . . Mr. Zatarain manufactures a root beer with which he is said to work cures." On the whole I regret never having seen this, even more than having missed (in Massachusetts) the imitation of the "Castle of Carcassonne built about 1934 for the daughter of Lydia Pinkham." Magnificently illustrated, with good maps, full of useful information, these guides have yet another claim to respect. They illustrate the richness of American life which the casual visitor too easily dismisses as monotonous and fundamentally dull. These guides show how wrong that is. They remind us of Walden Pond where "Emerson's intimate friend, Henry David Thoreau, the naturalist, fled from society, built his hut and studied the trees and birds." They also tell us of that eminent New Orleans figure, Edward Burke, who was "credited with having per-suaded President Hayes to withdraw federal troops from

Louisiana; indicted while State treasurer for fraudulently negotiating State bonds, but escaped to Honduras and became a banana planter." I cannot help fearing that, if we had a series of government guides, we should hear about the withdrawal of Mr. Thoreau to Walden but not of the withdrawal of Mr. Burke to Honduras!

XIV

CALVIN THE FIFTEENTH[1]

(1938)

To the prosperous classes in America the reign of Calvin Coolidge has naturally enough acquired a golden glow. They feel about it as Talleyrand felt about the *ancien régime*, that only those on the right side of the system under the old order have known the true *douceur de vivre*. Of course, under Coolidge, as under the King, there were less fortunate areas and classes. But these spots in the sun did not materially lower the temperature of America the Golden, when it held east and west in fee, and when a depressed and dazzled Europe was offered, by M. Siegfried, the choice between Henry Ford and Gandhi.

What part did Calvin Coolidge play in this farce that ceased to be funny so suddenly in 1929? Was he merely a symbol, and if so what kind of a symbol? That he was a symbol, Mr. White makes plain. Politicians and business men agreed that they were fortunate in having in office the shrewd Yankee who had said "the business of the United States is business." But Coolidge, if a symbol, was an apparently incongruous symbol of the flush times. No one less like the patron of the age of easy-come easy-go could be imagined than this meagre, economical, tight-mouthed, ungracious Yankee. As Mr. White suggests, it was his apparently anachronistic appearance and ways that made him so useful a front. And an America rapidly racing away from the moral moorings to which Messrs. Smoot and Fess were trying to tie her by law, wanted a reminder of the stern old days of the Republic, when an austere economy had made America what she was. Now, of course, in the magic

---

[1] *A Puritan in Babylon: The Story of Calvin Coolidge.* By William Allen White. (Macmillan. 16s.)

world of the new economics there was no real need for these qualities, the prophets were giving America congenial counsel:

> Lavish of your grandsire's guineas,
> Show the spirit of an heir.

And Mr. Coolidge was a most agreeable mentor to have around, for he openly approved of the national imitation of Coal Oil Johnny, while himself putting on so fine an impersonation of the Spirit of Thrift. He was the perfect partner for Mr. Andrew Mellon and, according to Mr. White, of Mr. Montagu Norman, in their disastrous policies of easy money for speculation. The smash, when it came, was so complete that it was hard not to blame Mr. Coolidge and to attribute to him an "after me the deluge" attitude which was only in part his. Yet it was his in part. For he was a Yankee after all. No Coolidge had gone west. Once they had got as far as Vermont, they had stayed at home and prospered. And no really optimistic and adventurous soul stayed behind in rural New England unless chained to that barren soil by accident like Ethan Frome. The Coolidges were people who had got as far as they had by watching their step, which was just what Coolidge's America refused to do. But Calvin Coolidge had reverence for people who had been much more successful in gathering gear than had his father and grandfather, and who was he to be less confident than Andrew Mellon, now seen as at best the Pompadour, at worst the du Barry, of the Coolidge era?

In any case, even had Coolidge been always as foresighted as it is possible that he occasionally was, it would have been an act of superhuman courage for him to have taken action that would have cut short the life of the great bull market. In one of his many ingenious speculations as to what really made Coolidge tick, Mr. White stresses the influence of the Professor of Philosophy at Amherst, Garman. Garman used Hegel as an earlier generation used Kant to restate the truths of the New England Primer in modern dress and Coolidge learned from him a respect for the *status quo* (dialectically interpreted, of course) that justified his inaction. The President who helped to blow up the balloon that burst under Mr. Hoover really heard in the tickers announcing that U.S. Steel had gone up another five points the march of God in the world.

But the chief interest of this book is the light that is cast in it on the workings of politics, on the mystery of how X becomes a ruler in the democratic State. For the task of showing this process at work Mr. White is peculiarly well fitted. In America, he is the rough equivalent of the late C. P. Scott. He has had the hard task of driving together his liberalism and his loyalty to the Republican Party and it is this "from the inside looking out" point of view that gives his account of how Coolidge became President its peculiar interest. The career of Coolidge, especially when studied under the guidance of so expert, friendly and critical a guide as Mr. White, is as good a case-history as we can get. It is not only that Mr. White was a witness and occasionally an actor during these years, but that Coolidge was so completely a politician. He was a lawyer and began his life practising law, but from very early years he was not only a politician, but a successful one—that is to say he was in office; he was a professional politician, associating necessarily with men practising the higher and the lower graft, the graft of the small-town politician and the graft of the great banker. He was an American party politician—that is to say he had to work within the framework of a party big enough to hold him and Henry Cabot Lodge and William Allen White and Hiram Johnson and Fiorello La Guardia. He got on by being reliable, by being personally honest (but not so much of a prude as to blow the gaff unnecessarily), by industry, by loyalty to his patrons. As he said, "while I have differed with my subordinates, I have always supported loyally my superiors."

That is how you get on in Russia or Britain or America, as long as the rules of the game don't change on you. Being loyal to his superiors meant backing Senator Crane against Senator Lodge; and opposing the late Senator Lodge was one way of being on the more generous and historically defensible side of most questions. But although Coolidge doubtless did wish success to the League of Nations, for instance, he was a party man and when he ran on the ticket with Harding in 1920 we may be sure that he did not succeed in deceiving himself (as more eminent people did) into the belief that the way to get America into the League was to vote the Republican ticket. It is this success of the politician in the regular game that makes this book so fascinating for anyone who is willing to take American politics seriously, which is one way of taking America seriously. Here you have the whole story, told in a racy if occasionally archaically racy style, of conventions and deals, party meetings and jobs, the daily dodges and the occasional intrusion of unwelcome truth. And it is told by a man who takes politics seriously if with humour (which makes it all the more surprising that Mr. White should have ignored the senatorial defeat of Coolidge's manager, Mr. Butler, in 1926). And it is told from Emporia, Kansas, about a man from Northampton, Massachusetts. So many Americans really worth knowing come from places like Emporia and Northampton. And they decide American policy quite as often as the people from Boston and Bar Harbour.

XV

AMERICAN GEORGICS [1]

(1939)

"O fortunatos nimium, sua si bona norint, Agricolas."

HITHERTO, the tag has always seemed rather irritating, because of the implication that Virgil and Maecenas and all the other urban preachers of the delights of rural life knew better than the farmers what was good for them. Why shouldn't the farmers know their own business best? *Sua si bona norint* indeed! Yet it has been possible for a holder of these views to read with pleasure and profit a book half of whose theme is the unsuspected joys of farming (unsuspected in many cases by the farmers) and a good deal of the other half is a series of cracks at urban life, politics, manners and ideals. Indeed the modern world has given fresh life to Virgil, for Mr. Smart is a stout anti-fascist and, if not a pacifist, at any rate an anti-militarist; yet to-day

Hinc movet Euphrates, illinc Germania bellum.

But in Ross County, war in Europe and war in the Orient are both far away. The first reason why Mr. Smart's defence of the joys and rewards of farming does not arouse the customary irritation is that he is frank about his own limitations as a farmer. It is not only that he admits that he knew little four years ago and that he has not learned as much as he should have done, if he was to make up for the lost years when he was learning about books and prints and boys instead of about bulls and rams and roosters and their mates. But he knows how far he still is from being what Americans call "a real dirt farmer." The farm that he works doesn't keep him and, even

---

[1] *The Adventure of an American Farm.* By Charles Allen Smart. (Oxford University Press. 8s. 6d.)

with the resources of his other inherited farm that he lets on a *métayer* tenancy to that admirable master of the rural arts, Mr. Kincaid, he has to have other resources, in this case the profits of writing. He and his wife are willing to go without many things that they had, including a bathroom; they miss a lot, including horse-riding, music and the arts in general; they are willing to work hard at dirty jobs that have to be done every day—and still, like the Jones boys, they can't make the damned thing pay. But they are getting nearer that ideal by the application of the principle—cut down your wants that have to be paid for and use as much of your own products as you can. Don't be a one-crop farmer, don't indeed be a cash farmer. Once you start computing your cash income, whether from eggs or wool, your books are going to look as unhealthy as if you were a big New York house a jump ahead of the Securities and Exchange Commission.

Mr. and Mrs. Smart have become better buyers of sheep and sellers of wool and beef, even when they don't rely on knowledgeable and kindly friends to save them from the wiles of dying owners of worthless sheep who recover speedily when the bargain is off, even without the trip to California which its being *on* might have paid for! The neighbours and the members of the Farm Bureau are beginning to forget that they are merely city people coming back to land they happened to inherit. Yet it still seems doubtful if the Smart farm is going to pay its way. So Mr. Smart is not giving aid and comfort to the Americans, who believe, as a great Chicago corporation lawyer told this reviewer in 1934, that the only solution of America's troubles is to get millions of people back on the land on "subsistence farms." That, if they only knew it, was what was good for them. *Sua si bona norint*, in fact, which said, the lawyer was driven off to his Sabine farm in Lake Forest. Farming is a skilled trade and it is more important for America to make the world safe for the people who really know their business on the land, a white Kincaid or a black James, than to make it profitable for retired schoolmasters like Mr. Smart or other modern representatives of Virgil, Horace, Goldsmith and the Neo-Agrarians. But though it would be wasteful for Mr. Wallace and the Department of Agriculture to think mainly in terms of the

Smarts, it would be a mistake to neglect them altogether. For the Smarts often bring in a little money and a willingness to try new things, both of which the real farmer often lacks. In their own moderately competent way, the bourgeois amateur farmer is useful, as that shrewd peasant, Émile Guillaumin, has admitted. When he has got through with his failures and half-successes, the professionals can use the results. But the Smarts can do more than that. Virgil knew the importance of the cultivation of the rural gods; some of them (Bacchus and even Pan) are cultivated enough, even in Ohio, but Apollo is neglected. The American countryside is from that point of view rather dull. Mr. Smart shows his good sense in disliking that synthetic legendary figure Paul Bunyan and in thinking kindly of the legendary Johnny Appleseed, who carried apple-seed in his pocket and swept over the West

> Planting the trees that would march and train
> On, in his name to the great Pacific,
> Like Birnam Wood to Dunsinane.

But the "days of President Washington" are long past and the modern Ohio farmer has not that pride in the achievement of his fathers that you find in Minnesota and the Dakotas. There were giants in his earth too, but they have been a long time dead. Mr. Smart laments the decline in cultural independence of the local town, Chillicothe. Its own life is dried up by the increasing urbanization of the country; it is near enough Columbus and Cleveland and even New York, and yet not near enough to have acquired urban tolerance. So an amateur performance of scenes from *Waiting for Lefty* awakens murmurs not only from that tiresome body, the American Legion, but from the mysterious "Americaneers." Chillicothe, indeed, seems to be full of the traditional old ladies from Dubuque who perform for America the functions of our Lord Chamberlain's office. Mr. Smart hopes, not unreasonably, that "immigrant" farmers of his type, now members in good standing of the Farm Bureau, may do some good. And in return? Well you don't find it necessary to get drunk as often as you did before you became a farmer. For, in modern America, if people don't get drunk any oftener than they do here, they are more candid about it. Then you get a sense of doing something useful. Mr. Smart is not stupid enough to think that writing a book isn't work, but he has his doubts about the vast mechanism of selling and buying bits of paper that was and is the work of so many intelligent Americans—and may not be, for long, if the machine slows down.

For the British reader it is perhaps a pity that the American title *R.F.D.* was changed, for it would have suggested something of the novelty of this life. Here we have the federal government, a few years ago so aloof, replacing or improving the sanitary work of the local Lemuel Putt. Here we have described the difficulties of keeping warm and alive at 20° below zero. We can note, too, the absence of such familiar landmarks as the parson and the squire. There is a real social democracy in this society, even though there is considerable economic inequality, and not everybody is really on visiting terms with everybody else, not merely because there are inherited feuds, but because there are barriers of different experience. After all Mr. Smart has, in his time, read both Mr. Eliot and the *Boston Evening Transcript*. *R.F.D.* does not preach a panacea and does not even quite reassure us about the future of Mr. Kincaid, even if the floods don't wash the farm away. But English readers will learn a great deal about a side of American life that is little known here or, for that matter, in America, except of course to the thirty millions who live it.

XVI

LITTLE OLD NEW YORK

(1939)

THE Federal Writers' Project was one of the boldest experiments in social salvage undertaken by the New Deal.
But faced with the task of compressing New York into one
volume, the anonymous federal writers have lost courage. So
this "Panorama" is not a guide-book, but a lively and, in many
ways, learned survey of the life of New York from subways to
swing. Geology, economics, ethnology, art are all called on to
explain and to illustrate the life of the city which, thanks to the
movies, is better known to the world, visually at least, than
any of its rivals from Babylon to London have ever been.

The attempt at a conspectus was a bold one, but it deserved
and has achieved success. There is only one serious omission
in the editing, though that is serious enough; there is no map.
End papers of a very general diagrammatic type are not
enough, for if it is easy to keep the topography of Manhattan
Island in one's head, it is harder to remember from what part
of the hinterland of Brooklyn came the latest Norwegian film
star. And outside the city limits are the suburbs which provide the female audiences for the matinées and the evening
audiences at home for lectures. A general map covering the
territory between Princeton and Westport, as well as a more
detailed map of the five boroughs, would have been extremely
useful. There are, as is inevitable in a long book by different
hands, some minor slips. It is not very important that Bakunin,
who died in 1874, is declared to have been impressed by the
strikes of 1877. An ambiguity in language may mislead readers
into thinking that burning Negroes alive was a regular, perhaps
an annual event. With various hands at work, there are natural
differences of interpretation and of language. The million

Russians with whom Miss Ertz credits the city, elsewhere appear more correctly as Jews, and the criticisms of the street plan that run from Frederick Law Olmsted to Mr. Lewis Mumford are scattered through various sections. One criticism made by G. K. Chesterton is, however, ignored, the difficulty of remembering a numerical address, such as 129 E 30th Street, compared with an address in the older part of the city, say, 12 Gansevoort Street. But all in all, this is a good job. It makes a beginning in explaining New York to visitors, and, even more necessary, to New Yorkers.

The great city is many things, but it is, above all, a harbour and a port. How it came to be the greatest port in the world is made plain in Professor Albion's most learned, acute and readable book which can be commended to all serious students. It is because of its greatness as a port that New York can house the Planetarium and Madison Square Garden; provide funds and students for Columbia University, to teach all subjects from "advanced calculus to plain cooking"; make the milieu for the large audiences at Roseland, and the small audiences at the Onyx; be the dream city of millions for whom New York is the "roaring forties" of night clubs, gangsters, chorus-girls and jazz, surrounded by vast apartment houses to which virtuous young women of various professions are lured, and from which they always escape suffering from nothing worse than a bad fright. New York is not America, and New York is not just an amusement centre, but it is that, and much of its glamour and its unpopularity in America is due to its reputation as a centre of sin. Dallas may outstrip Forty-second Street; Philadelphia sin in its own decorous way; but New York is still alone on its bad or suspect eminence. As is well stressed here, even Hollywood is only a suburb of New York; apart from films about the films, it does not provide its own background, it is parasitic on Park Avenue, and the lower East Side, on the writers and actors of the New York theatrical district to provide it with most of its raw material, and, in the great "first-run" houses of New York, the new films find their most profitable publicity. What is true of the films is true of most other arts, although New York is a great importer as well as exporter, importing Toscanini and exporting *The*

Women, for instance. Into this Tiber pours more than one Orontes, but unlike Rome, New York hits back.

In all this welter of tourists and sailors, adventurers and victims from the outside world, the native New Yorker is rather neglected. Yet he exists. Indeed, with the practical cessation of immigration he is becoming more numerous proportionately than at any time for three generations past. It is a pity, then, that the article on the vernacular is almost exclusively devoted to vocabulary, and to rather exotic aspects of that. Where did the New Yorker get the accent that produces such phrases as "I saw a boid called Berd on Toity-toid Street"? Is it really worth taking space up with "wanna buy a duck?" which is now surely only a signature phrase for Joe Penner? A more interesting part of the linguistic information in this volume is the learned discussion of swing terms; study of this may be commended to the statesmen who think that "jitterbug" means what Sir Samuel Hoare and other eminent authorities thought it did two months ago. The elaborate refinements of swing language are not to be mastered by a tired statesman or leader-writer! But the hysterical vigour of the city is well displayed in the conduct of the real jitterbugs whose vigour and abandon might startle savages; in the passionate sporting crowds who follow the basketball teams or Joe Louis, or the bearded wrestlers, as well as fill the bleachers in support of two of the three leading baseball teams that this volume mentions. For if only to show that even New York has topics too sacred to be discussed in public, the writer refuses to name the Brooklyn Dodgers. We read of and see the great bridges; we are told of, but not shown, such pioneer skyscrapers as the Shelton Hotel; the horrors of the slums are not hidden from us, or the inadequeacy of many social services. And we end with a brief account of this year's great exhibition, which has been built on a rubbish dump, and which will leave behind it a park where many blades of grass will grow where before there were only the wrecks of Model T's and other relics of progress.

XVII

ON READING AMERICAN FICTION

1940

IT is over a century since Sydney Smith, in the brisk dogmatic fashion that became an *Edinburgh Reviewer*, announced that no one read an American book. Of course that was simply the heightened way of putting things that was the style imposed on the writers of the great Whig tribunal of letters but, despite laudable efforts by *Blackwood's*, the literary relations between the Mother Country and her bumptious offspring were one-sided. Americans read innumerable English books, not only the classics but the contemporary stars of the literary firmament. Dickens had as many readers in America as at home and, as Oliver Wendell Holmes sadly noted, Martin Tupper had more. On both sides of the Atlantic the absence of a copyright agreement made it cheaper for the reader to study the literature of the other half of the English-speaking world than it was to study the products of his own hemisphere, but the literary balance of payments, if there had been any, would have been markedly in favour of the Mother Country. Eager citizens of the Brave New World awaited the latest products of the literary genius of the effete monarchy whose sway they had cast off and Jefferson Brick read and, possibly, recognized himself in the writings of Mr. Dickens— without any material profit to Mr. Dickens as that candid business man of letters pointed out with some heat.

Of course the traffic was not entirely one-way. Washington Irving provided not merely agreeable and flattering *pastiches* of Addison, but in *Rip van Winkle*, added to the corpus of childish legend and with the *Leatherstocking* novels of Cooper there entered the literature of the English-speaking world one of the great themes of popular diversion. As much as the

Arthurian legend of the Middle Ages, the *matière d'Amérique* became common property. And even in the England of 1940 it is possible to see in the fields and waste-lands round the housing estates, little boys with feathers in their hair and bows in their hands, doing the best they can to be Blackfeet and Sioux and, where raw materials permit, with fire and amateur wigwams made of old boxes, adding to the heart-warming illusion that they are on the trail of the Paleface. Cooper and his disciples made one part of American experience common property to the youth of both countries—indeed to the youth of both continents, for at least one eminent French lawyer learned English so that he might read of the deeds of the Braves, since his rigorous father forbade him to read of them in French, but was willing to overlook the literary defects of the *genre* if it aided in the acquiring of a command of another language.

Nor was contemporary American literature altogether neglected. In *Little Women* New England produced a classic and, even to-day, the "Provincial Lady" has gone on pilgrimage to Louisa Alcott's shrine. And to cite a greater name, many more Englishmen than the hero of *Trent's Last Case* could have replied if asked if they knew *Huckleberry Finn*, "Do I know my own name?" Yet these exceptions only tested, without breaking the rule. It may be said with some confidence that of the vast bulk of American literature, the English reader knew little or nothing and a few brilliant exceptions, *Uncle Tom's Cabin* or *Helen's Babies*, remained brilliant exceptions. There is, of course, a possible defence of this neglect, if a defence be thought necessary. American literature, in bulk, was anæmic, a feeble copy of English models; its authors unwilling, despite Emerson's counsels, to give up trying to import nightingales into the American fauna and studiously ignoring the existence of poison ivy in the American flora. Augustine Birrell noted rather tartly that even so urbane and witty a man as the elder Oliver Wendell Holmes strained our patience too much when he tried to illustrate points of literary practice, not merely from admitted masters, but from dim American imitators of them. *Omne ignotum pro magnifico* was certainly not the attitude of the British critic to the hardworking if uninspired literary gentlemen of New York and Boston. Willis and Paulding, indeed, who were they? And, to-day, few Americans who have not "concentrated" in American literature at college could reply confidently. Time has justified the supercilious Britons. These pinchbeck authors have proved a good deal less enduring than brass. So have many of ours, but we have many more genuine brass specimens, far fewer Brummagem geniuses in proportion than American literature has had until very modern times. The English reader who neglected American contributions to what Mr. Mencken in his elephantine and engaging manner calls "beautiful letters," did not miss much. The real stars, Hawthorne, Whitman and the rest were not neglected or if they were, as happened with Melville, were no more neglected in England than in America.

Fundamentally this situation had not changed by 1914. There were a number of American novelists who had acquired critical or popular reputations, James and Mrs. Wharton, Ellen Glasgow and Mary Johnson, Robert W. Chambers and the American Winston Churchill, Howells and Booth Tarkington. But compared to Shaw and Wells, Barrie and Belloc, Bennett and Chesterton, Conrad and Hardy to name only a few of the English team, the Americans were like a scratch cricket eleven or a modern cabinet, nearly all tail.

That is all changed. Without descending to the petty verifications of statistics, it may be asserted with some confidence that the balance of literary exports is now on the American side, that there are more American first-raters or, at any rate, best-sellers than there are English rivals to them. There are three living American Nobel prize winners in the field of literature; there are no English ones. The judgment of Sweden may not be infallible in literature any more than in finance or war, but that such a judgment should be possible at all is worth noting. Of course the popularity and prestige of American literature, especially in the field of fiction, is only one aspect of a general growth of American prestige. From the last post-war period, America has rivalled Russia as a modern Utopia; whether as the home of technology, of the "secret of high wages," of the movies, of popular music, of

Harvard or of Hollywood, the United States has filled the imaginations of the educated classes as the vision of "America the Golden" had long filled the imaginations of European proletarians, anxious to escape from their chains or to have them gilded more than was usual in Düsseldorf or Glasgow. Long before Hollywood had become the modern Thebaïd, with Messrs. Huxley and Heard as joint St. Anthonies, it has been the Abbey of Thélème for Europe as well as for America. Any source of information about the background of this enchanted scene was welcome. New York, Miami, Catalina Island, were more familiar to the eyes of the world than any other cities or regions had ever been and, when not looking at America, it was natural to be reading about it. With the coming of the talkies the American hold on our imagination grew, for our songs as well as our stories came from the same factory and Fletcher of Saltoun's wise friend would have found Messrs. Cole Porter and Jerome Kern worthy of the most respectful attention. *Time* and *Life* and still more the *New Yorker* illustrate the growth of American prestige. Coinages like "socialite" are laboriously copied in a social context that makes the literal imitation merely silly. Gone are days when an American magazine existed entirely on pirated English contributions. With us are the days when naïve imitations of American methods are the solution for all problems of popular journalism, when a popular daily has thought it smart to give the title "I Cover the Waterfront" to what had hitherto been known as "Harbour News" and when it is no uncommon sight in an Oxford Common or a Cambridge Combination room to see a don struggling desperately with the jests of the *New Yorker* and, if under forty, almost as ashamed to admit his inability to grapple with Peter Arno as he would have been ashamed, a generation ago, to fail to catch the point of a joke from Aristophanes.

With smart young people America is as much the thing as England was in the days of Parisian Anglomania, when Berlioz was young. "Swing" is as much a safe topic of vague conversation in bright undergraduate circles as Proust or Cézanne were fifteen years ago. Artie Shaw and Wingy Manone, Benny Goodman and Archie Templeton, their merits and their vices, especially their rival claims to æsthetic purity, are subjects for warm debate and to have heard "Stuff" Smith at the Onyx is to have a claim on the tolerance of the sophisticated young that could not be made even on the basis of the possession of a season ticket for the best seats at Glyndebourne. Indeed, since there is nothing like a broad assertion, it is here asserted that American life and culture is a main interest of all the bright young things not absorbed in the Talmudics of Marxism and the diversion of some who are. But it is not merely the bright young things who provide the market for the floods of American fiction with which our sagacious publishers irrigate our arid lands. The general reading public, free from the chains of *snobisme* in intellectual matters if in no other, provides the main market for the retailer of American fiction.

But to talk of American fiction in general is to simplify the problem of why the demand for it is so great. *The Grapes of Wrath, Headed for a Hearse, Northwest Passage, Kitty Foyle*, to name some recent successes, have little in common except that they are books by Americans about American themes. There is a market for the American social novel, the picture of contemporary America, for the American "tough" novel, for the American love story. But probably the readers who enjoy all four types equally are few and perverted, persons to whom the American taste on the palate is so strong that any dish with that flavouring is delicious. Contemplating the classification of American fiction given above, the chronicler is more baffled to account for the popularity of the American historical novel than for the success of any other line offered by the industry on the British market. No fact is better established in the publishing world than that the British public do not want to read American history; the British man in the street, the critic, the statesman are alike content to get along with complete ignorance of the history of the United States or to make shift with a few commonplace and almost always erroneous impressions. Allusions to American history in the public prints reveal a profound and complacent ignorance that cannot be easily paralleled. Persons who know nothing of the history of Yugoslavia do not, as a rule, make airy allusions to the history of that country, allusions which give them away at once. That kind of complacent ignorance we leave to our rulers. But persons who will firmly refuse to learn even the elements of American history from a text-book, will cheerfully read very long, detailed and often highly informative historical narratives cast in the form of fiction. With all allowances made for the talents of the best practitioners, such as Mr. Roberts, and even when all allowance is made for the curious sauces with which these historical dishes are sometimes served up ("curious" being used, as it was used by Mr. John Mair, in its technical bookseller's catalogue sense), it is surprising that America, from the Revolution to the Civil War, should now be what Scotland was in Scott's time, the best background for fictional history. From this class *Gone With the Wind* should be excepted. The success of that book is, as Americans put it, "one of those things," an event as decisive and unpredictable as a great flood or a great drought. Scarlett O'Hara could perform her tricks in any environment and although compared to some earlier fictional versions of the Reconstruction period such as *Red Rock*, G.W.T.W. is a model of scholarship, its chief appeal is not historical. There is enough truth in the poet's view that "every woman is at heart a rake" to have made the story of Rhett and Scarlett a sure-fire hit even if set in Wigan.

Can it be that the success of American historical fiction, where it is not merely a renewal of the success of Cooper with the forest and the prairie as the new Sherwood Forest of our boyish thought, is due to the unpleasant state of Europe? It is hard to-day to read history or historical novels without falling into day dreams of which the chief charm is the chance they give one of strangling most of the begetters of our present troubles at birth! It is possible to read of American generals and politicians making love and war without being pricked by the painful thought that all of their public activities have had immediate unpleasant consequences for us. In the Never Never Land of American history, the doughty deeds of the heroes are not for us represented by conscription, income-tax demands, a profound sense of insecurity and danger.

It is easier to understand the vogue of the American

sociological novel. We want to know about this strange and dazzling country. We may lament as romantics the fact that,

> Across the plains where once there roamed the Indian and the Scout,
> The Swede with alcoholic breath set rows of cabbages out.

But the son of the Swede, risen from cabbages and, if alcoholic, alcoholic in a more refined fashion, can have a lot to tell us about life in the cities that have, like Mr. Sinclair Lewis's Zenith, thrust their topless towers to the sky from sites where three generations ago, there were only the trader's hut and the tepees of the savages. The America of to-day is made more comprehensible to us by Mr. Lewis, by Mr. Horgan, by Mr. Steinbeck, by Mr. Faulkner, by Mr. Caldwell, by Mr. Wiedman and by many less competent describers of the American scene. American family life among the bourgeoisie and among the share croppers of Georgia, among Iowa farmers and New York garment makers; we are ready, it appears, to learn a lot about all of them. We are even willing to learn a lot from that very bogus literary *genre*, the dynastic "epic" or "saga" where an industrious young man, with the aid of a file of Sears Roebuck catalogues, a file of *Harper's Bazaar* and a justified trust in the uncritical ignorance of his audience, can illustrate the rise and fall of American society. The author need have no real powers as a novelist, he need not even (if one may judge from a recent and successful specimen) possess the minimum command of mere chronology that the reader is surely entitled to expect. But as long as the usual ingredients are present, sex, business, remarks on furniture and dress and vague rumblings-off, based on the technique of the "at that moment" school of historians, the British reader will patiently plough through a family chronicle which he could easily see through were the locale Wolverhampton and not Wichita.

Some of these novels are, indeed, only valuable as sociological descriptions. If you want to learn about the working of the mail-order business you can read a novel written to that end, a novel whose human beings are singularly dull and unindividualized. Miss Ruth McKenney, admired of all readers of *The New Yorker*, is wiser than Mr. Halper, the author of *The Chute*. Miss McKenney writes about "My Sister Eileen" with her right hand and about labour problems in Akron, Ohio, with her left. The creator of Hyman Kaplan, as a serious sociological student of the American press, writes under his own name, with no fictional fig leaf over the bare facts. If you want to understand modern American Society you can learn more from the objective and factual studies of "Middletown" made by Mr. and Mrs. Lynd, than from a bale of novels whose only real justification is the pill of information hidden beneath the jam of a love story or at any rate a sex story.

Where the novelist brings real imaginative power to bear, as is done by Mr. Steinbeck and Mr. Caldwell, then the propagandist and informative side of their work is given a power it would not otherwise have had. No mere accurate description of the working of the Fugitive Slave Law, no economic study of the fate of the migrating "Okies" in California could have done what *Uncle Tom's Cabin* and *The Grapes of Wrath* did— put a triumphant economic and social order on the defensive. But for one Mrs. Stowe or one Mr. Steinbeck, there are a dozen sociological novelists who would make fair Ph.D.'s, but who make very poor novelists. Yet poor as they are they are read here as well as in the United States. Why?

Because they write about something: the organization of trade unions, the social effects of the emigration to American soil, the clash of races, the conflict of classes and creeds. It is true that we have writers who, as well as all but the best Americans, deal with real topics, who escape from the crippling conventions of the English class structure. *Love on the Dole* in one way, the lighter life of the new industrial settlements of the Great West Road as revealed to us by Mr. McGraw in another, do what the Americans set out to do. But the popularity of the American may be due to the fact that our consciences are not pricked by the woes of the Okies as they might be by the wrongs of the "Special Areas"; we can read *The Grapes of Wrath* with the comforting feeling that we cannot do anything about it. But that is not the whole story. Our fiction is not as frivolous as our stage, but it is too frivolous all the same.

The limitations of English practice that help to make the market for American fiction are beautifully illustrated in that field where mass production is commonest, the crime story. The mere puzzle story, what the Americans call the "Whodunit," is bound to be a highly artificial *genre*. As Mr. Ogden Nash has recently pointed out, most detective stories would be a great deal shorter if the "Had I But Known" device were barred, the failure of the essential witness to tell all in time to save the detective and the reader a great deal of trouble. To get round this difficulty, all sorts of devices have to be employed, the chief one being building up the character of the detective in the fashion rightly condemned by E. C. Bentley. When it comes to bogus characterization, to the consecrated devices which attempt to conceal the fact that a short story is being spun out to 220 pages, the American practitioners are just as maddening as the English. Fictional detectives who ask to be hit sharply on the head with a blunt instrument are common on both sides of the Atlantic. And the writers who do manage to be entertaining, as well as more or less puzzling, are not all American. Miss Georgette Heyer can do the bright conversation trick as well as Mr. Marco Page, which is meant to be praise for both of them. But the American writer can take advantage of his freedom in a way barred to the English.

First of all he is freer in the matter of locale. Governed by rules as rigid as those of cricket, the English detective story writer is pinned down to London and the South of England— and abroad. Here the precedent has been set by Holmes. He worked for the Pope and the Royal Family of Holland, visited Khartoum and Mecca when both were barred to the infidel, but he never took a case north of Trent, except in the one instance of the visit to "The Priory School" which seems to have been near Chesterfield. The living "mistress of them that know," Mrs. Christie, observes the same rule; Poirot has detected in Mesopotamia but not in Manchester. What Holmes and Poirot do, does not matter; they need not abide our questions. But other are less free and the convention that murder takes place in London or the home counties, usually only among super-tax payers and in a general atmosphere of restrained gentility, is trying. Mr. Croft's Inspector French travels a good deal and the Coles's Mr. Wilson's cases sometimes involve slightly critical views of the social order, but that

is about all. The American detective is not so bound. Mr.
Queen, Mr. Vance, the latter happily gone to his reward,
practised as a rule in New York, but Cape Cod, Dallas, Los
Angeles, even Philadelphia have all eminent fictional sleuths in
steady employment. Then the American authors, as a class,
realize with De Quincey that murder, if not serious in itself,
often leads to open breaches of decorum and morality. Too
often in an English detective story, it is hard to regard the
murder as more than a technical device for beginning the game.
The American murderer and murderee (and often the
detective into the bargain) are quite often definitely *not nice*.

This point is better illustrated from another popular branch
of crime fiction, the "tough" story. The tough story of what
Mr. Cyril Connolly has called "They Shoot Postmen Don't
They?" type, in which the authorship of the crime is not in
question, merges easily into the tough detective story in which
the authorship of the crime is discovered after a series of
assaults, bumpings-off, torture scenes with as much sex and
soaking thrown in as the readers can stand (or maybe as the
author can stand; the reader can stand a lot). This *genre* is so
popular that we now have English imitations of it. But these
imitations suffer from a double weakness. The authors lack
gusto and conviction; their heroes and villains tend to be
heroes and cads in the tradition of *The Magnet*, only the
authors are much less good story tellers than is Mr. Frank
Richards. The English tough detectives, if they would not
break down and weep at the sight of a picture of their deceased
mothers, would definitely be embarrassed and blushing at the
thought of the descent on them of their headmasters. No such
weaknesses cramp the style of the American detectives. Of
course all American authors gain something from the extraordinary breakdown in the taboos once common to both
branches of the language. Gone are the not very distant days
when, as it was said, American authors had to pretend that
they thought adultery meant putting sand in sugar. Indeed,
liberty has become a new servitude. A linguistic convention of
brutal candour has grown up, the charm of euphemism is lost.
Nor is language all. Jokes of a bold type, that were all right
once, threaten to become stereotyped. One, in particular,

which was in place when used by the greatest master of this school, Mr. Jonathan Latimer, has since been worked to death by less skilful practitioners; it threatens to become as regular a device as the umbilicus in the early work of Walt Disney. But if you propose to supply "toughness," it is idle to try to provide it and, at the same time, to write a book that a solicitous young woman can let her mother read. It can't be done and should not be tried. To make a good "tough" crime story, sadism is not enough; normal sex must have its place, however distressing this fact may be to English gentlemen.

The real advantage of the American crime story writer over his British competitor is more serious. America provides better raw material. Of course, for the classical family murder we can hold our own with anybody. Glasgow with its magnificent record is, in itself, enough to enable us to look American boasters in the eye. But for the fast-moving shooting, knifing murder, America is an easy winner. Our crime kings who are demonstrating mathematical propositions in one part of London while their victims are murdered in another, require a lot of simple faith in the reader. But many a busy citizen of Chicago who was poking his nose into Mr. Capone's business *did* die of lead-poisoning while that master was relaxing in his little winter place in Florida. In English detective fiction witnesses are often removed just as they are about to tell all. But does that often happen in real life? In America, such a solution of the problem of dragging the story out is far from exciting incredulity. How to keep your witnesses alive until they can testify is a real problem for an American detective or District Attorney. Murder rings are common in English fiction—but there is a real one being uncovered in Brooklyn at this moment. It is true that a writer of exceptional talent can do a great deal with very little. Mr. Graham Greene showed that in *Brighton Rock*, where the actual crime would not have made the back pages of the Chicago press when the local gang business was brisk. In America, no crime writer need be afraid of running too far ahead of fact. Indeed, fact may run after him. The story of *No Orchids for Miss Blandish* has since been imitated in real life in the city and state where the fictional version was laid! English detectives should continue to play cricket; let

Americans play baseball, facing all the risks of the game, the bomb, the blonde, the bed.

In crime stories, as in more serious branches of the art, part of the popularity of American fiction is due to its close relation to reality. It is true that the English reader—and reviewer—does not always appreciate the degree to which he is being given sociological information about the state of Kansas City under the Pendergast machine, or the social life of Chicago's suburbs. For instance, no English reviewer, as far as I saw, noted the main theme of Mr. Christopher Morley's *Kitty Foyle*. That book was a great success in America, not merely because it was an ingenious re-telling of the old, old story of King Cophetua with a Hindle Wakes twist. It was a success at least as much for the light it cast on the life of the "Main Line" families of Philadelphia. That society is, or was, a mystery to the average American. Its Bostonian counterpart is not, for the best families of Boston are not merely exclusive, they are highly literate and expository. The Lowells may speak only to God but they have no objection to having their conversation overheard. Before such modern ironical accounts of the First Families of Boston, such as *The Late George Apley*, there was *The Education of Henry Adams*. But Philadelphia was another matter. Some fugitives from the "Main Line" chain gang like the present American ambassador in Paris tried to tell all. But although *It's Not Done* is a good political novel, it is too hostile to the society it describes to give the reader much sympathetic interest in it. When Edward VII. as Prince of Wales visited Philadelphia in 1860, he shocked society there by asking casually "What is a Biddle?" America waited two generations for an answer, but now it knows what the Philadelphia Guermantes are like. Mr. Morley, that is, was doing the work of a Malinowski or a Firth, as much as the work of a pure novelist and America was grateful to him, although few English readers saw the point, perhaps because they did not realize how fantastic in American eyes was a community in which cricket was taken seriously!

It is not maintained, then, that the popularity of American fiction is necessarily due to a conscious thirst for information; what it is that makes American fiction alive—and so readable

—often escapes the English reader. But consciously or unconsciously, he cannot help learning a great deal about America, which is something new. With the films, the American picture papers, the American novel, English knowledge of America is greater than it has ever been. Yet that may not make for sympathy or understanding, for the America displayed is often a good deal less attractive than a more balanced picture would reveal. The America revealed does not, as a rule, evoke warm emotions as was sometimes done in the past. A distinguished Englishman, two generations ago, complained after a visit to America that what he missed was the pleasure of association, the pleasure which Italy and France gave so abundantly. Indeed, he asserted, he only once got that pleasure; crossing a stream in Florida he asked the conductor of the train its name. "Why, that's the Swanee River." No modern American writer has done what Stephen Foster did for that visitor or what Mark Twain did for this writer when I stood on the bank of the Mississippi at Hannibal, Missouri, whence Huck Finn set off on his immortal journey.

XVIII

INSIDE AMERICA

(1941)

THE Oxford University Press has recently published a new batch of new Federal Guides,[1] and at a time when interest in America is deeper and more genuine than it has been for a long time, the value of the guides as a key to the American labyrinth is greater than ever.

Their very existence is of symptomatic importance. What British Government would have sponsored a "Writers' Project," would have made work of this kind for its marginal intellectuals? The British conviction that we have nothing to learn from America in the field of government, that our ways of doing public business are always the best, is one of the main obstacles to Anglo-American understanding. So the problem set by the Federal Guides is worth pondering. More than that; we are convinced for the most part that Americans are a nation of congenital boosters, and there is enough civic pride, even civic vanity, in these guide-books. But it is doubtful if a British Government would dare to sponsor so critical an account of our local government, of the appearance of our industrial towns, of the economic prospects of our great cities, as Federal and State Governments have sponsored. I should like to see as critical an appraisement of my native Glasgow as Cincinnati comes in for. And it is not only the social services or business prospects that are critically handled. There are fairly bold æsthetic judgments too. They are not, perhaps, bold by the standards of a bright young undergraduate fed on the honeydew of Le Corbusier, but they are much more critical of expensive local monuments than the average town councillor in these islands would think permissible. The missionary labours

[1] *South Carolina, Pennsylvania, New York, Ohio, Indiana, Michigan.*

of Mr. Osbert Lancaster would seem to be less necessary in America than at home.

But the Guides have another great merit; they are about the *real* United States. They devote space and labour and thought to the cities and towns where the majority of the American people live. It is a long time since England was a predominantly agricultural community. But the home guide-book treats England and Scotland as rural, picturesque, historical, ignoring the fact that Birmingham is far more important, representative and worth studying than Stratford, Glasgow than Edinburgh. Here every scrap of historical prestige is indeed saved; links with Europe are sought and found (although it is characteristic that the level of accuracy in the description of these old-world links is far below that displayed in the description of living phenomena). Youngstown (Ohio) is not Winchester (England) or Arles (France), yet the city is an important unit of American life. It is there that steel tubing is made by "plunging a hole through a solid cylinder of steel to furnish completed tubing far stronger than was possible under the old lap-and-butt welding-process." America was, and is, the great home of inventors, and here they get their due meed of praise. The mouse-trap theory of progress is exemplified again and again. It was the ingenious inventor of the separate collar that made Troy (New York) go ahead faster and farther than Ilion (New York); it was Eastman and the Kodak that clinched the claim of Rochester (New York) to its pre-eminence, which had once been threatened by Carthage (New York). It was Goodrich whose belief in rubber made Akron (Ohio) a more important city than Terre Haute (Indiana). Even South Carolina had its inventors, including the maker of the first practicable submarine.

Here in the man of ingenuity with a new idea (and in the vast plants where new ideas are welcome) is one of the greatest dangers to the Third Reich. But many Americans who rejoice in that ingenuity would resent its being too closely tied up with the perennial quarrels of Europe. For away from the ports, most of the inhabitants of the States here described are, or were, increasingly indifferent to Europe. Gone are the days when the chief rival of Cincinnati as "Porkopolis" was Dublin

(Ireland). For the citizen of Columbus (Ohio) 1913, the year of the Great Flood, is more important than 1914, the year of the Great War. To us it is merely an episode in the family history of Mr. Thurber; to Columbus it is the end of an era.

Yet Europe's shadow is thrown over these pages, more perhaps than the compilers realized. We talk of "the melting-pot," we know that the United States has long ceased to be "Anglo-Saxon," but we do not, and cannot, feel the fact as Americans do. And so we neglect one important and respectable source of American isolationism, the fear that American intervention, even American interest, in the quarrels of the Old World will delay the achievement of national unity in the New. Take Detroit, the most rapidly growing of the great American industrial cities. It has long since forgotten its French origin except as an historical ornament that justified calling cars after La Salle and Cadillac. But it cannot forget the great Polish colony of Hamtranck, the once German village that has grown into the city of 50,000, imbedded in the territory of Detroit, but firmly refusing to be annexed. There politics and social life, education and religion, athletics and dissipation, all have a deep Polish colour. Hamtranck, in a sense, is now what Cracow was in its brief life as the sole free Polish community. There the Polish wedding is performed with all its traditional jollity. The only sign of Americanization is that it is no longer the custom to throw coins into a plate, and, if the plate is broken, to claim the right to dance with the bride. Paper-money is thrown in instead. But at the small town of Posen, which is even more Polish than Hamtranck, there is no mitigation of the old custom, either because of a dislike of breaking dishes or of reverence for paper as apart from hard money. Before 1939 these customs were what "old Americans" love to call "colourful." But in 1941, with the long martyrdom of the Polish people still continuing, the American citizen may regret a little the closeness of the ties that bind the Polish-Americans of Hamtranck to their mother-country.

He will the more wonder apprehensively if he is a Catholic, and reflects that Hamtranck is not far from Royal Oak, where the Reverend Charles Coughlin does business. No one has given more glowing testimony to Father Coughlin's love for

justice and hatred of iniquity than has Father Coughlin himself, but the Poles of Hamtranck must have noticed that his
love of justice never incommodes the politics of the Third
Reich, and that their brethren in the faith who follow Father
Coughlin with such impressive, if not edifying, trust, seem to
think that the hatred of Jews is nearly the whole duty of the
Christian man, a practically complete substitute for the love
of Christians. And when they notice that Archbishop Beckman
of Dubuque, Father Coughlin's most august episcopal ally,
finds that his ancestral ties with Germany are not strained in
any way by the policy he commends to his fellow-Americans,
they, too, may be tempted to speak out of place, and interpret
their duties as American citizens in an excessively Polish light.

The Guides, with their customary and admirable candour,
make no bones about it. Such and such a town is predominantly
"American," such another is predominantly German or Polish.
It was because it was one of the most "American" cities that
Muncie, Indiana, was chosen for the investigation made
famous in "Middletown." Mr. Booth Tarkington's Indiana-
polis is far more American than Mr. Louis Bromfield's Cleveland. The belief in "Hexen" has survived in a more lively
form in rural Pennsylvania than in the Palatinate, and the great
Indiana abbey of St. Meinrad, set among the German Catholic
villagers, is a safer repository of German Catholic tradition
than its mother abbey of Einsiedeln can be to-day. Yet can
the American politician or statesman be sure whether the voters
round St. Meinrad, if they remember their origin at all, think
of Germany as the country where life in the old traditional
fashion is being made impossible, or as the holy land of which
they are missionary children?

Yet here they are, Poles, Irish, Germans, Maronites, Jews,
Negroes, Welsh (the Eisteddfod is naturalized in more States
than one), striving, and on the whole thriving, where a few
generations ago the Indian and the *coureur de bois* alone of
humans disturbed the forest. If we think of America too
simply, in too great masses, here is the corrective. *E pluribus
unum* indeed, but here are the elements in the compound.

XIX

AMERICAN HISTORY

(1941)

IT was, I think, Sir William Harcourt, who said around 1900: "We are all Socialists now." Something of the same mass conversion seems to have struck politicians and academics; the gainer being not socialism but American history. It is not very long since eminent persons could blithely refer to Alexander Hamilton as the author of the Constitution or even of the Declaration of Independence or could confuse the two documents with no qualms of conscience. Then all that was needed for a powerful speech on American problems was an acquaintance with the late F. S. Oliver's *Alexander Hamilton*. American history was the hobby of a few people but it was academically unprofitable. Few universities or schools even professed to do anything about it and of those that did, fewer still had anything like adequate resources for teaching or studying it. There were only two chairs of American history, in Oxford and in London and nothing that could be described as a school.

This indifference to American history, reflected in the stern refusal of the British public to buy books on the subject as much as in the disinclination of the really able undergraduate to take the subject seriously, has long been a subject of lamentation among the few zealots. Bodies like the Carnegie and Commonwealth foundations or the Rhodes Trustees have done a good deal to make library facilities better. The regular stream of graduate students sent to the United States by the great foundations has done more. It is not only that facilities have thus been given to intending historians to study American history in America, but an interest in the subject has been fostered in other academics, in chemists and lawyers. But it was safe to say that, other things being equal, knowledge of American history was a marginal unit in the intellectual equipment of the intelligentzia.

Nor was this all. While institutional efforts to increase in American history were more zealous in the last ten years, the facilities for developing that interest got worse. Before the great slump, American publishers could afford prestige budgets. All or nearly all important American books were published here or, at any rate, were sent for review here. That is no longer so. Only the university presses keep up the good old custom of sending over a few copies of each important book. But private publishers, especially those with no direct London connections, no longer bother. It is hard to blame either the American publishers or their British colleagues. Even before October 1929, the rewards of enterprise in this field were meagre. One of the best books on American history, already a kind of classic in the United States, was published at considerable expense here. Less than two hundred copies were sold while in America it sold many thousands. At least once a year I receive from publishers American typescripts or proofs or books with a request for my opinion of their value for the English market and in almost every case I am forced to state that even the best of them will find few readers—in a country where the Viennese industry of gingered-up history has found no difficulty in taking root.

To give examples of the difficulties of the study of American history here is only too easy. As far as I know, no volume of the admirable series of the American Political Leaders edited by Professor Allan Nevins has been published here or even reviewed. Yet that series includes such fundamental books for the study of Anglo-American relations as Professor Nevins's life of Hamilton Fish and so essential a book for the understanding of the reactions of conservative Republicans to the League of Nations as Professor Jessup's life of Elihu Root. Again, Mr. Pringle's life of Taft has not been reviewed here, although it is of the greatest interest for the inner story of American attitudes to the Peace of Versailles and the League of Nations.

It is natural, then, that the first-class books of more

technical interest like Dr. Buck's *Road to Reunion* should be unknown here. The case is worse if we reflect that there are only two good specialized American history libraries in this country, at Oxford and London. In other universities, the would-be teacher of American history has to order books unseen or come to London or Oxford or rely on seriously inadequate local resources.

It is against this background that the current campaign for the study of American history should be seen. That campaign is being directed with great energy, skill and good-will. On the efforts made to increase the amount of time spent in the teaching of American history in schools, on the training of teachers to do the job, on the production of text-books, on what may be called the tactics of the campaign, I do not wish to write here. The efforts are zealous and the first fruits promising. I shall attempt the more ungrateful task of point-ing out some dangers, dangers mainly of emphasis. It will be more than a pity if this campaign fails, in whole or in part, because of an undue simplification of the problem. That simpli-fication will not be the fault of the teachers or of the educational officials. It will be the fault of the public and of the politicians for whom " American history" is something a good deal simpler and more manageable than it is for the student or teacher. American history will have no educational, or social, or political value in our educational system if it is in any way treated as a "stunt," instead of being studied as a subject of great intrinsic interest. And there is some danger of American history being treated as a special aspect of British history, as having as its main theme war and diplomacy. Yet there must be a firm resistance to the temptation to explain American history in terms of British analogies. Some themes can be so explained. There should be no minimizing of the common legal, cultural, religious links, but a great deal of American history can only be understood in American terms and it must be studied with the same readiness to make the necessary effort as is expected of the students of any other country. And if British teaching of American history differs notably from good American teaching of American history, it is a pretty safe assumption that it is differing for the worse.

One problem that faces the " Americanist" in this campaign for the introduction of American history into British schools is the survival of the widespread illusion that American schools and colleges still teach American history in the spirit of Mr. Jefferson Brick, that twisting the lion's tail, that reviving all the bitterness of the Revolution or the War of 1812 is practically a prescribed part of the standard American curriculum. This is an illusion that dies hard. There are backward schools and colleges; there are backward states; there are stupid or even malignant teachers. But I should say that the educational systems of the great majority of the states of the Union are in this respect a model, not a horrible example. That American history is taught with somewhat less than the objectivity that one would expect from a visitor from Mars is true, but it is taught with a good deal more objectivity than it was a generation ago and certainly with a good deal more objectivity than British history was taught in Scottish schools when I was at school.

The belief that there is a fixed, anti-British *school* tradition in America is an obstacle to the teaching of American history in British schools because it fosters the belief that there is a common, "good thing" version of American history in which nearly all was for the best. It also confuses the issue in another way, for it implies that the main theme of American history is Anglo-American history—which is dangerously untrue. Thus a schoolmaster writing to the *Daily Telegraph* on August 20, 1941, complains that "while the story of the struggle for American independence has been taught for years in our own schools in an impartial manner, the teaching being accompanied by notes giving 'arguments for' as well as 'arguments against,' the American boy is still taught about this unfortunate episode in our history in a manner which too frequently gives him a prejudice against us."

The assertion about American education in general is, like all such assertions, far too sweeping to be safe. There is not one unified educational system; there are forty-eight. Indeed, even that is a misstatement for inside a state there may be important variations. But some indication of the bias of history teaching in America can be got from the inspection of

American text-books. Rightly or wrongly, American teaching depends more completely on the text-book than does ours. These text-books are more expensive, more lavishly produced, usually written by more formally eminent persons than ours. One result is that publishers and authors are conscious of the pressure of professional opinion and hesitate (they have no doubt higher motives as well) to make fools of themselves by naïve displays of chauvinism. Take for example a recent and admirable specimen designed for high schools. The statement by these experienced teachers of the Anglo-American controversy is certainly far from justifying the strictures of the letter-writer. "Even the most hurried examination of the factors in the controversy ending in the Revolution leads one quickly to discard the old theory that the Revolution occurred because an English despot was seeking to recover his lost power." What objection can be made to that? Other text-books of the same rank (as far as the eminence of their authors and publishers go) take the same line.

But the real danger in this view of how American history is taught in American schools lies in the attitude revealed in the last part of the letter. "The American boy is still taught about this unfortunate episode in our history in a manner which too frequently gives him a prejudice against us." "This unfortunate episode in our history!" But for the American boy it is neither an episode nor unfortunate. It is basic to the whole of modern American political history and institutions. It is not a mere case of deciding whether it is or is not unfortunate that George III. ever occurred. The problem for the teacher of American history in both countries is the same; it is not returning a moral verdict on the conduct of George III., Lord North, George Washington or even Benedict Arnold. It is explaining, not necessarily justifying, a great event which the Americans insist on calling not "the struggle for American independence" but "the American Revolution." And until our teachers begin to think as well as talk of it as "the American Revolution," the prolonged political, military and economic

---

[1] *America: Its History and People.* By Harold Underwood Faulkner and Tyler Kepner, Harpers. Professor Faulkner teaches at one of the best American women's colleges, Smith, and Mr. Kepner is Director of Social Studies in the public schools (council schools) of Brookline, Mass.

crisis which resulted in the establishment of the United States under its present constitution will remain unintelligible.

What is to be avoided is the illusion that teaching even enlightened views about those parts of American history which obviously impinge on British history is teaching American history. An analogy will show how absurd this view is. French history impinges more often and more dramatically on British history than does American history. But no history teacher (I hope) falls into the trap that study of the two great French Wars between 1793 and 1815 is the same thing as studying the history of the French Revolution and the Empire. That must be studied for its own intrinsic interest. Because there were no British troops involved, the Battle of Jena is not to be neglected in favour of the Battle of Maida—even in Maida Vale. The Code, the Concordat, the *Conseil d'Etat* are all worth study even though they have no obvious implications for the understanding of the younger Pitt or Lord Eldon or Wilberforce.

So with American history. The Americans call the crisis of which one dramatic and obvious consequence was the separation from Britain "the American Revolution." They do this because it *was* a revolution; the War of Independence was only a part of the whole. What light does moralizing about George III. cast on the contract clause of the Constitution? What light does admiration for the public spirit of the (English) Whigs cast on the land problem on the frontier? None or next to none. Even if the case of George III. in English history could seem as simple now as it did in pre-Namier days, the case of George Washington or George Mason is what should be studied in studying American history.

The error of judgment that reduces the complex and fascinating problem of the birth of the United States to a mere family quarrel that could have been easily ended by tact and understanding, is the most conspicuous example of the delusion that by American history we should mean the study of Anglo-American relations. But it can be seen in other less dramatic ways. The origins, the conduct, the results of the War of 1812 can be made to yield both interest and enlightenment in the hands of a scholar of the calibre of Professor

A. L. Burt.[1] But it can be freely admitted that a British school time-table has little room for the details of this episode. But what it must have room for is for understanding why it is not a mere episode for Americans. If time is so short that only ten minutes or so can be devoted to the two and a half wasteful years of war between 1812 and 1815, let it be devoted to explaining why the Democratic party in the United States holds its annual bean-feast on January 8; to explaining why, in normal times, the leader or leaders of the party meet in Washington to hear a pronouncement on party aims and on party fortunes. For nine years past the leader of the Democratic party has been Mr. Roosevelt and he is peculiarly fitted to speak on Jackson Day as he is a most fervid admirer of Andrew Jackson. And why Andrew Jackson and why January 8? Because on that day in 1815, General Jackson easily defeated a British army under the Duke of Wellington's brother-in-law, an army that was attempting to take New Orleans. To explain why Jackson became a political after being a military hero; to explain the fact that the recently French and Spanish city of New Orleans was involved; to explain the modern relevance of these facts; this would be to teach American history, not to teach "Anglo-American relations." And there are several good reasons why we should teach the first and not the second. It is a far richer, far more nourishing subject than "Anglo-American" relations. And the second, narrower, and more arid subject cannot be taught in anything but the most futile examination sense without a background of American history studied and assimilated for its own sake. We have, in fact, no choice. If American history teaching is not going to be just another burden on overloaded teachers and pupils, it will have to be studied for itself.

This is not, it is important to insist, that it should be taught and studied in isolation from general history, but merely that it should not be taught as a part of English history, that the United States should not be thought of as a lost dominion or as a laggard ally.

Another danger inherent in the situation was indicated by

[1] *The United States, Great Britain and British North America, from the Revolution to the Establishment of the Peace after the War of* 1812. (Oxford University Press.)

a friend of mine. He asserted that it would be one of the duties of the teachers and text-book writers to replace the picture of American life given by Hollywood by a truer and less dangerous one. This is to ask far too much of the teacher and the text-book. It is natural that teachers of all ranks should look with some suspicion and fear on the picture of any society given by the cinema. The simple themes of violence, luxury, movement, sex that make the movies so fascinating to the average adolescent are handled sometimes coarsely, sometimes stupidly, always too simply. But to imagine that they can be countered by simple appeals to the "better elements" of adolescent nature against the skilful exploitation of these passionate interests by the highly paid and highly skilled employees of the great film combines, is to suffer from professional delusions of grandeur. An open war against the picture of America given by the movies is a war bound to end badly—or rather to end in a complete victory for Hollywood.

It is far better to face the facts. For better or worse, the average boy is going to get his most vivid picture of American life from the movies as, a generation before, he got it from the "bloods" in which Buffalo Bill and his brethren for ever rode to do justice and endless Redskins bit the dust. In the United States, there is a constant stream of complaints from parents and teachers about the deplorable effects of the movies. I have talked with American grade and high school teachers on this theme and their remedy has usually been the encouragement of "worthwhile" movies. But, alas, there are so few "worthwhile" movies, that is movies whose values, sense of proportion, fidelity in detail, caution in the treatment of sex meet the standards of teachers and parents. Those which do have these qualities, too often have also a fault which makes their virtues barren; they are dull. I have been told with distress more than once how, in Zenith City, a worthwhile movie which some women's club or Parent-Teachers' Association had brought had played to empty seats, while some deplorably low-brow opus had filled all the local movie houses. Quite often the public was showing truer taste than its mentors; the "good" movie was an incompetent job; the "bad" one at least did what it set out to do.

Hollywood does distort contemporary American life and mutilate American history. But save in such special *genres* as "musicals," the average Hollywood film does attempt to be pictorially plausible. And as its main audience is American, Hollywood has to give an exterior picture of American life that an American audience will not find ludicrously unlike the real thing. Clothes, houses, cars, furniture, speech have to be at worst prettifications of the real thing. Hollywood still gives a more lifelike picture of America than the British film industry, even before the war, gave of Britain. The boy and girl who is being taught American history in a British school has his mind filled with visual images of American life that are not impossibly remote from reality. The average American may never have seen a gangster, but there are gangsters; he may never have seen a drought, but there are droughts. And it is absurd in such circumstances to pretend that he does not learn something of America (and of American history) even from movies set in contemporary America. It would be wrong, on these grounds, to regret that the pupil may have a more vivid memory of *High Sierra*, or of *Mr. Smith Goes to Washington*, or *The Grapes of Wrath* than of some more formally historical book or picture that he has been forced to study at school. And there is little or no need to excite interest in contemporary America. The movies do that; so do *Life* and *Time*.

But "this is not history"; that is, it is not past history. History is easier (both to teach and to write) when it is dead or when the actors are dead and the movements are classified and the end known. But even for that kind of history, for the study of great events, of great struggles whose end is known, it would be a mistake to ignore the help that can be given by the movies and the futility of ignoring the fact that, if the movies are treated as an enemy, they will be a certainly victorious enemy. The historical movie has often been bad enough in all conscience. Not only has it been comically inaccurate in detail but it has been profoundly unhistorical in theme and spirit. Hollywood has not totally reformed but at any rate its treatment of American history has greatly improved. It is true that Hollywood tends to take over existing best-sellers and best-sellers do not always show much historical sense in plan or writing. But the recent *engouement* of the American reading public with American history has created a market for serious historical novels and Hollywood has benefited thereby. It is true that *Gone With the Wind* still preaches the doctrine of Southern gentility and Yankee rapacity—but *Gone With the Wind* is a model of historical proportion compared with earlier Civil War novels and films and, as a counter to its saccharinity, even Hollywood has not been able to remove all the claws from the script of *Kiss the Boys Good-bye*.

Even the most critical and modernistic minded teacher of American history will not be content with commenting on films and on popular novels. He will need some dominant theme to hold the attention of the intelligent pupil who is not content with a chronological string of unconnected and rather boring facts. It has to be admitted that American political history bores most people; even most Americans bring but a tepid interest to it. Yet some political history is indispensable. We must not confine our teaching programmes to the Revolution, the Civil War and the World War. Nor will it be wise to treat the history of the United States merely as a successful exercise in federalism. All of these things have their relevance but they are only parts of a bigger pattern. That pattern is the territorial and economic growth of the United States.

Basically, American history north and south, like Australian and North and South African history, is the record of the expansion of Europe, of its peoples, languages, civilization into more or less open country. In some regions, North and South Africa, Peru and Mexico, the country was not quite so open. But all colonial expansion has certain characteristics in common and the common themes can be illustrated. The overflow of Europe from the sixteenth century on is the dominating theme of world history. The most striking and important example of that overflow is the United States.

American history, political and constitutional, occurred in space as well as time. Without overdoing the frontier theory, the territorial growth of the United States *is* American history.

"Westward the course of Empire takes its way." Seen from this light, the constitution, the parties, the Civil War, isolationism, the Revolution, all fall into place. Boys who are bored with mere narrative can be stimulated with map-making and there is a lot to be said for asking the geography specialist, when there is one, to take over the teaching of American history. Faced with American history in its more formal character, the pupil may react with no great enthusiasm for taking up his new burden of information. But generations of teachers have discovered (with modified rapture) that there is one theme that holds most boys from play and learning alike. Indians and cowboys are as popular as ever. Even adults of a high degree of sophistication found some of the old magic in *Stagecoach*. The Apache and the Sioux, there is the jam for the pill! The boys may be highly partisan; they may prefer the Indians to the Paleface, *victrix causa*, very rightly, is a theme that does not appeal to youth. But the fact that boys regret the defeat of the Trojans does not make the Iliad bad material for pedagogic art. Tell the boys how the Indians gave way to the frontiersmen and how they, in turn, gave way to the sedentary farmers who, in turn, gave way to the city population. For by that time the wheel will have turned full circle and in the fight between G-men and gangsters, the old theme recurs—with a more even chance for law and order to win sympathy than mere progress had in the story of the Indian wars. On the foundations of geography and Indian lore, how much can be built! George Washington will be no longer merely the intolerably veracious child or the intolerably virtuous man. He can be the youthful adventurer on the frontier who, at an age when in peace-time English boys are thinking of scholarship examinations or school cricket, was commanding on the frontier and firing the first shots in a great war, a very young man more like the heroes of the R.A.F. than like an animated bust.

American history is about roads and boats and railways, great rivers, great deserts, great lakes, explorers, adventurers, bandits. It is more than that, true, but let the boy get the sense of movement, of the march of the English into and through the vast eastern forests to the prairies and the plains, the march north of the Spaniards through the deserts and the mountains, the march south of the Russians over the ice wastes of Alaska; these are the themes that stir the admiration of the young. Once his interest is aroused, the political and constitutional themes can be made relevant and even exciting. And the puzzling and the irritating aspects of some American attitudes to Europe and the world will seem more comprehensible, if not less belated survivals of a once defensible historical tradition. The more thoroughly the boy grasps the truth that American history is profoundly American, that geology and climate play their part as well as *Magna Carta* and the Pilgrim Fathers, the better prepared will he be for an understanding of the American role in the modern world. *Tout comprendre* may not be infallibly followed by *tout pardonner*, but it often will be. And in any case, understanding of so great an historical phenomenon as the United States is a good thing in itself.

XX

THE DECLINE OF BOSTON

(1941)

INDIAN summer in New England is one of the climatic triumphs of the world. In those brief days the sudden glory of the fall foliage makes Brattle Street in Cambridge (where Longfellow lived) and even Sacramento Street (where Howells first lived) seem among the most attractive backgrounds for a poet or a philosopher that the world affords. But the Indian summer is short-lived; the "tremendous storm winds of the equinox" become bitter storms; winter follows and the bare austere landscape seems unfriendly to any rich growth of the human spirit. And the period in the intellectual history of New England that Mr. Van Wyck Brooks describes[1] was, like the Indian summer, short-lived. Long before the first signs of reviving life had aroused the hopes of the literary botanist, long before the terminal date set himself by Mr. Brooks, New England's cultural winter had set in.

In the famous opening chapter of *The Education of Henry Adams* the narrator describes the New England aristocracy to which he belonged in terms of the ancient Jews. To be an Adams, to be a Brooks, was to be as much marked off from the heathen as to have been a Cohen circumcised in the Temple by a High Priest of one's own blood. And it was not only the great families of New England that were thus marked off. The whole region was made by Nature, before it was made by the Puritans, the home of a peculiar people. Geology began what history carried on. Even the fertile valley of the Connecticut River is never far from the bare hills unto which Jonathan Edwards in Northampton or Emily Dickinson in Amherst could so easily, if they wished, lift up their eyes. After the first

---

[1] *New England: Indian Summer, 1865–1915.* By Van Wyck Brooks. Dent. 18s.

great wave of Puritan immigration New England was left
alone. There were newcomers like the Sullivans and Reveres
and Faneuils, but they were few. The same stock, with the
same equipment of blood and traditions, grew from being a
special type of Old Englanders into being New Englanders, in
a region where the special type became the normal type, where
a new climate, a new way of life, new hazards and new fortunes
turned the East Anglian into the Yankee.

In that long historical process it might well seem that the
Yankee was being bred into his type by a process of refrigera-
tion. He became an impressive but not an amiable variant of
the North European transplanted in North America. But
suddenly, just two hundred years after the settlement of the
Massachusetts Bay, the cold, rocky soil put forth fruit and
flowers. The sons of the Puritans, shaken out of their intellectual folkways by the scientific revolution (which Harvard
College had favoured) and by the Kantian revolution which
France passed on in a clarified form, put away the things of
their childhood—or tried to do so. And, for less than a generation, New England flowered: Emerson and Margaret Fuller,
Prescott and Parkman, Holmes and Lowell, Longfellow and
Whittier. It was not a new Periclean or Elizabethan age; but
the flowers were real flowers, they took the winds of March
with beauty—a serious, moral, moralizing beauty, but beauty
nevertheless. The new humane religion of the Unitarians, the
warm and optimistic natural religion of Emerson, these
brought forth fruit and flowers—but only for a generation.

Emerson himself noted that it was the men and women
who had become Unitarians who were productive, who preserved the old moral energy and added to it a less legal, less
shibboleth-ridden view of life. But those who had been born
free were not the men their fathers had been. They had neither
that faith in themselves, nor in New England, nor in the
possibility of remaking humanity that had marked the men of
the generation in which Lyman Beecher was still defending
the old orthodoxy in that Boston church which gave its name
to "Brimstone Corner." A Boston wit had attributed the
decline of the old New England Calvinism to the growth of
the general conviction "that a man who had been born in

Boston had no need to be born again." These were the days when Dr. Holmes could describe, with only half an ironical intention, the true Boston man as one for whom the State House was "the hub of the universe." It was another Boston wit who, less than a generation later, could with even less irony declare that "good Americans when they die, go to Paris." For a region, for a people marked almost as much as the Jews by their religion, it was no light matter that the sap went out of the Unitarians, the missionary spirit out of the orthodox and that the gap was filled by Moody and Sankey, by Mrs. Eddy, by the great Episcopalian preacher Phillips Brooks.

Boston in 1870 was not the home of poets and cranks, of reformers, and fanatics that it had been a generation before; there were many reasons for that: economic, political, historical, demographic. But one was obvious. Boston was no longer a community united by beliefs still held or recently shared and reacted against. It was ceasing to be Jerusalem; it was on its way to being Laodicea. And that change affected and was reflected in a dozen institutions; in Harvard College and the Latin School; in the Athenæum and the State House; as well as in the First Church in Cambridge or in Andover Theological Seminary. The unity of New England, or at any rate of its most vocal section, Massachusetts, was dissolving and soon Yale was to follow Harvard, if at a distance, in an acceptance of the frequent rightness of the outer world, the consequent frequent wrongness of the New England Way. And this is the main theme of Mr. Van Wyck Brooks's elaborate and subtle reconstruction of the cultural history of a region, of a minor nationality, in decline.

Had the decline only affected New England the theme would hardly have been worth the loving care devoted to it by Mr. Brooks. We might conclude that all that New England had to give had been given in the generation between the first proclamations of Emerson and the outbreak of the Civil War. The seed that seemed to have been cast on barren ground had borne fruit after all; but it was not surprising that the ground bore only one crop, that the sowers preferred more fertile soil.

But for American cultural development it was not so

simple. In the vast, sprawling, ebullient, boyish nation, fighting wars and building railroads, still loosely tied together, still living from hand to mouth in all departments of life, the role of New England was, or should have been, the preservation of standards, the insistence on the permanent, the bidding of the American nation take thought for the morrow. It should have protested against the democratic tyranny of King Number in all departments of life, not merely in politics. It was the duty, the special role of the New Englanders, to be the select band of Gideon, not the mere undifferentiated host. And that duty New England performed inadequately and prevented any other region performing it at all. Yet the second fault that can be imputed to New England in this generation, is hardly a fault. Where else could the new nation have looked for that kind of leadership? Not to booming New York or to somnolent and complacent Philadelphia. Not to the Middle West, despite such cases as the Hegelian School in St. Louis. Not to the ruined South.

Mr. Brooks reminds us of the awe in which the culture, the literary achievement of New England was held in other American regions. That reverence sometimes hid itself in jests. New England was a region where almost anybody you met read Sanskrit for relaxation—and, as is made plain here, Sanskrit was almost as much studied in nineteenth-century New England as Hebrew had been in the seventeenth—and studied not only by divines or scholars. But the rest of America did not only laugh at New England, it admired. It was in this period of decline that pilgrims like Hamlin Garland came to see the local Shelleys plain, that outsiders with a sense of the deference due took houses near the great men without daring to accost them. To see Dr. Holmes walk across Boston Common was to re-live the Autocrat's love story. To listen to Bronson Alcott discourse of divine philosophy in Concord was to breathe the air of the great days of *The Dial*. But by the middle of the period that Mr. Brooks has chosen to chronicle, death or infirmity was removing the giants and they were not being replaced. The reverence of the Middle West grew less as each year removed a great traditional figure. It was because Howells had seen and talked to the great, to Holmes and Lowell and

Emerson, that the future President Garfield in Ohio called his farmer neighbours in from the dusk to hear the returned pilgrim tell his story.

It is an episode that does credit to the values of those farmers of the Western Reserve. But then the Western Reserve was a New England colony, a Thurii eagerly awaiting news of Athens. Elsewhere the reverence for the New England achievement was increasingly artificial. In proportion as New England's achievement was racy of its own soil, it was foreign to the experience of the men in the Great Valley, in the fertile lands of Iowa or Illinois, far from the sea, from the rocky shores, from the stony hills that have coloured New England literature to this day. If Old England's landscape and social structure were alien to the experience of New England, so was the landscape, moral and religious as well as geographical, of the Central States to which New England for two generations had been exporting her most vigorous sons and daughters. But more sons than daughters. In all ranks of society the young men went off to seek their fortunes; sometimes with their women, more often without. Yet where a New England woman like Josiah Royce's mother went, even into the Alsatia of early California, she brought with her the standards of New England and, where there were enough of them, the pioneers were tamed.

But the women were even more successful in taming the men who remained behind, in imprinting on New England a feminine character. For New England culture in its post-meridian phase was predominantly a woman's culture. The most remarkable purely literary figure is a woman, Emily Dickinson; the most characterful of the characters is a woman, Mrs. Jack Gardner. It is not proven beyond all reasonable doubt that feminine dominance in these matters is a bad thing. There is a case for the Hôtel de Rambouillet. But the feminine domination of the intellectual life of New England went further than any civilizing of the uncouth genius in a *salon* or a special grace given to the language by a woman of genius. The age of Louis XIV. is not the age of Madame de Sévigné. Even Marcel's grandmother would hardly have thought that. But this Indian Summer was a woman's age in too many ways.

Mr. Van Wyck Brooks does not now feel so bitterly about this as when he wrote *The Ordeal of Mark Twain.* As Mr. Max Eastman has shown, Mark Twain's reverence for the society of that New England colony, Elmira, was not without justification. And both Henry Adams and W. D. Howells have testified to the fascination exercised over them by the American, especially by the New England, women of this generation; they were more interesting, better worth study, better worth commemoration than the men. Whether that judgment was just or not, that it could be so confidently passed was significant. Yet a generation later Mr. Marquand makes of the Boston women the symbol of the sterilization of the spirit.

Of course, not all the successful cultural enterprises were dominated by women; they did not dominate the Boston Museum, for instance, or the Massachusetts Historical Society. And it was a man, a distinguished soldier before he became a great banker, who provided Boston with its great orchestra. A symphony concert, with its faithful and zealous audience, sitting under a series of foreign conductors, listening to foreign music and foreign performers, as their ancestors had listened to Mathers and Emersons and Channings expounding the New England Way in terms of the logic of Petrus Ramus, was as near a representative of a cultural town-meeting as modern Boston could provide. Yet the music was as much an exotic as the Græco-Roman statues in the niches above. The Boston of Henry Lee Higginson was an importer of music, but the Boston of the great age had been an exporter of literature and ideas. It was now barely self-sufficient and its diet too often planned according to feminine tastes. It was always wholesome; it was often good; it was seldom delicious. The men were the Marthas, building, banking, emigrating, researching. The arts were accomplishments that fell to the Marys.

In a *rentier* society (as the upper class society of New England increasingly became) the women, as inheritors of wealth less likely to dissipate it than are men, had the economic as well as the social power to impose their standards. Culture in the sense of knowledge, of information useful for social purposes, useful for providing social hurdles that the newcomers could not jump, in a large measure replaced culture as a freeing of the spirit. It became backward-looking; the development of something learned at school or college; it became conservative and timid.

The result was not only bad in New England; it was bad all over the United States, where such things were left to the women, they were an ancillary to the social position of the wife of a successful man. Mr. Brooks notes how the changed economic position of Boston reacted on the spirit of the city. The transfer of the headquarters of the Cunard Line from Boston to New York was a symptom of a decline that affected more than the port. Boston was becoming a backwater. And the rest of New England was no better; Hartford, the only rival to Boston, was even more a *rentier* city; wild dreams and intellectual innovation do not flourish in a society whose main business is life insurance. It is not accidental that it has been with the second industrial revolution in New England, with the rise to dominance of the specialized machine industries, that New England in our days has again felt the breath of new life. Hartford is now a centre of the aircraft industry, the home of engineers as well as actuaries. And if rural New England now has a fresh crop of poets, of critics, of statesmen, it is in part because the long retreat of rural New Hampshire and Vermont ended in this century. The dairy farmers, the growers of Christmas trees, the men who have turned the tide in regions that seemed doomed to certain death a generation ago, have provided the minimum of healthy community life that a flourishing, non-elegiac literature needs.

The comparative sluggishness of New England life in this age was the necessary accompaniment of the nationalization of New England. The arrival of the Middle Westerner, Howells, to take over the inheritance of the *Atlantic Monthly*, like his later departure for New York, was symbolic. Henry James in Boston, like Henry Adams in Washington, illustrated the nationalizing of American life. It was the North British Railway, as much as anything else, that turned Edinburgh into a museum rather than a living creative capital. And neither Scottish nor New England cultural patriotism was lively enough, or had enough conviction of valuable difference, to make the fight against London and New York anything but a long rearguard action.

Mr. Brooks does his gallant best with the names of John Boyle O'Reilly and Louise Imogen Guiney, but in this period the forces that were making of New England, New Ireland, New France, New Italy were with hardly any effect on the formal intellectual life of the region. If, by a New England culture, we mean a literature and an art representing the ideas and experience of a society, the watered-down eclectic Puritan culture, flavoured by European sauces, could not mean much to a largely Catholic population. It is only in this generation that some kind of synthesis has begun to appear. Until that had been begun, New England culture, as far as it was set off from the total American culture, was bound to be increasingly dry and backward-looking. The failure of Maurice Barrès to make of his "Lorraine" more than a machine for his political and literary projects, was due to his ignoring of the real Lorraine of steel and ore. To think of New England in terms of Beacon Street and Harvard and Concord to the exclusion of Fall River and Holy Cross College was as doomed an undertaking as to think of Lorraine in terms of the Place Stanislas and Domrémy. It was worse, for Barrès was a more sensitive and more critical artist than, for the most part, were the defenders of the New England tradition.

Yet although the story told by Mr. Brooks is of a society increasingly cut off from its soil, obstinately refusing to come to terms with the real New England around it, it is not the whole story of New England—even as a culture. Long before Boston produced men of imaginative genius, it produced scholars and scientists. And in this Harvard and Yale and the other New England colleges were custodians of the oldest New England cultural tradition. President Eliot may have had unfortunately democratic ideas of the equal value of all academic studies. But the Harvard of the great lawyer, Thayer, of the great mathematical philosopher, Peirce, of the great chemist Richards, of William James, of Josiah Royce, was both a true *studium generale* and a very pure representative of the New England tradition. More Aristotelian than Platonic, more impressive than charming, it was the great achievement of the

Brahmin caste and of the community which, within a few years of its establishment in the wilderness, had set up a college.

And it was not only in science and scholarship that New England showed how far from decadent she was. If there was no Webster and if the Adams family ran to brilliant explanations of impotence rather than to positive political achievement, Senator Hoar and Speaker Reed were worthy of Massachusetts and her daughter Maine. And in one great figure the nationalizing of New England and her continuing gift of character and mental toughness to the nation were both exemplified. If the Boston here described was in 1865 "Dr. Holmes's Boston," the best of New England, its courage, its freedom, its sense of style in life and language found their exemplar in Dr. Holmes's son. And in his own life the young soldier, proud of ancestry, who became the great judge, the great citizen, the great man, showed that necessary adaption of the best of the old traditions to the necessities of the new life of New England and of the Union. That acceptance of the whole of life which Emerson's generation had preached, he practised. The society that produced Justice Holmes was not without its justification, and only New England, more specifically only Boston and Harvard, could have produced him or a score of original, if less famous, men.

XXI

THE WORDS OF PRESIDENT ROOSEVELT [1]

(1942)

THE publication of the papers and speeches, "The Works," of leading American politicians is one of the national traditions. There are not only editions of the papers of great statesmen which, like the Nicolay and Hay edition of Lincoln's "Works" or the Charles Francis Adams edition of the "Works" of John Adams, are themselves monuments in the history of American historiography. There are, too, elaborate editions of the "Works" of eminent politicians who, like Clay and Webster, never reached the White House; and there is even an edition of the writings of James Buchanan, whom his successor as head of the Democratic Party and President of the United States uses here as the classical horrible example of a President too infirm in purpose, too legalistically minded, to carry out in more than the barren letter, his oath to "preserve, protect and defend the Constitution of the United States." But it is rare, indeed unprecedented, for a President in office to sponsor his own "Works." For this great series is not to be compared with a comparatively brief collection of papers like "The Hoover Administration" of Messrs. Myers and Newton. That apologia for an ill-starred Administration was more like a traditional campaign tract than is the enterprise, magnificent in scale and elaborate in execution, of which the second series of four, unlike the first series of five volumes, is now made available to British readers.

---

[1] *The Public Papers and Addresses of Franklin D. Roosevelt.* With a Special Introduction and Explanatory Notes by President Roosevelt. In four volumes. 1937 Volume: The Constitution Prevails. 1938 Volume: The Continuing Struggle for Liberalism. 1939 Volume: War—and Neutrality. 1940 Volume: War—and Aid to Democracies. Macmillan. £6, 6s. set of four volumes.

The plan of the series is admirably designed to make the volumes available to the common reader, the student and the publicist. It is not merely a matter of making easy the "index lore that turns no student pale." Cross-references, classified lists, elaborate annotations make all readers in debt to Judge Rosenman, who compiled and arranged the material. And the material is of every kind that could reasonably be expected to be covered by the words "public papers." There are great formal statements like the inaugural address of 1937; there are special messages to Congress; there are diplomatic documents like the letters to Hitler; there are messages to all sorts of societies, to festive bodies of Irishmen and harassed bodies of Jews, to the organizers of Scout jamborees and to great and good neighbours like the jubilating Dominion of Canada. There are reports on special activities of the Federal Government and similar documents of the type familiar to users of Richardson's "Messages and Papers of the Presidents." Here is richness. But it is not only the richness of the varied subjects dealt with, it is the richness of the man who wrote and spoke these messages. And the impression of one guiding, powerful, nearly tireless leader of men is made more powerful, almost, by the characteristic notes contributed by the President than it is by the documents so annotated.

These notes are material for the future biographer and for the present historian. They are *ex parte* statements, but *ex parte* statements are among the most important materials of history. Of equal interest are the introductions to each of the volumes. These are more formal statements and defences of presidential policy and action. "Defences" is, indeed, hardly the word to use; they are reiterations of presidential convictions on more or less controversial subjects and appraisements of the degree of success which the President has had in putting his policy into effect. They are, with the notes, a kind of serial Monumentum Ancyranum, less complacent but not less valuable than the Roman prototype.

The most novel documents printed here are the transcripts of the interchanges between the President and the reporters at the famous press conferences. As is or should be widely known, President Roosevelt, by an even bolder innovation than Wilson's addressing Congress in person, has made these conferences something like question time in the House of Commons. Of course the differences are great. He is addressing not members of a body to which he belongs and of which he is the servant as well as the leader, but a body of employees, of unofficial persons, employees who are, for the moment, his guests. Not all that is said at the conferences is for publication in any form, and some of it is only to be published without direct quotation. But the role of the press conferences in giving the American people a constant feeling of being intimately informed of the designs and achievements of the President must rank second only to the presidential development of the potentialities of radio in creating that more perfect union between leader and led which has been so healthy a side of American political life since 1933. The informality and the unofficial character of the press conferences extend to more than the membership. It is not customary in the House of Commons to ask questions about the Prime Minister's teeth, or, even when the source of the question is feminine, to reply "Oh, judge for yourself, sweetness!" But the range of questions asked and answered, the give and take of journalist and Chief Executive, the light cast on the workings of the Presidential system, make these records of the greatest interest and value. Unfortunately, they are just the part of the volumes where the English common reader will most miss a little editorial help. He will not know that Senator Sherman Minton was Administration Whip or that the *Star* is the great Washington evening paper, or even that Senator Vandenberg's "given name" is Arthur. But he will be able fully to appreciate the continuous testing of presidential quickness, acuteness and parliamentary skill that is a part of the system—and to have a more intelligent pride in the fact that in his one experience of this ordeal by question, Mr. Churchill proved himself as much a master as his host. It is these records that the future biographer will prize the most.

The most remarkable and characteristic of the introductions does not deal with foreign affairs at all but with the great issue of the role and powers of the Supreme Court. On no policy of the Roosevelt administration was opinion more bitterly divided; no proposal coming from the White House in modern times has been more violently received. One must go back to Lincoln's proclamation of Emancipation and Jackson's veto of the new charter of the Bank of the United States to find a parallel for the boldness of Presidential action and the violence of opposition to it. As may be remembered, the President proposed, in addition to many more technical reforms in federal procedure, that, for every justice of the Supreme Court who attained the age of seventy, had served for "ten years continuously or otherwise" and who did not resign, an additional justice should be appointed, although the total additions to the Court should not raise the number from the present nine to more than fifteen. In short, the President, as his enemies put it, proposed to "pack the court."

If that was the Presidential plan, it was not without provocation. According to Mr. Dooley, the "supreem coort follows th' iliction returns." But that was in the remote days of the Insular Cases. In more recent times the Court had notably failed to follow or even to notice the election returns. The Court had struck down nearly all the New Deal legislation, and in the Court itself the action of the majority had provoked protests from the minority marked by an unjudicial candour which is rare in that exalted atmosphere. Justice (now Chief Justice) Stone reminded his brethren that "Courts are not the only agency of government that must be assumed to have capacity to govern. Congress and the Courts unhappily may falter or be mistaken in the performance of their constitutional duty." And Justices Stone, Brandeis and Cardozo did not hide their opinion that it was the Court and not the Congress that was faltering or being mistaken. What the dissident justices said, was said more vehemently by other eminent lawyers and the unstatesmanlike rashness of the majority was resented by prudent conservatives who wished the Court to remember the counsel of John Marshall that "it is a *constitution* we are expounding." But the proposal to recognize that the Court *was* a political body, and that the accident which had filled it and kept it filled with the representatives of a political and economic order which the march of events and the will of the American people had condemned could not be allowed to delay for an unknown period the implementing of the mandate given to the President by the voters, was shocking to a reverent people. Some way round the constitutional obstacle must be found, but not that way. And so the President's Bill was defeated in a Senate in which his party held three-fourths of the seats. But while the controversy was going on, while the stream of witnesses, more or less expert, with testimonies more or less relevant, poured through the Senate's committee-room, the Court did listen—or so the vulgar thought. It reversed itself. It accepted legislation whose difference from the legislation it had condemned was invisible to the lay eye, and, with statesmanlike courage, it even openly reversed its not too recent past in casting overboard the doctrines of *Adkins* v. *Children's Hospital.*

The President had lost the battle but had won the campaign. So the man in the street said; and so the President believes. More still, death and retirement gave him the chance to put on the bench Judges who thought with him concerning the commonwealth. On the Court to-day only one member, Justice Roberts, does not owe his present position to Mr. Roosevelt. It was Justice Roberts who by his change of position enabled the Court to reverse itself—and it was Justice Roberts whom the President, with the approval of the American people, so recently chose to head the investigation into the disaster at Pearl Harbour.

Another man than President Roosevelt might have been content with his substantial victory. But it was noticed during the Court fight that he "had his Dutch up," that all his immensely combative temperament was engaged. So the introduction to the 1937 volume fights the battle over again. There are minor confessions of error in tactics. The President regrets that in his initial message he did not state frankly that his aim was not merely to improve the technical efficiency of the Court. "I made one major mistake when I first presented the plan. I did not place enough emphasis upon the real mischief—the kind of decisions which, as a studied and continued policy, had been coming down from the Supreme Court. I soon corrected that mistake in the speeches which I later made about the plan." He did, indeed, and one Democratic Senator returning

home from Washington, primed with iron resolution to oppose
the Bill to the death, found that the wife of his bosom had been
converted by the arguments used by the President in one of
the most skilful of his "fireside chats."

The President defends his refusal to accept any compromise by declaring that no compromise which would both
have had any real effect and could have been enacted, was ever
proposed to him. He is ready to rejoice openly in what Mr.
Robert Jackson, one of the two persons consulted in the
making of the "Court plan," has called "a retreat to the Constitution" by the Court. But we may surmise that, however
sincere the President's rejoicing over the change in the tone
and in the personnel of the Court, he still regrets that the
issue was not settled on a basis of principle, not of persons.
For to quote the most skilled legal servant of the New Deal,
now himself a Justice of the Supreme Court, "the Court has
renounced no power and has been subjected to no new limitation. The effect of the attack was exemplary and disciplinary,
and perhaps temporary." The President may well agree with
Mr. Justice Jackson. Whether he does or not, he is too much
of a fighter to make appeasement an internal or external policy,
or to admit error in anything but tactics. Mr. Dooley defended
the ebullient self-satisfaction of Theodore Roosevelt by saying
that no man who bore a grudge against himself would ever be
Governor of New York. And no man anxious to placate his
enemies or critics could have been elected President of the
United States three times, or inspire in Hitler and his jackals
the hate and fear that is inspired by Mr. Roosevelt. At such a
moment it matters little that the Dictionary of American Biography does not support Mr. Roosevelt's belief that the chief
maker of the Constitution, James Madison, was not a lawyer
or that the interpretation given by him to the phrase "promote
the general welfare" in the preamble to the Constitution, is not
universally accepted. The law, like the Constitution (and the
Presidency), is a servant of "We, the People of the United
States," and the People is endangered by more formidable
enemies than doubtful glosses on legal terms.

Although the main theme of the first two volumes is home
policy and of the last two foreign policy, the interweaving of

the two themes is constant from 1937 to 1940. The President had no hesitation in commending his domestic policy by calling attention to the lesson of the collapse of democratic Governments abroad. On April 14, 1938, he told the nation in a fireside chat that "if by democratic methods people get a Government strong enough to protect them from fear and starvation their democracy succeeds; but if they do not they grow impatient. Therefore, the only sure bulwark of continuing liberty is a Government strong enough to protect the interests of the people and well enough informed to maintain its sovereign control of its Government." But the power of any Government to do its duty by its own people was limited by the pressure on it of external events. On October 5, 1937, in his famous "quarantine" speech at Chicago, the President had stated this truth:

> The peace, the freedom and the security of 90 per cent. of the population of the world is being jeopardized by the remaining 10 per cent., who are threatening a breakdown of all international order and law.

And a few days later, in a fireside chat, the President declared: "Nor can we view with indifference the destruction of civilized values throughout the world. We seek peace, not only for our generation but also for the generation of our children." But the American people was not yet ready to follow the President as fast and as far as he wished to lead it. The so-called "Ludlow amendment," which would have made it impossible for the United States to declare war until after a referendum, was soon to darken counsel. The President himself, under pressure from Europe, as is explained in what is almost an apologetic note, had prevented the purchase of arms by the Spanish Government. If not in vain, then with less than the deserved measure of success, the President warned the American people in his speech at Kingston, Ontario, that "We in the Americas are no longer a faraway continent, to which the eddies of controversies beyond the seas could bring no interest or harm." And with a true appreciation of the incapacity of the American people to control its generosity of heart, he went on: "We cannot prevent our people on either side of the border from having an opinion in regard to wanton brutality, in regard to

II

undemocratic regimentation, in regard to misery inflicted on helpless peoples, or in regard to violations of accepted individual rights." This was one reason—though not the only or the main reason—why the "realist" policy of Messrs. Lindbergh and Nye was impossible. The defenders of this policy were, by the event, to be pushed, no matter how "liberal," how "radical" their origins and intentions, into the position of apologists for tyranny, as well as preachers of national blindness.

In Volumes III. and IV. the main theme is one well known to us. We have here the story of the unavailing attempt to get the Neutrality Acts of 1935 and 1937 amended while their amendment would still have some deterrent force. And we are shown Senators, some of them still living and still talking, whose sense of the times in which they were living was as inadequate as was that of President Buchanan in 1858–61. With the outbreak of war in Europe, the sense of doom—and of intelligent, courageous and foresighted leadership—increases. The "good neighbour" policy in Latin America, the increase in the defence programme, the beginning of the transformation of the United States into the "arsenal of democracy" are seen here in high-lighted detail, in new perspectives. There are not merely great moments like the Charlottesville speech in which the assassination of France by the imitator of the venal *condottieri* of the worst Italian traditions, was for ever stigmatized in terms worthy of the crime. There is the record of the day-to-day movement of American political opinion, revealed in the Presidential campaign as well as in Congress and in the Press. By the end of Volume IV. the President has received the unprecedented honour of a third term, and the way is prepared for the enactment of "Lease-Lend" and the realization by the Axis that the United States would not permit the destruction of freedom in the world, since only in a world in which other peoples were free could the Americans themselves remain free.

There is one special message, sent on a formal occasion but of poignant interest to-day. On August 1, 1937, the monument to the American dead at Montfauçon was dedicated in presence of a gathering that included the President of the French Republic, the American Ambassador, General Pershing—and

Marshal Pétain. To that gathering President Roosevelt spoke by radio. And in words that are an ironical commentary on Vichy, though not on France, the President of the United States recalled to his own and the French people the great, traditional link that bound them.

> Though the seas divide us, the people of France and the people of the United States find union to-day in common devotion to the ideal which the memorial at Montfauçon symbolizes. That ideal, to which both nations bear faithful witness, is the ideal of freedom—under democracy, liberty attained by government founded in democratic institutions. . . . France is carrying on in the tradition of a great civilization, a civilization with which our own culture has had full communion from our very beginnings as a nation. We, of this country, have not forgotten nor could we ever forget the aid given us by France in the dark days of the American Revolution. Our historic friendship finds apt expression in the quotation from a letter which Washington wrote to Rochambeau, and which is inscribed on the base of our monument to the great Frenchman: "We have been contemporaries and fellow-labourers in the cause of liberty, and we have lived together as brothers should do, in harmonious friendship." . . . All of the past speaks to us in the living present, and out of the shadows of a thousand years emerge the glory and the achievement which are France.

And turning, as Lincoln had done, to the dead buried on the battlefield, the President prayed that no cloud should fall on the friendship of the two republics.

> In their name, for their sake, I pray God no hazard of the future may ever dissipate or destroy that common ideal. I greet the Republic of France, firm in the confidence that a friendship as old as the American nation will never be suffered to grow less.

That friendship between the nations survives; but the American people, no matter what reasons of policy govern the actions of the State Department, will not willingly give to the men who have abolished the very name of the Republic and who trample on the body of liberty with what energy their years permit, the disposition of the assets accumulated by Rochambeau and Lafayette.

There is an immediate, obvious and important connection between the two main themes of this book. It was not merely as a prudent administrator of the executive Government of the United States, concerned to see that no harm befall the commonwealth, that President Roosevelt saw in Nazi-ism a menace to the American way of life, while less far-sighted politicians in the United States and in Britain saw in the policy of Hitler's Germany a mere matter of internal concern and hoped, perhaps unconsciously, that the paranoiac brutality of the régime would exhaust its malice and glut its appetite on the Jewish and other victims of the rebirth of the autochthonous Teutonic tradition. But as the custodian of the American political tradition, as the official successor of Jefferson and Jackson, both as President and as head of the Democratic Party, Mr. Roosevelt could not but see in the Nazi madness a menace to the peace and liberty of the American people.

Over a century before, Jefferson had rejoiced that in America "the mass of mankind has not been born with saddles on their backs, nor a favoured few booted and spurred, ready to ride them legitimately by the grace of God." All over Europe in the succeeding century the naïve legitimist doctrine here condemned had been in retreat. But when the victory appeared won the heresy re-emerged from the caves ten times more odious and more dangerous as the right of a *Herrenvolk*, in Europe and Asia, to dominate and exploit the inferior people not chosen by God to rule. The reversal of the apparent course of history was so sudden, so ominous, that it was natural, in America as here, that millions of the led, hundreds of the normal leaders, should have shut their eyes to the terrible truth. But President Roosevelt did not shut his eyes, and little by little, with infinite tact and patience, he opened the eyes of others.

But it was because he had not been a sayer of smooth things when he spoke of domestic troubles, because he had not feared to carry the battle, with all his energy, to the enemies of his view of the good life, of the essential American tradition, that the run-of-the-mill American, however slow to grasp the full meaning, the full weight of the President's warnings, never took seriously the propaganda that made of those warnings mere rhetorical exercises by a baffled politician. The comic implausibility of the Berlin picture of the President as the agent of plutocracy, as the spokesman of the money-changers, frustrated a propaganda campaign that otherwise might have told.

To represent President Roosevelt as the mere defender of

the *status quo*, as the champion of vested economic interest, as the timid conserver of a dying economic and political order, was, except for the doped victims of the Goebbels machine, merely to waste ink and breath. And the recent rage of the Führer is noisy if not eloquent testimony to the German recognition of that failure. For all its faults, for all its inadequacies, for all its empiricism, the domestic policy of the Roosevelt administration was the essential foundation, inside the United States and out of it, for the trust of the weak, the oppressed, the disinherited in the spokesman of democracy. For him and for them it was not a mere instrument of government but a way of life.

Jefferson ended his contrast between the free American and the tyrannically ruled European peoples with words that in our own day have become inspiringly prophetic: "These are grounds of hope for others." In these four volumes the grounds of that hope for all the peoples of the world are made plain, and in that hope, here expressed in so many varied forms, the United Nations will fight and conquer. The nations "shall have a new birth of freedom" and this world must be what, in his message to Hitler on the eve of Munich, Mr. Roosevelt declared that the American people wished it to be, "a world of neighbours." In that phrase the American frontier experience of common co-operative effort under law found its expression. To the making of such a world possible the immense strength of the United States, under the uncontested leadership of the preacher and practiser of the policy of good neighbourliness, is now dedicated.

XXII

HOLMES AND POLLOCK[1]

(1942)

SIR JOHN POLLOCK tells us that on one occasion Andrew Lang attempted to score off the eminent lawyer who was still Oliver Wendell Holmes, junior. "So you are the son of the celebrated Oliver Wendell Holmes." "No," replied Holmes promptly, "he was my father." It would have surprised many of the Bostonians who took pride in Dr. Holmes's pride in them, to think that the younger Holmes would live even longer than his father, and, towards the end of his days, be as great a figure in all the United States as his father had been in New England. For by the time Justice Holmes retired from the Supreme Court, he was America's Grand Old Man, known not only as a great judge but as a great character, as the embodiment of the Yankee virtues, a living reminder that they were not the narrow, prudent, unattractive things that Calvin Coolidge had made them appear to be. Holmes would never have said or thought that "the business of the United States is business." Business was not the main business of any man or nation, and the law was business, part of the man but far from being the whole man. And it was characteristic of him that in the great professional and national celebration of his ninetieth birthday, he described his role on the bench as "a little finishing canter before coming to a standstill." It was round the perpetual youth of Holmes that legend wove its tales, some of them none the less admiring for being ribald. He did right to quote "Copa": "Death plucks my ear and says, 'Live, I am coming.'"

---

[1] *The Pollock-Holmes Letters.* Correspondence of Sir Frederick Pollock and Mr. Justice Holmes, 1874–1932. Edited by Mark De Wolfe Howe. With an Introduction by Sir John Pollock. In Two Volumes. Cambridge University Press. 36s. net.

In considering this remarkable correspondence, it is not unjust to begin by stressing the share of Holmes. He was not a greater lawyer than Pollock, not perhaps as great. (That is for his brethren learned in the law to say.) Nor was it that he was concerned directly in great causes that Pollock only saw from the stage-box of the jurisconsult. Pollock was deeply concerned in at least two great legal-political problems, the Venezuela case and the abdication legislation of 1936. And the Pollock clan was deep in the fight over the Prayer-book, a fight that naturally interested the grandson of the Rev. Abiel Holmes and the son of the author of the "*One-Hoss Shay*." Pollock was a fencer, a traveller, no cloistered bookworm. Yet the dominant impression of the correspondence is that of a duologue between the man of action in life and the law and the scholar who, from time to time, issues forth into the world of action where exactness, scholarship, the prudent reserve of the man who knows how much is still in doubt are rather a handicap.

It is inevitable and right that most of these two volumes should be devoted to law and lawyers. Holmes and Pollock were men, wits, scholars, but they were soaked in the law. And so we have discussions of cases in which Holmes, as Chief Justice of Massachusetts or as Associate Justice of the Supreme Court of the United States, discusses what he and his brethren have done well or ill, where he and Pollock comment on the doings and misdoings of the most august courts of England and the United States (and, in one case, of Scotland). As they exchange highly critical views of some eminent judges, the reader is tempted at times to think of Bowen's amendment of the address to the Queen that began "Conscious as we are of our unworthiness" to "Conscious as we are of each other's unworthiness." But there is nothing smug or complacent in the criticism of the House of Lords or the Supreme Court. And there is not too much of that appetite for praise which the elder Holmes admitted to in himself, and noted (as a naturalist) in all other authors. Holmes and Pollock could continue to differ on contract to the end of their long lives without thereby quarrelling, or failing to purr agreeably when stroked by a skilled and friendly hand on the other side of the Atlantic.

Agreeing on the importance and the fascination of the law, Holmes and Pollock yet approached it in different attitudes. In Pollock, far more than in Holmes, there is a passion for legal elegance, consistency and depth. Holmes is continually expressing his admiration for his friend's never-failing erudition, but he shows no signs of reproaching himself for a comparative lack of it. As he told Pollock, his closest friend on the Supreme Court, Louis Brandeis, in vain tried to get him to improve his mind, that is to fill it with the mass of sociological facts that were meat and drink to the author of the great brief in *Muller v. Oregon*. But Holmes determinedly went his own way; he did not need an immense apparatus of learning, legal or general, to apply the few general principles that were his constitutional doctrine. He could make a legal distinction with the best of them, but he was not obsessed with the importance of deciding every case that came before the Supreme Court as though all the future of human or American happiness depended on it. In the Herbertianly named case of *Haddock v. Haddock*, he began his dissent with very characteristic words: "I do not suppose that civilization will come to an end whichever way this case is decided." (Characteristically, again, Holmes regretted that he had "only succeeded in irritating" Justice White, whereas he had only written his dissent to modify "White's mode of putting the case.")

It was against another type of legal solemnity, the hangover of Puritan prejudice, that Holmes protested much later, when he upheld the right of the New York legislature to control the theatre-ticket brokers, the "ticket-scalpers" of New York City. Mr. Justice Sutherland had laid it down that "it may be true, as asserted, that among the Greeks amusement and instruction of the people through the drama was one of the duties of government. But certainly no such duty devolves upon any American Government." It was the son of Dr. Holmes, the fellow-Bostonian of Tom Appleton, who replied. "It seems to me that theatres are as much devoted to public use as anything well can be. We have not that respect for art that is one of the glories of France. But to many people the superfluous is the necessary, and it seems to me that Government does not go beyond its sphere in attempting to make life livable for them."

In the popular, though not in the professional reputation of Holmes, he was pre-eminently a "liberal" in the American sense of the term. There was, of course, truth in the public identification of Holmes with liberty. But there was not much truth in the identification of Holmes with liberalism, in the sense it has acquired in modern American usage. He was no great believer in the power of the State to remedy the results of economic inequality. Indeed, he was impatient with Socialist argument that thought it had made a decisive point when it pointed to the fantastic inequalities of income that the industrialization of the United States had made a commonplace. Holmes had no more admiration for some of the mere robber barons than had most critically minded Americans. But he thought that some of the magnates, James J. Hill, for instance, the great railroad entrepreneur, had earned their fortunes, that the commonwealth had gained far more from their enterprise than they had taken as their price. To make things difficult for future Hills was not wisdom, it was sentimentality. And even where the inequality of fortune had no such pragmatic justification, its effect on the social structure was not serious enough to justify so much anguish of mind and so much legislative interference as it provoked in many of Holmes's admirers. What serious harm did such inequalities of fortune do? This was a question he asked again and again. At a time when conservative critics in the United States were lumping Holmes and Brandeis as the great twin brethren who were making the way plain for the destruction of economic freedom in the United States, Holmes preserved his sceptical preference for the existing social order. So it was natural that he should have sympathized with one of the theses in Mr. E. S. P. Haynes's *The Decline of Liberty in England* (it is not pointed out by the editor that this book was written by a close kinsman of Sir Frederick Pollock and so had other claims on Holmes's attention). "The whole collectivist tendency seems to be towards underrating or forgetting the safeguards in bills of rights that had to be fought for in their day and that are still worth fighting for."

But the name of the sender of *The Decline of Liberty* suggests one answer to the problem of why conservative

Americans did not see that Holmes was as much, or more, a conservative than they were. It was Mr. H. J. Laski, not Sir Frederick Pollock, who had sent the book, and from the moment that the young Harvard instructor appears on the Holmes side of the correspondence, the faculty, the almost superhuman Holmesian faculty, of admiring the author while being totally unconverted by his views, is fully displayed.

Holmes and Pollock both devoted time to persuading the other of the merits of men and books that for some reason were more visible on one side of the Atlantic than the other. With Pollock it was naturally books rather than men. With some exceptions (like Shadworth Hodgson, whom Pollock may have encountered during his tenure of his chair at Corpus Christi College, Oxford) Pollock was content to state the merits of the doctrine rather than of the author. But Holmes did not separate a man from his books, if any light on the books was cast by the personality of their maker. Brooks Adams could not be understood merely through his books, neither could the author of *Authority in the Modern State*. Only a book-hunter with a scent for the hidden rarity could take so much interest in doctrines for which he had no native sympathy. And so Professor Laski adds himself to the team of persons determined to get Holmes to improve his mind by extending his reading.

In fact, of course, Holmes's mind was remarkably well filled. He might hesitate to test the judgment of his friend Canon Sheehan of Doneraile on the merits of Suarez and reserve judgment on the merits of the Canon's own novels, but he was remarkably willing to try anything, any author or doctrine, once. The efforts of Pollock to get him to estimate more highly the merits of the classical authors had this measure of success. Holmes re-read them, but still thought that classical simplicity was merely a polite phrase for a rather boring naïvety. Thus Holmes was delighted with the President of Corpus's *Greek Genius and its Meaning to Us*. "It puts more forcibly and strikingly what one knew in a general way. . . . The book is delightful. I would rather read it than Plato, but I frankly prefer the modern straight through." Pollock was more orthodox in his literary tastes, although there is at least one indication that he did not apply to the classics that he knew so well the rigorous standards of scholarship that he expected from editors of Year Books or Reports.

The same difference of temperament and taste is to be seen in their respective approaches to philosophy. Holmes and Pollock did not differ very deeply, but Pollock had more patience with the efforts of the too ambitious philosopher than had Holmes. He had, too, more dialectical acuteness (which was perhaps simply a fruit of his greater patience). Holmes disliked attempts at making the universe more emotionally tolerable such as he thought he detected at the basis of William James's preaching of the power of faith. He saw in James his Irish blood leading him into preposterous positions, and he greatly preferred, at any rate in reasonably small dozes, the unfaith of Santayana. But each new doctrine, Russell and Whitehead, Bergson and Bradley, are fit themes for men who held Holmes's view that "the chief end of man is to frame general propositions and that no general proposition is worth a d——"

The exchange of views and news of books was not confined to those which formally treated great themes of public import. But it is worth noting that the author of the great dissent in *Lochner v. New York* had a high opinion of Herbert Spencer, although later he did not approve of the action of his brethren in legislating him into the fourteenth amendment. Holmes read Marx, but he also read Proudhon—or about Proudhon. He enjoyed P. G. Wodehouse, and he tried, without much visible success, to "sell" George Ade and Milt Gross to Pollock.

Holmes's indifference to that Bostonian sexual prudery which was and is notorious in the rest of the United States, was one of his claims to popular fame. And although the best joke of the type that it has been agreed to call Rabelaisian in these volumes is Pollock's suggested address to Ferdinand of Bulgaria on his assumption of the title of Tsar, there is abundant evidence that Holmes's own reputation was not wholly apocryphal. It is in character that he took much more pleasure in reading *Colette en ménage* than in reading *L'Education sentimentale*. "There is humour of a sort not usual in French books. Well, to be civilized is to be potentially master of all possible ideas." But his taste was too good not to notice the difference in quality in what had gone out under the name of Willy in this case and in *Jeux de Prince*, which Holmes had hoped would be improper, but had found too tedious to read. Here Holmes was his uncle's nephew, for John Holmes used "to smoke 5 cent cigars for fear that his taste should become too refined."

On one side of life, this correspondence shows Pollock to more advantage or, at least, more fully, than it does Holmes. Both were interested in public affairs, but, whether Holmes preferred not to write on them or felt that it was unbecoming in a member of the Supreme Court to give his opinions on them, there are far better materials for commentary on history, in its usual sense, in Pollock's letters than in Holmes's. Holmes does tell a characteristic story of Theodore Roosevelt's anger at his vote in the Northern Securities case, and it may be fairly surmised that he was not an admirer of Woodrow Wilson, but in the main the reader is left to infer Holmes's views from Pollock's letters. This is not very satisfactory. For example, it seems unlikely that whatever views Holmes held on the Sacco-Vanzetti case, they were as simple as those set out by Pollock. Pollock saw the hand of Moscow everywhere; Holmes may have seen it too, but he must have seen in the making of the problem something of Massachusetts procedure and of the temperament of Judge Webster Thayer, as well as a Communist stunt. And even if Holmes shared Pollock's contempt for Wilson, he might have set-off against the President's alleged ingratitude to Elihu Root and William Howard Taft, the power of sophistry which enabled those eminent lawyers and unreconstructed Republicans to persuade themselves, and a large number of well-meaning Americans, that the way to get the United States into the League of Nations was to vote for Warren Gamaliel Harding.

On one great problem of the last twenty years, Holmes had strong views. He disliked reading about war and especially about the Civil War, in which he had taken a distinguished part. But the old Adam stirred in Colonel Holmes, not merely forcing him to defend the tactical knowledge of General Sumner at Antietam against the criticisms of Pollock, but to dislike the questioning of the value of patriotism and the writing-off of the claims of war as a solver of otherwise insoluble historical problems. As he grew older Holmes grew even better looking and there remained to the end something pre-eminently military, something Gascon, in that moustache and that spare soldierly figure. "He may be a better lawyer than I am, but I was a d—d sight better soldier," so the legend runs, he commented on the criticisms of an eminent jurist who had attained Holmes's military rank behind a Washington desk in 1917–18.

Both Pollock and he, at the ends of their lives, had troops of friends, and Holmes had praise from his which Pollock, in vain, tried to get the son of "The Autocrat" to agree was excessive. Holmes, as he admitted in the case of an article by Professor Laski, was too much touched to wonder if the butter was a little thick. He was, in the twilight of his life, as much *felix catus* as any member of the Saturday Club who had purred under his father's stroking.

Because of the great practical and symbolical place that Holmes occupied in American life, as well as because of his more forthcoming character, this correspondence is more a monument to Holmes than to Pollock. And, very properly, it is edited with an American public mainly in view. This means that English readers who do not know who Evarts was (and they, alas, are many) and those who do not know what Edward Atkinson was (and they, more reasonably, are even more numerous) must go unsatisfied. Some other allusions have been left obscure to the common reader in both countries who may not identify the pragmatist of Volume I., page 138 as F. S. C. Schiller or the cardinal of Volume I., page 162 as Merry del Val. Holmes could probably have told Pollock that the application of the term "Lost Cause" to the South was the work of E. A. Pollard (Volume I., page 9). And the emendation of "not Lester Ford" into "Paul Leicester Ford" is ingenious but probably superfluous. The context makes it likely that Lester Ward was what Holmes meant to write (Volume I., page 186). There is danger of a confusion between Professor J. B. S. Haldane and his father on page 213, Volume II., and Holmes's reputation for critical judgment might suffer if it were true that he had so poor an opinion of the complete

Greville. What he was complaining of was a shortened and rearranged version of the Reeves edition with some new matter (Volume II., page 216).

At the end of their lives, honours had come thick upon both Pollock and Holmes. Pollock was not merely a Privy Councillor but, out of all custom, a K.C., and, what apparently pleased him even more, he had been received as " *docteur en Sorbonne*." Holmes, when he retired, had the great satisfaction (thanks to the good judgment and political magnanimity of President Hoover) of being succeeded by Cardozo, whose fitness for the Supreme Court bench he had long before pointed out to Pollock. Both preserved their intellectual energy to the end. Holmes was not to be converted to Pollock's admiration for the *Testament of Beauty* and Pollock was led on by a short review to a defence of Montesquieu against Holmes's criticism. The elder Holmes had once written.

> there's nothing keeps its youth,
> So far as I know, but a tree and truth.

It was their joint and several pursuit of truth that made both Holmes and Pollock exceptions to this law.

XXIII

THOMAS JEFFERSON [1]

(1943)

THE city of Washington is a vast Westminster Abbey, with memorials to the illustrious dead scattered all around. But there are three that lead all the rest, the memorials to Washington, Lincoln and Jefferson. And it is not accidental that Jefferson should complete the trinity, nor that his monument should have been erected only a few years ago. For the claims of Jefferson to be one of the most important Americans have never been disputed; what has been in dispute is his claim to a beneficent importance. For Jefferson, in the Declaration of Independence and all through his long life, was, and is, the inspirer of the indigenous American revolutionary tradition. That special mark that Acton noted in the American Revolution, "Sons wiser than their fathers, ideas rooted in the future, reason cutting as clean as Atropos," that is Jefferson's mark, the mark of that "great beast," the People, loved by Jefferson and hated and feared by Hamilton. Jefferson is still a theme of controversy, not only as the planter of the revolutionary seed in the welcoming American soil, but as a person, as a statesman, as a party leader. Every few years the subject tempts an American author; there are no successes complete enough to frighten off competitors. The latest entry is Mr. Padover's, whose book is a very odd combination of rare virtues and common faults. The faults are striking enough. Jefferson's ideas are simple, so normally is his style, but Jefferson was not in the least naïve and Mr. Padover often is. Some of his *obiter dicta* are what Americans call "sophomoric," and his knowledge of the general history of the times, of its language and its temper, is very uneven. Readers who come to this new life of Jefferson with the standards of Professor Becker or

[1] *Jefferson.* By Saul K. Padover. Cape. 21s.

Professor Chinard in their minds will be disappointed and if they are pedantic enough they will be shocked.

Yet the serious faults of the book are more than set off by its merits. For Mr. Padover has the undefinable gift of the story-teller. He is not a distinguished stylist; nor does he show profound scholarship. When he leaves the straight path of simple narrative he often gets lost. But this life gallops on; Mr. Padover may not be an elegant rider, but, like his hero, he is a good rider and is never thrown. This is more a scenario than a life, but it is a most lively and readable scenario.

Mr. Padover makes it plain, what is often obscured, that Jefferson's private life was as interesting and, to Jefferson, more important than his public life. We learn a good deal about Jefferson the lawyer, Jefferson the Governor, the Secretary of State, the party leader, the President; but we learn more about the man, the indefatigable writer, rider, questioner, talker and theorist, who could make only the most ineffective public speeches yet led or vanquished great debaters and men of action.

In action Jefferson had great successes and great failures. As organizer of the "Republican" party he thwarted the "monarchical" designs of Hamilton in the early days of the constitution whose chief author was his devoted disciple, James Madison. And as President, by the purchase of Louisiana from Napoleon, he not merely doubled the territory of the United States but gave the Union and the Presidency a new character. But, as Governor of Virginia and in his second term as President, he was baffled by the problems of war. His semi-anarchical and anti-militarist theory of politics did not stand the ordeal well and he ceased to be Governor of Virginia, and, a quarter of a century later, ceased to be President of the United States, with genuine relief.

That both offices had been made burdensome by European wars was one cause of Jefferson's profound conviction of American superiority. If there ever has been a 100 per cent American it was this man of the world, who knew Europe so well. It was no accident that he (and not Washington, as most Americans believe) coined the term "entangling alliances." And some of his judgments on England, France and Germany are almost comic in their bland conviction of righteous superiority. It was not entirely without justice that Mr. and Mrs. Brick chose him as the eponym of their son. It was his indignation at the theory of Buffon and Raynal that animal species degenerated in America which gave warmth to the "Notes on Virginia"—an aspect of that famous tract which Mr. Padover oddly ignores. Politics, even American politics, were only the barely necessary condition of the progress of the American rural republic. And almost morbidly sensitive to criticism, Jefferson gladly abandoned politics for the delights of his farm, his library and his experiments at Monticello.

Politicians more often affirm their desire for retirement than show that they really mean it. For Jefferson there were things far better worth doing than discovering with how little wisdom and goodness the world was ruled. There was the endless delight of curiosity about the world of nature; there was the endless campaign against the forces that fought the light, above all the "priests." There were Greek plays and Roman historians to study; there were the essential teachings of Christ to be extracted from the New Testament; there was an immense correspondence to be answered. It ranged from applications for political jobs, for whose answer he had a form letter printed, to the letters from his old friends, friends never lost, friends regained.

Chief of the friends regained was John Adams. His ruffled pride was smoothed now. He and Jefferson were no longer actors on the public stage and his son, John Quincey, had been admitted to the dynastic succession and was in due course to enter the White House. The two old men had many tastes and many memories in common. The Republic was no longer infant and there was no danger that it would be monarchical or even aristocratic (as Jefferson had feared) or that it would be reduced to impotence (as Adams had feared). Adams had more leisure than had Jefferson at Monticello, and he wrote more and at greater length, but it is in this correspondence that the vitality and intellectual versatility of Jefferson are best displayed.

Jefferson had less leisure than Adams because he was, much

12

more than Adams, the great symbolic figure of the Republic. His party was dominant all over the Union; his fame universally accepted in America and in Europe. This fame had its penalties. Monticello was another Abbotsford. Every American who had political or intellectual ambitions made it his duty to pay a visit to the great man. So did all important foreign visitors, German princelings and British savants alike. Monticello was more than Abbotsford; it was Ferney, it was Weimar as well. And combining the role of Scott, Voltaire and Goethe was ruinous. Nearly all the Virginia gentry were land poor at the turn of the century and became poorer. Even that most prudent plantation manager, Washington, might have found himself pinched had he lived another ten years. And Jefferson was an indefatigable and successful farmer but not a good manager. He did not economize easily; there were always horses and books to tempt him and wine for his guests. He had a growing family of grandchildren and his was a class and type to which thrift did not come easily. He could keep careful accounts, but he could not balance them.

It was a man nearing bankruptcy who launched out on his last great enterprise, the founding of the University of Virginia. For the future of the free republic, a general educational system which should open to the youth of genius (a term lavishly used as was the eighteenth-century custom) was an indispensable foundation for the society Jefferson dreamed of. At first sight, Virginia was not a hopeful place to launch such a scheme. It was getting poorer; the gentry, the buttress of the old culture that had produced Jefferson and Madison, were weaker, politically and economically, than they had been. And as far as Jefferson's schemes for an educational ladder were concerned, they failed. Priest-ridden New England, for all its surviving Church establishment, had more faith in popular education than had the greatest State of the South. With the projected university, Jefferson had more luck. His prestige was immense in his own State, and it was to the *Genro* of the State, Jefferson, Madison, Monroe, that the formal supervision of the project was given. But it was Mr. Jefferson's scheme. It was his dearest project, too. He could not evade visitors, he could not evade being called to national council by his disciples in great crises like that which preceded the declaration of the Monroe Doctrine. But the main charge on his time was the university. To squeeze funds out of the reluctant Legislature, to make sure that it would be located near Monticello, to try to secure its professors from clerical inquisition, to these ends the master politician employed all the arts that had made his party supreme. A few thousand dollars to complete the building, a favourable answer from a scholar in Geneva or Edinburgh, these were triumphs sweeter than the purchase of Louisiana or the discomfiture of the Monarchists. Jefferson rode over from Monticello every day and, when any accident forbade his daily inspection, watched the work through his telescope. Jefferson was indefatigable in preparing a fit habitation for the elect who were to be the philosopher-kings of the new Republic. His university was to be based "on the illimitable freedom of the human mind," a principle of academic conduct that he hesitated to follow when it was a question of exposing the minds of the young men to the damnable political heresies of his kinsman Chief Justice Marshall. In 1825, the university was at last ready; like a new Simeon, Jefferson was almost ready to say "Nunc dimittis." Almost but not quite. His own last years were clouded by anxieties. Congress had bought his library as the nucleus of its own, but that had not made him solvent. He was reduced to asking the Virginia Legislature to pass a special Bill to allow him to sell his lands by lottery. The Legislature agreed, but the news stung the American people to action and a public subscription saved Jefferson from experiencing the traditional ingratitude of republics, but did not save his family.

Eighteen hundred and twenty-six came and the old man clung on. There were only three survivors of the bold band who had launched the new Republic in 1776, Charles Carroll, John Adams and Jefferson. It seemed unlikely that either of the two ex-Presidents would survive to the day of jubilee. But with magnificent efforts of will they did and, with a perfection of coincidence that would have struck a Greek or Roman with awe, on July 4, 1826, Jefferson and Adams died.

It is one of the affectations of good Virginians always to refer to "Mr. Jefferson   But there is one place where this implication of his perpetual presence is no affectation, on the Lawn of the University of Virginia. There Mr. Jefferson is still present. And that is the immortality that he would have cherished most, for he has told us in his own epitaph what he thought were the most memorable achievements of his long life. So he lies in the earth of Monticello under a simple shaft that tells the pilgrim: "Here was buried Thomas Jefferson, author of the Declaration of Independence, of the Statute of Virginia for Religious Freedom, and Father of the University of Virginia."

It is too simple a view that sees in Jefferson a contemner of public honours. His self-chosen epitaph has a deeper explanation. It represents his scepticism of the permanence of any political form. So the United States, as a unified nation, had less permanent importance than had the axioms declared in the Declaration. New Orleans and Richmond and Boston might cease to be under the same government, but self-evident truths remained true. As a proclamation of the necessity of spiritual freedom, the statute of Virginia might well have exemplary power after the Commonwealth that enacted it had gone the way of other republics. And the view of life embodied in the University of Virginia might survive Virginia as the Republic of Plato survived the Athenian Republic.

XXIV

THE CONQUERING TONGUE

(1943)

EVERY few years someone sounds the clarion and fills the fife, calling on us to man the breaches and repel the assailing hordes of Americanisms that threaten the chastity of the pure well of English undefiled. Sometimes the invaders intend to clip off the strong verbs, sometimes they threaten to enrich our language with new and horrid words. Whatever they do, or threaten to do, it must be resisted. But despite all the rallying battle-cries, the battle, when it is delivered so far forward, is always lost. We may regret that the battle is so ill-conducted, but we should not hide the truth. "Even our newspapers, hitherto regarded as models of correct literary style, are many of them following in their wake; and, both in matter and phraseology, are lending countenance to what at first sight appears a monstrously crude and imbecile jargon; while others, fearful of a direct plunge, modestly introduce the uncouth bantlings with a saving clause." So wrote John Farmer in 1889. So, with very slight modifications, could our contemporary viewers-with-alarm write to-day. In vain they belittle the merits of the importations from America ("belittle" is one of them). In vain they forbid Americanisms to darken our doors (and "darken our doors" is another). However talented as controversialists the defenders of the old English tongue may be, they will find facts too much for them, such facts for example as the American origin of "talented."

There is nothing surprising in the constant reinforcement or, if you like, corruption of English by American. And there is every reason to believe that it has increased, is increasing and will not be diminished. If American could influence English a century ago when the predominance of the Mother

Country in wealth, population and prestige was secure, and when most educated Americans were reverentially colonial in their attitude to English culture, how can it be prevented from influencing English to-day when every change has been a change of weight to the American side? That the balance of linguistic power is upset is hard to doubt. Of the two hundred million people speaking English nearly seven-tenths live in the United States, and another tenth in the British Dominions are as much influenced by American as by English English. Nor is this all. As an international language, it is American that the world increasingly learns. The grammatical simplicity of English, its hospitality to new words, its freedom from the purist fetish that afflicts modern German for instance, make it a good international language. Its handicaps are its spelling and its pronunciation—and American is in some degree less erratic in spelling and less troublesome in pronunciation than is standard English. It is easier to learn to speak like Raymond Gram Swing than like Alvar Liddell. Whether it be true or not that Pius XI. said he could understand spoken American but not spoken English, it is *ben trovato*.

To understand what is happening to the language in whose ownership and control we are now only minority shareholders is an object of curiosity worthy of serious persons. It is also an object worthy of less serious persons, for the study of American is rich in delights and surprises. And this is especially true when we begin by slang. It was Mr. Dooley who said that when the Americans were done with English it would look as if it had been run over by a musical comedy. To-day, we should substitute the talkies for the musical comedy, for it is the latest of the arts that most affects English speech and, in America itself, is the main vehicle for the spread of general slang, as apart from the trade slang of special groups or crafts, such as tramps or railroadmen. It is an error, it is true, to think of "American" as merely a regularized form of slang; it has other roots than the luxuriant undergrowth of slang. But slang not only plays a great part in the growth of any language, it plays an especial part in the growth of a language like American, where the pressure of a uniformly accepted standard speech is less than it is with us and where such standard literary speech as there is, is further divorced from the living tongue than it is with us.

So that even if the merits of the *Thesaurus* just launched on the world[1] were less great than they are, its interest would still be considerable. But Messrs. Berry and Van Den Bark have produced a first-class survey of current American slang, a growth as rapid and rich as Iowa corn in a good June. It is not a dictionary but a thesaurus. Under a head like "religion" and under "sect; cult" we start with nudism and end up with astrology, which is sociologically as well as linguistically interesting. Then under "Attractive Person: I. Attractive Young Woman," there are fifty lines of synonyms, but under "Handsome Man" there are only two and a third lines and three of the synonyms are merely the names of film stars (Messrs. Valentino, Gable and Taylor). This may prove nothing more than that men not women make slang, but it may reflect the general American view of the relative distribution of pulchritude between the sexes.

Relations between the sexes naturally get a great deal of space. If the makers of slang are fertile in terms of admiration for female beauty, they are equally fertile in derogatory terms for the sex. The most misogynistic Father of the Church could read some of this section with approval, and, indeed, with some self-criticism: "Why didn't I think of that one?" As is necessary, if a book of this kind is to have any real value, it includes many words that will shock the middle-aged, and may even, in a few cases, bring a blush to the cheek of the young person. Without taking the evidence of college slang too seriously, it is obvious that to some American college lads and lasses, praise of chastity might well come as almost as much of a novelty as, Mr. C. S. Lewis tells us, it recently came to the young men and young women of Oxford.

There is a good deal of humour, and a good deal of wit, in the slang reported here. The extravagance of American popular literature that Professor Krapp noted as a stylistic mark is not dead. The countrymen of Paul Bunyan are still inventive,

[1] *The American Thesaurus of Slang: A Complete Reference Book of Colloquial Speech.* By Lester V. Berry and Martin Van Den Bark. (Constable. 40s.)

especially in the field of sport and personal physical achievement. The early American who was

> The uncle of the sun
> Half alligator and half hoss,

is still doing business at the old stand. At times he is not quite convincing. He recalls those excessively virile literary men of whom Mr. Max Eastman said that they "have false hair on their chests." But more are like Luis Angel Firpo, whose toughness was defended by a Press agent: "Really tough? Why, he's got hair on his teeth."

Of the utility of the *Thesaurus* it is hardly necessary to speak. A command of current American is for the politician what a few Latin tags were a century ago. No false quantity dropped in Parliament under Pitt could have caused more shock than Sir Samuel Hoare's famous mistake about the meaning of "jitterbug." It showed that he (and the Government he was defending) were not on the beam, were not cooking with gas. It is characteristic of the difficulties of authors of books like this that neither of these slang terms has been noted in time for inclusion. Nor has such a symbol of the slang-making spirit as "zoot suit," the material embodiment of jitterbug Weltanschauung. Yet (the defenders of English should note), the "zoot suit" is so well known here that a song about it was used recently as a clue in the B.B.C. programme, "Monday Night at Eight."

No slang dictionary or thesaurus can be really up to date or completely convincing. (There are several important words or phrases whose source and meaning seem to me to have been missed.) A great deal of slang is synthetic, made deliberately by talented journalists like the staff of *Variety*, or the Hollywood script-writers. And it is given artificial currency by the movies and the columnists. Messrs. Runyon, O'Hara and the rest are makers. The hoofers and Broadwayites, might well say like Oscar Wilde, "How I wish I had said that," and receive the classical answer, "You will." Much of the synthetic slang invented by lesser lights is mechanical, and fortunately ephemeral. But there are living growths here that will push above the weeds and become trees.

Whether we like it or not, much of our future speech is listed here. So we had better go to school and avoid provoking the violent reaction of Mr. Ogden Nash:

> Boy, you will certainly throw your lunch
> When you glim an Amurrican joke in *Punch*.

If anyone is foolhardly enough to try to write idiomatic American, he is given indispensable assistance here, and the wiser majority, who merely want to understand the movies, are richly catered for.

XXV

THIS IS AMERICA

(1943)

AMERICANISM, its meaning, its potentialities, its very existence are constantly discussed in America and outside America. What to us and to them is meant by Americanism, the American spirit, the American view of life and the world? Fortunately, the Americans have been highly literate from the first settlements, given to explaining themselves to themselves and to the rest of the world. And there is more reason, therefore, to look for the meaning and limits of Americanism in the written word than would be true of any other country. An admirable anthology of American prose and verse, lately published in America and now made available to readers in this country,[1] sets out boldly to discharge this formidable task of interpretation—and with a remarkable degree of success.

What are the American voices it calls up? Among the items in this admirable collection is the famous poem by Mr. Archibald MacLeish, "America Was Promises":

> America was promises—to whom?
> Jefferson knew:
> Declared it before God and before history:
> Declares it still in the remembering tomb.
> The promises were Man's; the land was his—
> Man endowed by his Creator:
> Earnest in love: perfectible by reason:
> Just and perceiving justice: his natural nature
> Clear and sweet at the source as springs in trees are.

---

[1] *The Pocket Book of America.* (Pilot Press. 3s. 6d.)

In all current discussions of Anglo-American relations and of the role of the United States in the modern world there has been too little attention paid to the promises made by America to the world, to its role as the "last, best hope of earth." America *was* and is promises, and promises not only to Americans. These promises are set forth here, with warmth, with eloquence, with power; in the Gettysburg speech and in Whitman's "When Lilacs Last in the Dooryard Bloom'd" with that additional power which we call genius.

But America is dogmas, too. Political and social dogmas. And they are set forth in two classic documents, the best statements of democratic faith and ordered liberty that I know in any modern tongue; in the Declaration of Independence and in the Constitution. A nation "conceived in liberty and dedicated to the proposition that all men are created equal"; a nation whose political established church lays it down in the creative text: "We hold these truths to be self-evident, that all men are created equal; that they are endowed by their Creator with certain unalienable rights; that among these are life, liberty, and the pursuit of happiness"; such a nation asks for the judgment of the world on a different plane. It has stirred the hopes of the world since 1776. It is not only Shelley (here happily quoted from "The Revolt of Islam") who has seen in the United States a ground of hope that he could not find in Europe. It is because of the generality of that hope that Ruggles at Red Gap or Mr. Smith at Washington are not merely convenient Hollywood symbols of exploitable patriotic emotion. It is because America has been, for over a century and a half, these promises to all mankind, that we and the other less happy peoples resent with what is, in truth, a flattering surprise, the betrayal of American principles by Americans. We may be wrong and naïve in so expecting, but we do in fact expect something better from the countrymen of Jefferson and Lincoln, something better as a system than Darlanism, something better than ostentatiously hard-boiled power politics, something better than meaningless banalities with no current content.

It was for this reason that the defeat of Wilson was such a moral blow. That Lodges should beat Wilsons, that was

lamentable. That Americans should think it not really regrettable or even a matter calling for serious reflection that the
ghost of the elder Lodge should still walk and the ghost of
Wilson be almost apologized for by his political heirs, that is
another disillusionment. Every American soldier, here,
whether he knows it or not, bears with him a burden of hope
that still springs in European breasts that man is

> . . . perfectible by reason;
> Just and perceiving justice: his natural nature
> Clear and sweet at the source as springs in trees are.

It is because of these beliefs, these "illusions," that people
are shocked by some manifestations of the less admirable sides
of American life, by an ostentatious indifference to politics.
The United States was made by politics, on and for a political
theory. "We, the people of the United States, in order to form
a more perfect union, establish justice, insure domestic tranquillity, provide for the common defence, promote the general
welfare, and secure the blessings of liberty to ourselves and
our posterity, do ordain and establish this Constitution for the
United States of America." It is not Colonel McCormick who
disillusions us. He is, after all, a traditional figure, the irascible,
suspicious, arrogant rich man lapping up flattery and morbidly
suspicious of having something put over on him. His performance is an unconscious refutation of the academic view that
the Comedy of Humours of Plautus or of Ben Jonson
has no relation to life. No, it is more subtle, more ingenious
nibblers at the American foundations who shock us and
shake us.

This anthology gives us abundant grounds for being
shocked, and abundant hopes for not being shaken. For we
cannot be more shocked than Emerson was when he painted
his bitter picture of the subservience of the Federal Government to the Slave Power. We cannot be more shocked than
Langston Hughes or William Vaughn Moody were, or than
Jefferson and Franklin and Paine would have been, at much
that shames America and us. But the shame of America has
deeper roots than ours, for her birth pangs and birth claims
stamped her from the beginning. It is that birth claim

which gives a super-national meaning to the bridge at Concord:

> By the rude bridge that arched the flood,
> Their flag to April's breeze unfurled,
> Here once the embattled farmers stood,
> And fired the shot heard round the world.

It is still being heard round the world and it resounds in almost every page of this anthology. Not quite in every page. Mr. Norman Corwin's excellent radio programme, "We Hold These Truths," is not quite good enough to keep the very exalted company it is given in this book—perhaps no radio programme can be. (And this would be true even if Mr. Corwin showed a clearer grasp of what the First Amendment does and does not do.) There is more justification for third-rate patriotic poetry like "Sheridan's Ride." Such balladry is justified by its history—and anyway, it makes plain what a first-rate patriotic ballad Longfellow wrote in "Paul Revere's Ride."

Only one section has no justification at all. The task of writing the history of American patriotic songs has been entrusted to a well-known naturalized American, Dr. Hendrik Willem van Loon. Dr. van Loon is an expert in *moyenne vulgarisation*, in which useful field of labour his books have gained him, like Joseph Finsbury, the respect of the shallow-minded. But it is possible to have quite a high opinion of some of his work in this field and still be several light-miles away from Dr. van Loon's own opinion of himself. At best, his contributions to this book are smart and amusing; at worst, they are naïvely jingoistic, inaccurate, and, as far as Britain is concerned, malicious.

One last thought has been provoked in me by this primer of Americanism. The men who would make Americanism not promises but promissory notes, can do many things with American history. But they cannot make the poets, the orators, the people, speak their language. It is not American language. They can go outside this book, to Vachel Lindsay and Robert Frost and other poets, to the great judges and the great preachers, but they cannot find material even for a shorter book than this is. And that justifies our hopes; for good causes defeated in America, buried by the wise, the good, and the rich (often with the rapturous applause of the poor) do not stay dead. And this truth was never better stated than by the poet of a cause—far from wholly good and so far wholly dead —by a poet of the lost cause of the South:

> In seeds of laurel in the earth
> The blossom of your fame is blown,
> And somewhere, waiting for its birth,
> The shaft is in the stone.

Here are inscriptions for the shaft and reasons why it will be hewn from the stone.

XXVI

AFTER BABBITT

(1944)

LITERARY historians, like political historians, want landmarks, dates and events as definite and identifiable as
July 4, 1776, or July 14, 1789. The preface to *Lyrical Ballads*,
the preface to *Cromwell*, the first night of *Hernani*, Emerson's
Divinity School Address—these are convenient landmarks. But
history seldom fits the chronological pattern, and literary
history even less than political history. Thus it is easy to see
that the literary movement in America, whose rise and maturity
Mr. Kazin chronicles,[1] is ripe for historical treatment, but it is
not so easy to see when it began or when it ended. Is it to be
dated from the Dreiser novels that caused the scandals, or from
the automatic and general acceptance of *An American Tragedy*?
Is it to be identified with Mr. Mencken's editorship of *The
American Mercury* or must we go back to *The Smart Set*? From
the conversion of Stuart Sherman to the new writers down to
the conversion of Mr. Van Wyck Brooks to the old?

This very inadequate list of beginnings and endings shows
how far from simple the movement was, how many issues were
involved, how mixed the causes and how far from homo-
geneous the armies that fought over freedom of utterance,
again "Ku Klux criticism," for the "inner check" or against
the "wowsers." Mr. Kazin, among many other merits, stands
above these battles and makes it plain that some of the battles
of the twenties were sham fights, some of the victories not
worth winning, some of the laurels withered before being
clapped on the brows of the authors of *Nigger Heaven* and *The
Hardboiled Virgin*. In an age which either treated literature as

---

[1] *On Native Grounds*. An Interpretation of Modern American Prose Literature.
By Alfred Kazin .Cape. 21s.

mere amusement like the Follies or the movies, which chatted of the *Seven Lively Arts*, or which was as concerned with the war against the Methodist Board of Temperance, Prohibition and Public Morals as with the artistic value of a novel or a play, Mr. Kazin's æsthetic interest, like his insistence on the importance of knowledge in criticism, would have been revolutionary. They are rather revolutionary still.

For despite Mr. Kazin's devastating attack on "proletcult" and the attempted dictatorship of the intellectual proletariat to be exercised through the " New Masses," the Communist was not the only party line, or the first effective party line, nor will it be the last.

One of the few serious omissions in this tight-packed book is Mr. Kazin's refusal to discuss the effects of prohibition on American literature. Later generations will find many things in the America of Harding, and Collidge unintelligible. Prohibition will be one of them and so will anti-prohibition. For the fight of wets and drys was almost as devastating as the fight between anti-clericals and clericals in France. Indeed, the prohibition fight *was* between anti-clericals and clericals. It mixed up Catholics, romantics, expatriates, libertarians, art-for-art's-sakers in a battle for free drinking, evolution, free thought, free love, Al Smith, Freud, Joyce, Karl Adam, Karl Marx, Russian movies, against traditionalists, Jew-baiters, Catholic-haters, political and social conservatives, moralists, legalists. Critics—or so-called critics—ceased to ask "What is he saying? How well does he say it?" and fell back on the simpler "Is he on our side?" It was possibly a greater crime in Stuart Sherman to defend prohibition than to be an academic critic and disciple of Paul Elmer More. Bad critical habits were formed which have not been shaken off to this day. But these habits have hardly any hold on Mr. Kazin, who is not taken in by pleas of social significance or by nationalism or anti-nationalism. His heroes, the great men by whom he tests the claimants for recognition to-day, are James and Howells, and he does not think it seriously matters that James preferred Rye to Cambridge (Mass.) or that Howells was frightened of sex.

This healthy bias not only gives Mr. Kazin a measuring-rod against which serious American writers can be measured, but it keeps him from being taken in by bogus claimants to immortality. Indeed, so far as his contemporaries are concerned, he is almost too severe. No author who is here discussed at length is taken too seriously. Some are given rather hard treatment, but the absence of gush is very stimulating to the palate. It is not quite so certain that Mr. Kazin does not take some of the ancestors of modern social problem novelists too seriously. The Populist novelists who lamented the hard lot of the farmer in the hard times had no more to say to the outside world than had the Populist leaders. American radical agrarianism is self-regarding to a degree that would startle a French peasant, and Hamlin Garland and the rest gave an impression that there were few human problems in the mid-west that dollar wheat wouldn't cure. We gladly turn to rural novelists who wrote about human beings, minor writers like Miss Ruth Suckow, and still more to important writers like Miss Willa Cather. The women knew more than the men and had something better to do than turn Bryanism or La Follettism into fiction.

And the modern grim chroniclers of the South, prone as they are to parody themselves, at least do not try to persuade us that the human problems of the rural slums of Georgia or Mississippi are mere raw material for the social worker.

One other weakness, not a very serious one, marks Mr. Kazin's treatment of European literature and society. He is too intelligent and too learned to be either anti-European or pro-European. He is rightly critical of the decline in purely *critical* standards in the work of Mr. Van Wyck Brooks. He prefers the earlier literary historian of great men, even if that historian was open to the factual corrections of Mr. de Voto and Mr. Max Eastman, to the antiquarian of to-day. But the lumping together of Newman, de Maistre, Lammenais, presumably because they are all " Catholic" writers, like the failure to follow out the very promising parallel between Irving Babbit and Charles Maurras, suggests that Mr. Kazin, in European literature, is too prone to go by labels. Another odd example of this is the denigration of American business men as patrons of the arts inferior to their European compeers. Walther

13

Rathenau may pass, but why Stresemann? In what way was
Berlin less an importer of exotic art than New York? In what
way was the elder Morgan, descendant on the distaff side of a
great New England Brahminical family in which learning was
hereditary, intelligent collector if not original patron, promising mathematician when at Göttingen, inferior to Stresemann,
son of the Berlin lower bourgeoisie whose graduation thesis
was on the bottled-beer trade? It is again a little disappointing
to see Mr. Kazin missing the point in his attack on Paul Elmer
More's uncritical and ill-informed adoration of England and
Oxford. For the comic revelation of the deeply un-English
mind of this learned Anglomaniac was his attack on Morley,
not merely for seeking to "'undermine' the English aristocracy while moving in its company" but for supporting the
Parliament Act although he had been made a peer! This
reduction of the House of Lords to a kind of Union League
which would rightly censure a member who voted the Democratic ticket is, indeed, a revelation of that naïvety that made
More more ineffective for good than a wiser if less learned
man might have been. And when Mr. Kazin deserts his own
good principles to imitate Mr. Van Wyck Brooks's composition of place, he ought to note that in Mrs. Wharton's childhood, Bulwer was already Lord Lytton, that there is no Duke
of Nottingham and that the sewing-machine heiress whom he
presumably has in mind married a prince, not a marquis.

But Mr. Kazin is at his best in discussing the central
writers who present the central problems. He is perplexed by
the problem of Scott Fitzgerald, by his astonishing inequality.
Hollywood is the easy explanation, but it is too easy. For the
problem is present from the beginning. It is the problem of
how the author of such a superficial pastiche as *The Beautiful
and Damned* could so soon write *The Great Gatsby*. Scott
Fitzgerald has another interest. His reputation as a "daring"
author, as the chronicler of reckless girls who kissed and
smoked without their mother's knowledge, seems comic to
readers of *Butterfield* 8. Judge Woolsey's judgment releasing
Ulysses for general circulation had many merits, legal and
literary, but it had one great beneficial effect: it made it
unnecessary to admire authors who might fall foul of the

Boston Watch and Ward Society, but who were otherwise no obvious improvement on Harold Bell Wright. Mr. Cabell's Poictesme was merely Graustark treated with the technique of the strip-tease, and it would have been seen as such sooner if the censors had left it alone.

Another problem which is still with us is Mr. Sinclair Lewis. Mr. Kazin has great and deserved admiration for his talent, especially for his talent as a recorder of speech. He compares him with a Red Indian stalking his prey, but he at least as much recalls Red Grange. He makes touchdown after touchdown while thousands cheer, and against big league teams, too, against organized medicine and private enterprise religion, against youth, against Europe. But the most permanent victory was not won against anybody; it was won for the human being, George F. Babbitt, whom Mr. Lewis liked.

The success of *Babbitt* was one of the cases where permanent judgment is likely to confirm the contemporary applause. But it had its comic side. For loudest among the applauders were the Babbitts and their wives. Rotarians reformed and subscribed to *The American Mercury*, laughed over "Americana" and talked of "men with both feet on the ground" as contemptuously as any of the *literati* in Greenwich Village. Mr. Kazin is fully aware of the funny side of a rebellion against bourgeois conformism that was warmly applauded by the bourgeoisie, and not only applauded but paid for more lavishly than any kings or oligarchies had ever in the past rewarded the most skilful flattery. It was difficult to keep angry as long as the victims kept so good tempered.

The year 1929 changed all that. Mr. Van Vechten's age of parties was over and many of the leaders of the twenties were now abused by their former idolaters. Many of them deserved all they got, but some had their real services ignored and denied. Mr. Mencken, for instance, had not taken in anybody who did not want to deceive himself. He was a robust, reactionary, Germanic materialist of the Haeckel school. It was only because he was against Harding, against Coolidge against the Klan, against the organizers of Red Panics that he was associated in the indiscriminating public mind with liberalism. He was denounced as a lost leader of a cause that was not merely not his but which he had warmly opposed. Even Mr. Kazin is a little unjust to Mr. Mencken's services and talents. His line of comic abuse became too early standardized and was imitated by the young men of the *Mercury* in a devastatingly competent way. But the comic talent was real, German not French, beer rather than champagne, but real Munich all the same. And the pretensions to learning were surely never meant to be taken seriously? When the poet sang

> of Mr. H. L. Mencken
> Who interlards his choice *Gedenken*
> With scraps of high-school German prose,
> To show the world how much he knows,

it is pretty certain that Mr. Mencken laughed, too. And as for his Latin, it was not a matter of displaying a few tags from Horace but of making a few schoolboy jokes from the anatomy text-book.

With the collapse of prosperity the comedy turned tragedy or, at least, melodrama. Gone were the days of Warren Harding's normalcy (Mr. Kazin does not note that the President who succeeded Woodrow Wilson was stylistically influenced by Edgar Saltus.) Authors hurriedly hewed to the party line—at least the men did. Miss McKenney, although an ornament of *The New Masses*, had more sense. *Industrial Valley* and *My Sister Eileen* were kept apart. But there was a sudden flood of confused Marxian waters through the private gardens of the literary world. The merely negative "debunking" history and biography of the twenties were now replaced by a Marxian or pseudo-Marxian version of history, literary, political, economic. Mr. Kazin is rightly scornful of most of the criticism and literature produced under the compulsion of the depression, but even he takes the critical antics of Messrs. Freeman and Hicks too seriously. As far as the stocktaking *was* serious and relevant, it owed more to old American traditions than it did to European theory. Mr. Beard, whose *Economic Interpretation of the Constitution* was one of the gospels of this time, was right both in protesting against the abuse of his thesis and in asserting that its ancestor was James Madison and not Karl Marx.

The tide of despair ebbed as dramatically as it had risen.

It became fashionable to see the bright side of the American past and then of the present. Novelists were a little behind-hand; they were still writing grim and powerful accounts of American life while most lawyers and doctors were writing autobiographies that owed more to Dr. Pangloss than to Messrs. Caldwell and Steinbeck. But the great and unparalleled work of revision of the classical tradition of American history, the product of two generations of laborious and honest scholarship, was suddenly exploited by men of letters who were pleased to be able to redeem the villains of the past. Benedict Arnold is no longer all black, and the time is at hand for the Republican leaders of 1866 to be whitewashed.

Mr. Kazin's plan excludes the theatre, which is a pity, since the sudden rise of the American drama to maturity is more astonishing than the revival of the novel. Messrs. Lewis and Dreiser had Hawthorne, Melville, James and Howells before them, Mr. O'Neill nothing much besides *Uncle Tom's Cabin* and Clyde Fitch. And the critics, above all, Mr. Edmund Wilson, deserve more space than they get here. *On Native Grounds* is primarily a history of the modern American novel, learned, critical, intelligent, and it is not unworthy of comparison with Mr. Matthiessen's *American Renaissance*.

Mr. Matthiessen, indeed, had an easier task, a more clearly defined and more unified literary movement to chronicle and analyse. Mr. Kazin has had to deal with a period in which the American abroad has changed from Daisy Miller to Henry Miller, from the age of Silas Lapham to the age of Studs Lonigan. It is too early yet to aim at final assessments, too early to see clearly the connection between American fiction and other American artistic achievements and social and political problems. But Mr. Kazin's learning, absence of party or clique bias and resolute adherence to artistic standards make him an admirable chronicler of a strange, eventful history and a sober critic of a confused but rich and rewarding period of literary achievement.

XXVII

FACTS ABOUT AMERICA

(1944)

"I<small>N</small> this catalogue of books which are no books—*biblia-a-biblia*—I reckon Court Calendars, Directories . . . the works of Hume, Gibbon, Robertson, Beattie, Soame Jenyns and, generally, all those volumes which 'no gentleman's library should be without.'" It is pretty certain that Charles Lamb would have classed *A Handbook of the United States of America, Pertinent Information About the United States and the War Effort* (Hutchinson, 10s. 6d.), as a specimen of the *biblia-a-biblia* that he detested. But there are tougher souls for whom this mass of information will be nourishment and who will have reason to be grateful to the Office of War Information and its Overseas Branch for making it available here. It is true that little has been done to conceal that this is roughage. Grim pages of small and unattractive print may put off the mere idler, the lounger in the flowery fields of statistics and crude, unprocessed information, but the reader who is in good training will be very amply rewarded. In short, this is a book which every editorial library should possess, and which by its very factual sobriety does a better job than many more lively impressionistic works have done.

First of all, it makes clear how great have been the changes imposed by the war on the American governmental structure. The old simple division into executive, legislative and judicial branches, the division of the executive into the great Cabinet departments and the independent agencies, the division between the Union and the States,—these classical landmarks are hidden beneath a deep, lush growth of new bodies, under unclassifiable heads, exercising new powers in all kinds of relationship with the old units of government, from harmonious

symbiosis to civil war. Much of the permanent growl of dis-
content from Washington comes from innocent and lost way-
farers who hope to find their way through the war capital with
the comparative ease of 1939. There was in Washington, two
years ago, an information bureau designed to help people like
these, and it did help them, but this book, even more effectually
than what was unkindly called "Mellett's madhouse," will do
the job both for the bold explorer who dares the risks and
discomforts of a journey to Washington and the fireside
traveller who simply wants to know what is going on and is
content with vicarious experience.

By the very elaboration of the picture painted in detail by
the first section of this book, it is made easier for British stay-
at-homes to understand some of the American irritation at
what, by the national tradition, is superfluous bureaucracy.
For many Americans still dream dreams of the days when all
men were masters of all political trades and when business was
supposed to have secrets hidden from the politicians and
bureaucrats. They are wrong—how wrong this book, unconsciously perhaps, makes clear. But it nevertheless is a source
of irritation to a patriotic and indignant citizenry to discover
that somehow the bureaucrats stay and grow. It may in time
(after this year's elections perhaps) be learned that you can
have good and bad bureaucrats, but that you must have
bureaucrats—which is a lesson for us, too. Whitehall may be
less of a hot-house than Washington, but Whitehall does not
publish guides to its own Kew Gardens of new departments
and old ones re-done.

But there is a larger and more interesting section in this
book; the collection of basic facts. We learn a great many
things that ought to interest us, even if we do not always come
easily to believe that figures prove or even suggest as much as
a Chamber of Commerce hand-out suggests. There are, taken
at random, such figures as 22,500,000 books published,
216,000 degrees conferred by universities and colleges, nearly
4,000,000 college graduates and a yearly average expenditure
on elementary and high-school pupils of $105 per head. Fifty
million visitors entered museums, and 1,250,000 pints of blood
had been collected for plasma by the end of 1942. There are

56,000,000 radios (nearly two for each family group) and 6000 television sets. There were 21 major short-wave stations and 15 more under construction. "Under centralized control, they direct transmissions to all parts of the world, in nearly 40 languages and dialects." There were 24,250,000 telephones, "about half the world's total."

Basic facts of a more important kind are here, too. We learn of that decisive dividing-line between the adequately watered and semi-arid zones. It runs roughly up 103°, usually simplified into the short-grass and long-grass divide of 100°. East are the farmlands, west are (or should be) the ranches. "For sustenance, each head of cattle needs from 12 to 320 acres of grazing land, depending on the quality of the range. Approximately 263 million acres of grazing land sustain the West's livestock production, an area about five times as large as Great Britain." But more surprising is the limited amount of good farm land available.   "There are about 460 million acres of good arable land, of which about 350 million acres were in crops in 1942." And only about 130,000,000 acres of land were entirely free from erosion—whose chief cause is not the tearing wind, but the pounding, sudden, heavy rain. We are assured that this time everything possible is being done to prevent that reckless ploughing-up of what was really non-arable land that did so much harm in 1917–18. Can it be that there is a lesson for us here?

And, as we contemplate the tide of American production flooding in, we should always remember the great peace-time industry that beat its electric razors into tank parts, its refrigerators into 'planes. "January 1942, saw the last gaming-machine produced; February the last passenger automobile; March, the last piece of metal office-furniture for civilian use. In April, production of civilian trucks, radio-receivers, gramophones, refrigerators, amusement-machines, slot-machines and vacuum-cleaners halted. In May, production of household washing machines, automatic ironers, residential coal-stokers and oil-burners, commercial laundry equipment (except for military use), metal household furniture, safes, vaults, electric roasters, toasters, waffle irons, grills, razors and a dozen smaller items stopped. June saw the last metal casket and burial vault, the last lawn-mower and commercial dry-cleaning machine for other than military use. In July, production of bed-springs, bicycles and household sewing-machines ended." This is the reverse of LendLease; it was the turning over of this productive capacity to military uses that was decisive. (It illustrates the American inflationary problem, too.) This turn-around could not have been achieved but for Pearl Harbour. Hitler may well curse his Japanese ally. He and the Third Reich will be buried in that last metal "casket" which is the coffin of his illusions and hopes.

XXVIII

THE BULLDOZER

(1944)

A FEW months ago the sky over my office in London was filled, day after day, with majestic flights of Flying Fortresses, and, however familiar the sight, crowds never failed to stop and look at this demonstration of American power. Over Oxford I had seen a great rehearsal of gliders assembling from all points of the compass like giant birds in a Homeric simile. And people still recall the roar with which the sky was filled all over south-east England on the eve of D-day. No one living in England now is likely ever to forget these preliminaries to the great assault, or to underrate the power that struck from 3000 miles away to batter down the ramparts of the Third Reich. Nor are soldiers like those in Italy, who saw the "ducks" land and move and swim with far better-controlled power than their kinsman Donald displays, likely to forget that either.

But it is possible, more than possible, that the most significant impression has been not that made by instruments of war—the Sherman tanks, or the admirable American carbines—but by instruments of peace turned to the uses of war. The bulldozer is politically mightier than the tank, for in the bulldozer western Europe has seen an instrument of power made directly by American civil society, serving indeed a military purpose, but bringing to the Old World a flavour of the New, of that world of repeated mechanical novelty in which wars are not quite episodes, but are no more than great but manageable crises of American production. The bulldozer, the jeep, the great American locomotives pulling tiny English freight cars, the immense parks of vehicles, the new roads and camps—these have suddenly reinforced with visible works a faith in

America as the land of miracles, shaken during the long depression years and only kept alive by the repeated sermon of the movies.

That faith had been shaken and it was not fully restored by 1939 or by 1941. With the Russian war and resistance, the courage of the Soviet people, the dearly sold defeats and then the first victories of the Red Army, the peoples of western Europe, defeated but resisting, the people of Britain, resisting but weary, saw a star in the East. The Russians had what it took, had the secret of success in war. And there is no use denying that success in war has, for most peoples, a magical prestige. We are not far enough removed from our ancestors to be philosophical about the claims of victory, about the debit side revealed by defeat. Disasters like Singapore or Tobruk, Pearl Harbour or Bataan were compared, in Europe at least, with Stalingrad or with the repulse of the Germans at the gates of Moscow.

More than one premature imitator of Goethe hastened to see both in the defeats and the victories a new world-wide Valmy condemning the old unplanned or semi-planned Western society. The Russians by our standards, had given up a great deal, but maybe that was the price of the survival of a modern society. Maybe we in the West were as belated adherents of nineteenth-century ideals and institutional practices as the Greeks of Alexander's time or the feudal nobles of the sixteenth century had been belated adherents of ways of life condemned by history.

On paper it certainly looked like it. There was nothing much to set against this view as the Russian war took a greater and greater toll of the Wehrmacht and Hitler and his mouth-pieces alternated between explaining in terms borrowed from demonology the victories of the Russians and indulging in Wagnerian laughter at the military amateurs in the West who talked of attacking their Atlantic Wall.

But while the talk and the writing were going on, preparations for the attack were going on too, and those preparations necessarily took a form that prepared millions of not very credulous, not very hopeful, battered, resolute English men and women to believe that the Americans now moving in and taking over had something—that maybe the movies were right after all.

First came the bulldozer; it came into parts of England which had been left outside the main stream of mechanical progress, into East Anglia, into the southern rural counties. It came in and did more to change the face of the land in a few months than had been done at the same speed since Roman times. "You have no idea," said the father of a friend of mine, an East Anglian squire, "you have no idea how they make roads; they lay the concrete down like toothpaste."

It was an engineer, who was also a farmer, who told me the delighted shock which he got in his double capacity when the American Air Force ran up overnight a new airfield. "They did all the main work in eight days. A change from our methods."

"What were our methods?"

"Eight Irishmen leaning on spades looking at one Irishman working."

This no doubt was something of an exaggeration, but roadmaking and construction in general are the most backward parts of British technical practice. And the latest American devices were demonstrated in parts of England more backward than most.

But even more important than the bulldozers, than the roadmakers, than the gigantic trucks negotiating the perpetual traffic bottleneck of Carfax at Oxford, were the drivers of the bulldozers and trucks. Where did they come from, these manipulators of these miraculous machines? Where did they learn their magic? A friend of mine, a chemist to a great industrial corporation, said he had never seen anything like the speed and competence with which the American Negro drivers delivered coke to a great war plant for whose technical performance he was responsible. The young man who built the airfields gave the same impression of effortless superiority. Where did they come from? Where were they trained? Was this an hereditary craft?

And the next shock came when it was discovered that often, perhaps in most cases, these wonder-workers were new to the job, that they had learned their techniques in a few

months in the Army since they had been snatched from the
tractor, or the less impressive machinery of the soda fountain,
or even from non-mechanical jobs. They were the same young
men who either did not know or preferred not to say what
they thought they were fighting for; they were the same
young men who chewed gum all the time and had such undis-
criminating taste in girls, the same young men who at first
seemed more tongue-tied and standoffish than the traditional
Englishmen, the same young men whose politeness and con-
sideration when they were doing the job of transforming the
face of so much of England did more to win friends than tons
of public speeches. They did such a wonderful job, and they
did it with the anxious courtesy of a college student trying to
avoid spilling tea on the drawing-room carpet. What society
was it that had produced them as well as the bulldozers?

Now western Europe is asking the same question. General
Patton's ride is, from a European point of view, more important than Sheridan's. It is no longer in the East alone that
victories are won—brilliant victories casting all the light and
glory that victory can cast on the societies that win them.
Whatever Tobruk and Pearl Harbour once proved is, at least,
disapproved, even more than disproved. In that common glory
both the Americans and the British share. But the British are
not newcomers to Europe as the Americans are, for despite
the original A.E.F., the Americans *are* strangers. And the
bulldozers, the bulldozer drivers, the G.I. in battle and behind
the fast moving lines are the novelty.

It is this that makes the difference from the boom in
Americanism that lasted from 1922 to 1929. Then America
exported machines and tourists, both welcomed for economic
reasons, but there was no equivalent of this export of Americans
at work, fighting, destroying, building. Then André Siegfried
said Europe had to choose between Henry Ford and Gandhi.
It chose neither. Both were too remote, abstract, inhuman.
Ford was a car, a method of production. Gandhi was a remote,
terribly alien solution to a problem that Europe did not feel
keenly about (perhaps not keenly enough, but that was and
is a link with America).

But now it is "Fordism" with the boys from River Rouge

and Willow Run visible in action as well as the machines they produce. There was always Hollywood and, of course, Hollywood had been in person to the war. But the real, constant work of Americanization done by the movies was not done by the most glamorous stars. The man and woman in the street might delight, and did and do delight, in the kind of diversion from this hard world they get from contemplating Miss Joan Fontaine, for instance, but Miss Fontaine and her colleagues are now performing the function once performed by the fairy tale aspect of royalty, and an important and necessary role it is too. But it was the background shots, the picture of American life, as a world in which ordinary miracles, miracles within the grasp of the ordinary man, are possible, that kept alive interest in America even during the dark days of 1932. It couldn't be all true, no, but it couldn't be all false.

And now in England, in Italy, in France, in Belgium and in Germany the movies have arrived. The movie characters in millions—the garage men, the taxi driver, the farm boys—are there, cheerful, enterprising, complete with all those devices that win wars and make life easier. The very homesickness of the average G.I., his total lack of any Kiplingesque desire "for to observe the world so wide," if a political nuisance at times, is the most permanent and convincing tribute to America. They all want to go home. Alas, in Europe, not all exiles want to go home even if they can. The victors don't want to stay and exploit victory, they don't want to transform Europe for good or bad reasons. They want to go home, to the only country fit to live in.

Of course, this passionate desire to return home may irritate Europeans who feel that their continent is not uniformly inferior, even at the technical level, to the United States. There is the Bailley bridge and the Spitfire as well as the bulldozer and the Sherman. But this conviction of superiority, this evident superiority in many cases, this ease and self-confidence are the most effective means of bringing home to Europe the fact that there are societies that can win this almost unconscious assent without the violent means of coercion and indoctrination that other societies competing for European adherence have used and use.

American democracy has long been under a cloud in Europe. It was seen, for a generation past, as the mere instrument of high and soon-to-be-decadent capitalism. It was better represented by the Sacco and Vanzetti case than by Jefferson or Lincoln. Since the genuine democracy of American life, the awful fight the rich have to put up to buy an adequate amount of never uncritical reverence, the easy optimism of the young, even the exaggerated hopes of the young, are things to be experienced, not demonstrated on paper, it was easy to make a picture in which American democracy was one of the world's great shams. And that attitude is not wholly dead, any more than is the other attitude which sees in Americans spoiled, rich children.

Not everything that American soldiers do in Europe runs counter to these two hostile views. The, to a European, unintelligible passion of race pride in so many Americans reinforces the first view: the occasional revelation of a belief that money or what money can buy in the way of gadgets will cure most or all of the world's ills reinforces the second. But the bulldozers and the bulldozer drivers are there to say different. And if Europeans thought life in a small town in America was bound to be deadly and intolerable, well they have learned better from the sight of young Americans in London and now I am sure, in Paris, whose only desire is to

> pick the morning gloria
> right off the sidewalks of sweet Peoria.

If the social democracy of American life seemed a fraud or an unimportant alleviation of a fundamentally exploiting society, well, the ease, self-confidence, good manners and good-humoured nostalgia of the G.I., of the bulldozer driver, have told us that there is something in it, that in the pursuit of happiness these young Americans have a flying start. Of course, she won't be caught; she never is (even in California) for more than a brief period, but it is something to begin the race with hope instead of resignation. Maybe it is that optimism, so easily demolished by any skilled literary wrecking crew, that produces the bulldozers and their drivers.

The English and, still more, the European method is

summed up in the war-time slogan, "Make do and mend." Well, it is a necessary attitude in a small and overcrowded island, but you can have too much of it, and in England a lot of people have learned that you can make do and mend too long, that when the seat is definitely out of your pants you had better hustle and get a new pair. The lesson is even more necessary in France, where the sense of the "patrimoine" to be saved rather than of the new assets to be created helped to weaken France in face of her greatest ordeal. And both England and France have lost so much of their patrimony in this war that there is a real chance of starting so many things with little regard to how it was done in the past—in fact, of going American.

There is one last result of this American attitude. It has made German propaganda ludicrously unsuccessful in creating suspicion of American motives in European breasts. (I could easily name half a dozen Americans who could give Goebbels ten pounds and a beating at this game.) What was the use of telling the English that the Americans were playing them for suckers and were really proposing to take over the empire? Even the dullest Englishman could see that empire-builders or empire-stealers must be made of sterner stuff than these permanently homesick young men.

What was the use of representing the United States as the centre of a spider's web of high capitalism when it was a fifty-fifty chance if an American officer could speak of "That Man" with the decorum due to a Commander-in-Chief?

And even that disconcerting political indifference of the American technician has its good side. It is not necessarily inferior to the dogmatic, uncritical, fanatical package of political ideas issued by many would-be remakers of Europe. For one thing it makes it plain that the average American soldier, whatever his Government or worried columnists in Washington may think, has no desire to remake Europe or Europeans. The fiercest passion of the European peoples now is to be left to manage their own affairs. They have had unpopular strangers in the house and they want to do their own house cleaning.

That they will do in their own way. But they have a lot of

house repairing to do, too, and maybe they will get, and certainly they would like help from the country of the bull-dozers, the country of humane miracles. Nobody knows what the future of Europe is going to be; there are too many im-ponderables. Among them is the mass American impact. But that impact can be a great, undoctrinaire dissolvent of out-moded ways of production and of life.

The bulldozer has cleared away more than ruins; there have been worse ways of winning friends than inscribing on tanks, "Hi, chum, no gum." The operative word is "chum."

14

XXIX

BRICKS ACROSS THE SEA

(1945)

So all day long the noise of battle rolls—not merely in the Ardennes or Alsace or on the road to Eleusis or beyond Ravenna, but across the Atlantic whose sky is dark with flying epithets and whose air is thick with imputed motives.

Traffic of this type has been heavy for years, but the Monsoon of Anglo-American controversy has normally blown only one way. Now the breeze from east to west has almost equalled in velocity the old blast from the other side of the Atlantic. And nervous nurses are busy feeling the pulse of that perpetually ailing patient, Anglo-American relations.

With so much else to worry us—in Greece, on the Western Front, in Poland—it is easy to write down the importance of this campaign of winter discontents:

O passi graviora, dabit Hitler his quoque finem,

or to put it into Scots:

Sticks and stanes will break ye'er banes,
But words will never hurt ye.

But although a powerful leader from Chicago (or London) is less disturbing than a V1 or V2 in the neighbourhood, it can be disturbing all the same. It is difficult to preserve a sense of proportion, or a sense of humour, when some of the recent controversial developments are contemplated. Yet it must be done, even when it is a case as flagrant as the suggestion that Field-Marshal Montgomery was complacently discounting the troubles of General Eisenhower in furtherance of his alleged ambition to succeed him as Commander-in-Chief.

When all allowances are made for the source of this slander it is, at first sight, impossible to take it quite calmly. Reflection produces more calm. There is an historical excuse for the authors of the slander. It is that American military history has been full of charges and counter-charges of this kind. There was the possibly mythical "Conway cabal" against General Washington; there was the undoubtedly treasonable plot of General Benedict Arnold. A few years later began the long and surprisingly untroubled career of demi-treason of General Wilkinson. There were the conflicts in the Mexican War between Generals Taylor and Scott and the still unsettled dispute as to whether General Frémont was a fool and knave or merely a fool.

In the Civil War there was the disputed role of General McClellan and the bitter political and military feud, lasting for a generation, that arose out of the court martial on General Fitz-John Porter. The musical-comedy atmosphere of the Spanish-American War was diversified by the virulent dispute between the partisans of Admirals Sampson and Schley.

In cheerfully imputing the worst motives to Sir Bernard Montgomery, the American critic is indulging in a national form of all-in wrestling of which the normal victims are American generals. We should be surprised, not at the campaign, but at its small scale.

President Wilson and President Roosevelt were victims of far more outrageous suggestions, but they have been able to keep politics out of the Army, with minor exceptions like the "persecution" of General Leonard Wood in the last war and the "neglect" of General MacArthur in this.

This is only a special case of a general law of American life that internal political controversy is still conducted on the robust lines of Eatanswill. The American people are still told, like the electors of that famous town, that "a more enlightened, a more public-spirited, a more noble-minded, a more disinterested set of men" never existed than themselves. If this sad world is not an earthly paradise, the fault must lie elsewhere.

So it lies with us. But the free and independent voters of Eatanswill took all this as something less than gospel truth and so do the American voters. They are still used, as we used to be to the full, warming rhetoric which Dickens found it almost impossible to parody and was reduced to reporting.

It is not a very long time since our own politics were not entirely dissimilar. Moderns emollified by the gentle tea-interval politics of the Baldwin-MacDonald era, may forget sterner days, but we may be sure that neither the present Prime Minister nor Mr Lloyd George do. It is less than a generation since they were accused of planning a pogrom of the Protestants of Ulster—among many other crimes recalling the darker pages of Tacitus. They were not much the worse for it. Neither are we.

Of course, we have changed all that. Our politicians and publicists are much subdued since the days when Chesterton took the hide off F. E. Smith, who was busy skinning somebody else; since Maxse and A. G. Gardiner did their best to gibbet the betrayers of their country and the parties who then ruled us. We are all much more responsible now.

Of course an irresponsible newspaper may be a public danger just as, the American would say, a too responsible journal may cease to be a newspaper. And the Americans are not quite wrong. We have lost as well as gained by the gentility that has sprung up, both the spontaneous kind and that engendered by the Official Secrets Act.

The decline of church-going has much to answer for. A generation ago, people were accustomed to docile acceptance of sermons from persons who, in fact, were saying: "Don't do as I do, but do as I tell you." Parsons were our columnists and their privileged position was accepted. Now they repent their own sins instead of ours, leaving the fine old damnation sermons to the (American) Fourth Estate.

Has the spirit of Mr. Podsnap died out completely? I seem to remember his voice being raised by journalists, cartoonists, M.P.s no longer ago than the storm in the Lebanon teacup. And if some Frenchmen, then in London, now in Paris, have succumbed to the temptations of *Schadenfreude* as they contemplate our situation in Greece, well, it is very sad, but very human.

Ghastly good taste has a lot to answer for and now that the explosion has come, real discussion may well do great good. No great harm was done by the Whitman parody of Sir Owen Seaman's, fifty years old, but still so topical:

> Spontaneous Us!
> O my Camarados! I have no delicatesse as a diplomat, but I
>   go blind on Libertad!
> Give me the flap-flap of the soaring Eagle's pinions!
> Give me the tail of the British lion tied in a knot inextricable,
>   not to be solved anyhow!

It is quite useless to expect either the British or American peoples to give up their passion for moral judgment, for the giving of political good conduct prizes. Both might remember the jest of Lord Bowen who amended the fulsome opening of an address by the judges to Queen Victoria into "Conscious as we are of each other's unworthiness."

And before, in the words of the worst of all American patriotic songs, they decide that "the baffled tyrant spurns amain," they might try to remember, that it is easy to spurn in words; it may be hard, with all the will in the world, to do it in deeds, except at intolerable expense.

"In the Archey Road," said Mr. Dooley, "when a husband and wife find they simply can't go on living together—thev go on living together."

XXX

THE AMERICAN LANGUAGE

(1945)

I T is a little difficult to say when a learned work becomes an institution; one suddenly realizes that the debate is closed, that the work in question has joined Liddell and Scott or John Glaister's *Forensic Medicine* among the immortal reference works that escape the deep damnation of Charles Lamb's *biblia-a-biblia*. But there is one unmistakable sign, the demand for and the supply of further materials; a supplement is the final proof, and the appearance of the first part of the new *Supplement One to ' The American Language '* (Knopf, $5) is proof, if any proof were needed, that Dr. Mencken's pioneer work has been crowned with deserved *immortelles* (*anglice* everlasting flowers). Although the new work of learning is designed for that great and dignified band who possess the fourth edition of *The American Language*, it is perfectly usable and enjoyable by those readers who come in here, as they say in the lesser movie parlours. The nourishment is abundant and the pleasures of the palate are not sacrificed to mere nourishment.

A pedant might wonder why it is necessary to discuss the Maryland and rival theories of the nature of the mint julep or the manufacture of floating soap; the darker arcana of politics or the oddities of such types of human behaviour as bundling. But the pedantic would be wrong; language is living, is the mirror of life and only he who refuses to regard anything human as alien from him, even the theology of wowsers or the moral ambitions of do-gooders, could possibly hope to write worthily of the American language. Mr. Mencken, at what cost to himself it would be profane to speculate, has plunged into the jungles and the swamps of religious, political and reformist literature and has come back, muddy, weary, but triumphant, bearing to shore "barbaric pearls and gold."

A considerable part of the *Supplement* is devoted to fighting and winning the old battle against the English and the Anglomaniacs who both deny the existence of an independent American tongue and/or (to use a horrid verbal device) the claim of American speech to rank above some pidgin tongue or thieves' cant. Again the pedants are rolled in the mud, with a few kind words for early preachers of the truth and the light like Noah Webster, John Pickering and Timothy Dwight. But the "birchmen" decidedly get the worst of it, as they well deserve to do. Haunted by the idle dream of "correctness," dominies and schoolmarms have tried to keep the brawling giant-child inside a tidy, clean and well-ordered nursery. The new Gargantua has insisted on taking to the range and producing a language worthy of Mike Fink and the Mississippi.

But there is something to be said for the pedagogues; the fact that they fight a battle that they are sure to lose and deserve to lose does not mean that they are wrong to fight it. A language which was made every day, not tied to its past, would have many merits, but it would be in some danger of losing the serious merit of intelligibility between generations and, though this risk is not great in the United States, between regions. Startled British educationists (or educators) have just reported on the linguistic genius of the peoples of West Africa who are busy making several new languages out of English; this is very creditable to their talents, but it makes more difficult the role of English as a *lingua franca*.

The school influence normally is seen, it is true, in deplorable forms, in the passion for impressively noisy Latinisms, for "realtor" and the like, but though the pedagogues do "accentuate the positive," they do more than that. I am sorry they seem to have lost the battle over "disinterested" so that the rising generation will not know what used to be meant by a sentence like this: "All the Senate is totally disinterested." And I propose to go to the grave fighting the already lost battle for the "correct" use of "like" and "as." Like the Spartans at Thermopylæ, we know we are beaten but, as we were right, what of it?

Mr. Mencken is in fine condition and so has more than enough vigour left to take on the Anglomaniacs who cling to the old superstition that English usage is *right*, that there are Americanisms but not Briticisms. Here the victory is already won, more completely than Mr. Mencken is willing to allow, perhaps because to admit it would prevent his fighting the battle over again. There has been a great change in the English attitude in the last twenty years, both among the *literati* and the commonalty. Mr. Mencken's picture of the attitude of the Literary Supplement of the London *Times* has been out of date for quite a long time, not for the deep political reasons he suggests, but because of a change in the personnel of the reviewers of that great journal (of which, by the way, John Bailey was never editor). Nor is the affected ignorance of English judges proof of much. They are a pampered race, as well provided as a movie director with "yes men" and "nodders," and the sycophantic laughter with which these flatterers greet "Who is Charlie Chaplin?" or "What is an automobile?" need not be taken too seriously.

But there is a controversy over the rapid Americanization of English which is real but whose sociological implications are not dealt with here. In no country known to me is mere speech of such social importance as in England (and I mean England, not Britain). In no country are so many prosperous, successful and worthy persons distressed by the fact that the moment they open their mouths they will reveal the fact that they weren't born even in "the second drawer from the top." On the other hand, in no country do flops, dead-beats and social failures, reeking with b.o. and conspicuously refusing to eliminate the negative in their behaviour as men and citizens, take more real comfort from the fact that their speech shows that they once knew better things.

In such a society, Americanisms are really revolutionary. They shake the established order, not of the pedants, but of all who benefit by this order, It is not merely speech in the sense of accent; it is vocabulary and, equally important, as Professor Pear, of Manchester, has been pointing out, the physical attitudes that go with mere enunciation to make up speech as a social phenomenon. To speak English well is not merely a matter of aitches, of avoiding Cockney vowels or the revealing "nothink" that is worse than either—almost. It is knowing a jargon that is continually being changed and a way of speech and associated habits that it is practically impossible to learn after adolescence. The socialites know this; the others feel it and resent it.

A generation ago, Chesterton attacked this new mysticism and the tricks associated with it. The middle classes had, as he pointed out, no sooner learned to say "port" and not "port wine," than their betters began to say "port wine" and not "port." In the new and remarkable novel of Mr. Evelyn Waugh, one of the tricks of his very high-well-born heroine is just this mockery of the vocabulary of the climbers just below her.

American destroys this monopoly in restraint of social ease. Here we are all learners, and since American is egalitarian, democratic and changing at the lower levels, there is reason for the belief that lower orders learn it quicker and better than the denizens of the stately homes of England. Why worry about "port" and "port wine" when the really smart thing is "rum and Coca-Cola?" What the irate enemies of American-isms are defending is not the rights of King George III., threatened by the American rebels, but the social structure of the realm of King George VI., at least as much in danger from Hollywood as from Moscow. When the populace laughed at the ignorance displayed by Mr. Neville Chamberlain *in re* "jitterbug," it was laughing at Rugby School as well as Munich. And it is a well-established fact that a young man, properly brought up, who yet takes to the American language, is very likely to reveal, under pressure, that he finds cricket boring, not worthy of an aspiring candidate to the proud adjective "groovy."

One last point before I pay final tribute. American has made more progress in England than Mr. Mencken admits. So his invaluable list of words that differ in the two countries is too long. For example, the English for "battery" (of a car) is battery, not "accumulator"; to this I will testify on Webster's Unabridged. And in justice to the taste of my fellow Britons, it is untrue that *The Specialist* failed in England. It has been a

best-seller for fifteen years; it is now in its twenty-second
edition and bids fair to rival *The Wide Wide World* in popularity. But having said this, what remains to be done but praise
the author of this great work and contemplate the irresistible
advance of the new *lingua franca* of the world? "What will
come of it all, knows God"—as was said in another connection.

XXXI

GENERAL JACKSON: REHABILITATION

(1945)

IT is only at the end of a most remarkable re-writing of a
decisive period in American history[1] that Mr. Schlesinger,
for a brief moment, departs from the attitude of the rigorous
professional historian and states the doctrine that the study of
a turning point in the history of a great modern society may
have immediately didactic uses. All through the narrative the
parallel between the dilemma that confronted General Jackson
and his associates and that which confronts the remaining
adherents of the liberal tradition in the western world is
implied, but it is when the triumphs, the failures, the *splendeurs
et misères* of the Jacksonian revolution have been chronicled
that the lesson of modified optimism is drawn.

> In a time like the middle of the twentieth century, when the pressures of
> insecurity have driven people to the extremes of hope and anxiety, the
> Jacksonian experience assumes special interest. Its details are, of course,
> obsolete, but its spirit may be instructive. In an age dominated by the com-
> pulsive race for easy solutions, it is well to remember that if social catastrophe
> is to be avoided it can only be by an earnest, tough-minded, pragmatic attempt
> to wrestle with new problems as they come, without being enslaved by a
> theory of the past or a theory of the future.

There are among us academic historians of the greatest
acuteness, learning and probity who will regard this appeal
from the present to the past, this search for the light, even if it
be only the light of analogous experience, as a kind of treason
to the craft. It may seem, indeed, a double treason in one

---

[1] *The Age of Jackson.* By Arthur M. Schlesinger, junior. Boston: Little, Brown
& Company. London, Eyre & Spottiswoode.

whose book shows such a command of the skills of the craft as is displayed here, skills that have been learned in the austere Harvard school and observed in a family that is now a dynasty of historians. But the men and women out in the world who want something more than the cold comfort of historical technique will find in this brilliant reconstruction food for thought, for hope and for delight in good narrative and bold and convincing portraiture. This will be true of the English as well as of the American reader; indeed, the English reader (if he is given a chance to read this masterly performance) will, it is not improbable, start with some advantages, above all the advantage of never having heard of General Jackson.

For it must be admitted that Andrew Jackson is the least known of all great Americans in this country, even the name hardly touches the public memory. It is true now; it was true a century ago, as that good Jacksonian, Nathaniel Hawthorne, found when, as Consul in Liverpool, he adorned his office with a portrait of General Jackson looking as formidable and as military as when he crushed the Creeks or wiped out Pakenham's Peninsular veterans before New Orleans. But, Hawthorne found, his English visitors fell into two classes, an older generation, which thought that Jackson was an American general who had been beaten somewhere, and a younger, which had never heard of General Jackson. Even less is known to-day.

There is an advantage in this ignorance. In Britain, at least, we have not to clear our minds of the old anti-Jacksonian legend that has survived the efforts of Benton and Parton, the testimony of young Josiah Quincy, or the laudations of William Cobbett or Walter Savage Landor. Of all the great men who have occupied the White House, Jackson has had the least generous praise. His importance has been above denial, but too often his role has been seen as disastrous and, when more historical comprehension *has* been revealed, there has been a rather grudging acceptance of him as an important, inevitable, representative but half regrettable phenomenon. Woodrow Wilson was not untypical in his cool and superior commendation or acceptance.

A man of the type of Daniel Boone, John Sevier, and Sam Houston; cast
in the mould of the men of daring, sagacity, and resource, who were winning
the western wilderness for civilization, but who were themselves impatient
of the very forces of order and authority in whose interest they were hewing
roads and making "clearings." . . . He impersonated the agencies which
were to nationalize the Government. Those agencies may be summarily
indicated in two words, "the West." They were agencies of ardour and
muscle, without sensitivity or caution. Timid people might well look at them
askance. They undoubtedly racked the nicely adjusted framework of the
Government almost to the point of breaking. No wonder that conservative
people were alienated who had never before seen things done so strenuously
or passionately. But they were forces of health, hasty because young, possessing
the sound but unsensitive conscience which belongs to those who are always
confident in action.

Mr. Schlesinger would object to almost every statement
an implication of the Wilson portrait. The "unsensitive conscience" of Jackson is a myth and, as for the Jacksonians, in
what way of conscience were Benton, Taney, Silas Wright
inferior to Clay or to that eloquent mouthpiece of the Bank of
the United States, Daniel Webster?

One of the achievements of this profound reconsideration
of the Jacksonian era is the rescue of Jackson and his associates
from the artful denigration of the opposition. Here we have a
highly critical examination of the story that Jefferson had foreseen—and feared—the ascendancy of Jackson as Lenin is
supposed to have foreseen—and feared—the ascendancy of
Stalin. At best, the statement is now to be marked "not
proven." So with the reports of the violence with which
Jackson approached political questions, his highly personal
view of his functions, his passionate hates and loves. The
picture is not totally false; Jackson could be too loyal and he
was a good hater, as ready to talk of hanging as a moral remedy
as Lord Braxfield. But, it is made very plain here, a good deal
of that public violence was a device of government. To frighten
or scandalize a delegation from the friends of the United States
Bank into leaving the White House in peace was a trick of the
trade, and the President, storming and threatening, was, in a
moment or two, perfectly at ease and amused at the success of
his stratagem. That the delegation went off convinced that
national ruin was at hand and that the White House was
occupied by a monster of irascibility and violence worried him
not at all. The "good, the wise, and the rich," the remnants of

the old Federalist party and the leaders of the new money power might lament, like Talleyrand on Napoleon, that a man in so great an office should be so badly bred. But Jackson did not waste time conciliating his enemies. And we have abundant evidence that General Jackson was with his friends and, on non-political occasions, even with his enemies, a model of old-fashioned courtesy, having far more in common in manners and social graces with General Washington than with General Grant or even with President Lincoln. His friends, his associates, his slaves, even his mere visitors all tell the same story.

But this manufactured reputation was not without its importance. It created the hostile Jackson legend to which even Mark Twain paid homage. It is one cause of the astonishing defect in *Democracy in America*, the total failure of Tocqueville to see the dramatic and permanent change in the character of the Presidency that began with Jackson's administration, the creation of that plebiscitary monarchy for a limited period which makes the President of the United States the agent and leader of "We, the People of the United States," as Congress, or either House of it, can never be.

Thanks to Professor Pierson, we know what kind of impression Jackson made on Beaumont and why Tocqueville saw in the Presidency an office far less powerful than the constitutional kingship of Louis Philippe.

> General Jackson . . . is an old man of sixty-six years, well preserved, and appears to have retained all the vigour of his body and spirit. He is not a man of genius. . . . Of a certainty, the power of the King of France would be nil if it were modelled after the power of the President of the United States.

So wrote Beaumont and Tocqueville, who was in America during a bitterly contested presidential election, could yet write. "Nul candidat, jusqu'à présent, n'a pu soulever en sa faveur d'ardentes sympathies et de dangereuses passions populaires."

It is Mr. Schlesinger's thesis that the strength of "dangereuses passions populaires" was the strength of Jacksonian democracy, that it was in close contact with those passions that the new Democratic party grew in strength and in political effectiveness, and that in the abandonment of the constant contact with the masses, especially the masses of the new eastern industrial cities, lay the causes of those divisions among the political heirs of Jackson that created the conditions in which civil war was the only way out.

In Wilson's account of Jacksonism it was the vague entity "the West" that explained Jacksonism. It was the view set forth by Turner in his almost too celebrated essay on the "Significance of the Frontier." "It was this nationalizing tendency of the West that transformed the democracy of Jefferson into the national republicanism of Monroe and the democracy of Andrew Jackson." As Mr. Schlesinger points out, there are many obvious reasons for doubting if it was as simple as all that. Henry Clay represented the West as much as Jackson. Many of Jackson's early western allies deserted him as soon as the character of the Jacksonian revolution became plain. And Turner himself, a page or two later, is compelled to note, or notes without noticing its implications, that the West was the home of "soft" money, of all sorts of inflationary schemes, while the central doctrine of Jacksonism was a fanatical hostility to paper money, to the control of national credit by banks, to all alliances between the Government and the private speculator. What the western farmer wanted was plenty of cheap credit; he was a speculator, hoping for the best, for a constant rise in land values. What the eastern industrial worker and small tradesman wanted was freedom from the violent oscillations of the price level, from the too desperate swings of the trade cycle, from imprisonment for debt, from judge-made law that forbade combinations of workers when the whole legal system was a combination of employers, from the rigours of *laissez-faire* in the wage market.

Jackson was a westerner, a planter, but Jacksonism's leaders and theorists alike were not typical westerners. The West was only formally loyal to the Jackson tradition, the South, under the pressure of its insoluble problem, formally disowned it. It was in the cities of the East that the true sense of the movement was understood.

It is in his rehabilitation of the two types of Jacksonians, the politicians, Van Buren, Benton, Silas Wright, and the intellectuals, Orestes Brownson, George Bancroft, William Leggett, Robert Dale Owen, Theodore Sedgwick, and even some less creditable but occasionally clear-sighted radicals, that Mr. Schlesinger's talents for the historical portrait are best seen. These men have been neglected by the historians of the dominant Federalist-Republican school. Their insights, too, have been ignored or dismissed by modern radical theorists, as convinced as were the Avelings, that Marxian analysis was first bringing light into a darkness of American social and economic complacency. Mr. Schlesinger is at home in the polemical literature of the thirties and forties and he has been able to bring out of forgotten pamphlets and periodicals some admirable discussions of the impact on American and, especially, Jeffersonian optimism, of the new class structure.

It was the Jeffersonian view that suffered most. The Utopian dream of a farmer's republic, shunning foreign trade and urban luxury like a new but pacific Sparta, was revealed as a mere dream long before Jefferson died. His own policy of economic coercion of Britain by embargo during the Napoleonic war, not only fostered American manufacturing but stretched and strained federal authority. There was a brief period of optimistic illusion; perhaps the old fears of the rise of a city proletariat, of a dominant merchant and manufacturing class, had been exaggerated. In the "Era of good feelings" it was only too true, so the faithful original Jeffersonian Republicans felt, that "we are all Republicans, we are all Federalists." In such an exchange of political labels and principles there could be no doubt which side would win and it was a formally Jeffersonian administration that chartered the Second Bank of the United States and created that leviathan of financial power and political influence which Jackson was to attack and to kill.

By the time Jefferson died there was no room for further illusion and the surviving Jeffersonians were not victims of further self-deception. The time came when the soldier from Tennessee entered the White House at the head of an army recruited in part on the model of the Cave of Adullam, but with more internal coherence than its enemies believed it to have.

That coherence was provided, in the first place, by loyalty to the President and trust in his will and in the political equivalent of that *coup d'œil* which had stood him in good stead on the battlefield. But there were other grounds of union. The money power, centred in the Bank of the United States and the new merchant and manufacturing oligarchy, was a novelty, and an unpleasing novelty, to many old Federalists. It was unpleasing, also, to the new class of professional men of letters. One of the oddest examples of the way that the history of this period has been transformed into a contest of ignorant and violent men opposed by the *élite* of the nation, is the resolute ignoring of the fact that all the important men of letters of this period with few exceptions were originally Jacksonian, even the amiable and easy-going Washington Irving, even the proud and class-conscious Fenimore Cooper. From Bryant down to Whitman, it is the same story. Hawthorne and Melville were stout Jacksonians, Emerson and Thoreau, at most, inclined to call a plague on both your houses. Only Poe was temperamentally and intellectually hostile to all democratic claims.

What was the content of the movement that united so many diverse talents, interests and passions? It would be going against the spirit of Mr. Schlesinger's book to insist on reducing to a formula a political movement as diverse and human as Jacksonian democracy. But there was one central doctrine, the necessity of controlling, by political means, the central economic power which, in the 1830's, was the Bank of the United States. In the days of Jeffersonian agrarianism the problem had been seen negatively. Don't have any central economic power at all. "No man should live," Nathaniel Macon used to say, "where he can hear his neighbour's dog bark." But that sentiment had no applicability in the slums of New York or Philadelphia, or in the new mill towns of Lawrence or Lowell. Indeed, it was not even adequate for the planter and farmer in the new days of steamboat and railroad. So, still using Jeffersonian language, Jacksonian democracy had to be positive, not negative, in its politics. Strengthen the Federal Government of the people, by the people, for the people, against the rival government of and by and for the bank.

15

The second battle was won, but the victory was not followed up and the party of Jackson split. It is another sign of the originality and courage of Mr. Schlesinger's mind that he revivifies the older Republican tradition which saw in the formation of the party a moral protest. We are reminded, what is easy to forget, that the mass support of the anti-slavery cause came from the Jacksonian rank and file. And not only the rank and file. The names of David Wilmot, Martin Van Buren, Gideon Welles and such allies of the Democrats against the Whigs as Charles Sumner and Salmon Chase should make absurd the view that sees in the Republican party in its first years a mere conservative continuation of the Whigs. Logical Jacksonianism meant opposition to the extension of slavery. The Van Buren "bolt" of 1848 was the revolt of the true believers against the time-servers, the true Locofocos were opposed to the slave power. But destiny was against them. The moral assets of Jacksonian democracy passed over to the party that soon came to serve the interests of business more effectually than had the too doctrinaire Federalists or the more ingenious Whigs. The party of Big Business was now, in American tradition, "the party of moral ideas."

The economic and social solutions of a century ago have not, as Mr. Schlesinger insists, any detailed lesson for us. But there is a general lesson of the spirit. The central, encroaching economic power of the day may not be a bank or even business. The need for a political, if you like, amateur control of the final economic decisions is not less than it was in 1832, nor is the danger of contempt for the average man less. Basically, there was faith and scepticism in both the Jeffersonian and Jacksonian view, and with that mixture of scepticism and confidence Mr. Schlesinger ends.

XXXII

GIVE UP HOLLYWOOD?

(1946)

THERE are certain themes that recur in every controversy. And one of them is the nefarious influence of the films, above all, of the American films. So, when an economic crisis like that which now afflicts us becomes the topic of discussion, the permanent crusaders against Hollywood see their chance.

We need dried eggs; we can't pay for dried eggs *and* American films, so cut out the films. So runs the argument.

It is a valid argument; it would be folly indeed to sacrifice bread (or its equivalent) to circuses (or their equivalent). But, behind the defenders of dried eggs, lurk the permanent enemies of Hollywood. Even if we were rolling in what Americans call "folding money," they would still be in favour of restricting to the narrowest limits the importations of American films.

Since we shall not be insolvent for ever, it is worth while pondering the question of whether it is in itself a good thing that American supplies of the stuff that dreams are made of should be reduced or cut off totally. If it is a good thing now, would it not be a good thing at any time in the future?

There is, it must be admitted, something totally exceptional in the role of the American film in the world. There has never been anything like it in history. Other arts have influenced countries remote from their place of origin. One culture has deeply influenced another since time began. But the American film is universal in a way no other art has been in so short a time.

It is not a matter of a slow seeping-in over centuries. The

hair-do, the slang term, the ideas and ideals of Hollywood are the currency of the world in a year or two after the fashion has been set. The world thinks to-morrow what is thought and said on "the Strip" to-day. And a vigilant defender of a national culture and way of life is naturally alarmed at this state of affairs. He may be too alarmed but he is not foolish for being alarmed. An intelligent seventeenth-century Scot, Fletcher of Saltoun, quoted the opinion of a wise friend of his who cared not who made the laws of a country if he could make its ballads. The wise friend had something and the modern equivalent of the ballads are the films (including their theme songs). All over the world, not always consciously, the native ballad is giving place to the American ballad.

The wise Scot had *something*, but not everything, for laws are important, too. The Stewarts had all the good ballads but it was the House of Hanover that kept the throne. Neither "The Red Flag," nor "The Internationale" are soul-stirring tunes, but international Socialism and Communism have got along. And it is not, I fear, the banality of "Giovinezza" or "Horst Wessel" that accounted for the fall of Mussolini and Hitler. I don't think that the British national character will be totally changed even if the whole population sees American movies (and no others) two or three times a week. National character should be made—and is made—of sterner stuff.

But the films have an important influence all the same and we should note what it is. And they have a special influence in Britain. The American film is the great competitor of the native film in all countries, but in France or Germany it is a foreign film; its competitive position has been weakened since the coming of the talkies. In Britain it has been strengthened. Who now remembers the foolish persons who thought that the talkies would be an automatic tariff barrier, that no nice people would care to listen to "those horrid American accents, my dear?" They *were* a bit of a shock in some cases; Mr. Adolphe Menjou became a less plausible Parisian figure once he spoke. But the innocent snobs, who thought that good standard American speech was more foreign or distasteful to the ears of the English man and woman in the street than the upper-class bleat of Oxford or the B.B.C., showed themselves strangely ignorant of the world they lived in. And they are still strangely ignorant, which is one reason why their campaigns against the American movies fall flat.

They say, for instance, that Hollywood does not illustrate English life truly. No more it does. But does it illustrate it any more falsely than do English films? The vast majority of English people live in big, drab, industrial towns. The films don't illustrate their local life, whether those films are English or American. They don't illustrate that type of American life, either, as a rule. But do the customers want them to?

I have called films the stuff that dreams are made of. That is what most of them are. When there are exceptions, like that most admirable film, *Brief Encounter*, they are not necessarily the most popular films. The average film-goer goes to the pictures to be amused, to be diverted. And the great superiority of the American film is its superior power of diversion. English films about fox-hunting, county society, dinner at eight or even at seven, are just as remote from the life of the average film-goer as films about the same level of life in America. It made and makes no real difference whether say, *A Yank at Oxford* or *Mrs. Miniver* is made at Denham or Hollywood. It is fairyland in either case.

A more serious objection is that historical films, films with a political or ideological flavour, are mainly American, and that, when an admirable film like *The Way Ahead* is produced here, it doesn't get adequate attention in this country and next to none at all in America. This is true and regrettable. But the success of the American film dealing with some episode in American history is only part of the story.

As England got orderly and respectable, its sober and law-abiding citizens began to dream of America as a land where anything could happen. Long before there were any movies, Buffalo Bill had made America a dream land for aspiring youth. The films benefited; they benefit still. But it is a sad fact that we haven't got a Wild West. True the United States doesn't have one *now*, but she had not very long ago. And if our gangster and crime movies are not as good as American crime and gangster movies, that is because our gangs, even in Glasgow, are not nearly so good as their American counterparts.

As long as the customer is given any choice, he will go to see American movies. And as long as he goes to American movies, some American ideas or ways of life are bound to become familiar, often appealing. Often, not always.

The British housewife in 1945, as a survey showed, still clings to the open fire and suspects central heating in spite of technical, economic and health arguments. Those housewives have seen, in their millions, American houses where indoors, with bitter weather outside, it is possible to move around clad in a fashion that would invite pneumonia in our much less rigorous climate. They have been amused but not impressed.

A great deal of the life shown on the American films is looked at with no belief in its relation to any possible life here and with no more intention of imitation than is provoked by the latest instalment of Tarzan or of Donald Duck. But a good deal does sink in. The films are one cause, only one, but an important cause, of the changes in the general views of marriage, careers, ambitions and the like. But there is not much to choose between British and American films. One type, the animated pin-up show, insists on the fact that young women are bipeds and mammals just as much when it is British as when it is American. The variations on the Cinderella theme, the good little girl whose beauty and charm ends up in marriage with the modern equivalent of the fairy prince, the millionaire, is more effectively done in America, because the story happens in real life more often in America than here and there are many more fairy princes, *e.g.* millionaires. But the ethical level is not any different.

The farce is, if anything, "rawer" when manufactured here; the "naughtiness" less subtle, if degrees of subtlety have any meaning in this context. But an American or British bedroom farce are (dollar exchange apart) so much alike that patriotic moralists should save their breath.

Where the American films make a permanent impression is in their background. The American houses, shops, cars, trains, gadgets, all suggest new demands to the British housewife—or girl-friend. Of course, not all American houses are as efficient as those in the movies. Many a G.I. bride is now finding that out. And the movies have done more to cause illusions to enter British female breasts than even the most seductive line spun by American lovers. But it *is* true that, on the whole, American life is organized to make running a house easier than it is here. If the movies make the British house-wife demand revolutionary changes in house-planning, I'm all for them, though I fear that British female conservatism is not to be shaken, even by the films.

The American film shows a more egalitarian society, with far more social flexibility and ease. Well, the American film is telling the truth about America (comparatively speaking) and is preaching a desirable lesson to England. (It doesn't preach, successfully enough, the high price paid for this energetic climbing or the hard work Americans put into their pursuit of happiness.) The American film shows a society full of energy, faith, industry, and hope. Well what's wrong with that? We must not, I think, give up American films for economic reasons and then pretend we are doing it for cultural reasons.

XXXIII

AMERICA'S LITERARY PAST[1]

(1946)

IT is almost a quarter of a century since Mr. Van Wyck Brooks ended *The Ordeal of Mark Twain* with an appeal to his literary brethren to escape or to break out of the trap that had closed on Mark Twain. "Read, writers of America, the driven, disenchanted, anxious faces of your sensitive countrymen; remember the splendid parts your *confrères* have played in the human drama of other times and other peoples, and ask yourselves whether the hour has not come to put away childish things and walk the stage as poets do." That invitation was accepted; no one could complain, to-day, that American literature is suffering, or has suffered for some time past, from inhibitions or from indifference to themes of social significance. Few aspects of American life have escaped being anatomized; few areas of groups have escaped the scalpel or the fluoroscope. But although toughness, candour, a grim resolution not to let cheerfulness come creeping in are fashionable still, they are now not the only fashions. The great pioneer has gone home to Minnesota to defend the domestic virtues whose possibly stifling effects he had once examined with a critical eye. George F. Babbitt is replaced by Cass Timberlane. Mr. Mencken has turned from castigating the imbecilities of the "booboisie" to studying the manifold felicities of the language they make and use, and Mr. Van Wyck Brooks has turned an increasingly affectionate eye on the literary past of America. It is no longer a matter of calling on the American *literati* to take up the standard long carried by their European comrades; it is a matter of recalling them to an appreciation of their historical inheritance.

[1] *The World of Washington Irving.* By Van Wyck Brooks. Dent. 15s.

The World of Washington Irving is the first volume of a literary history of the United States into which the existing volumes on New England will be fitted. It is a ripe, fully considered specimen of the *genre* which Mr. Brooks has made his own. It is not literary history in the sense that (in very different ways) Taine or Brandes or Professor Matthiessen or Mr. Alfred Kazin wrote and write literary history. There is none of their predominant interest in ideas and in literary achievement seen from some general standard of values. Perhaps Mr. Van Wyck Brooks has most affinity to Taine, but his close-woven, highly detailed account of the background, the geographical, social, political, economic milieu, is not in reality linked in intention or achievement to Taine's principles or practice. For it is the matrix, not what comes forth from it, that is the real subject. Some of the writers dealt with are important from an æsthetic point of view: one, Poe, is more than merely important. Cooper, by his creation of the classical form of the *matière d'Amérique*, the addition to literature of the West, the Indian, the prairie, is worthy of comparison with Scott. Irving himself wrote one minor masterpiece and the magic of *Rip van Winkle* in part lies in its evocation of the charm of the Hudson; it is the Catskills and the great river as much as the mild humours and white magic of the legend that preserve the tale. And in the political and economic writers of that age there is abundant material for reflection.

But, take it all in all, the age of Washington Irving (Poe apart) is not an age of masterpieces or even of any very substantial addition to the permanent stock of American (and English) literature. It may be that in Royall Tyler America had produced a distinguished comedy writer. It may be that *The Contrast* was "lively, witty and real—one could read it generations later, as one reads Sheridan and Goldsmith." Perhaps one could, but one doesn't, and the works of art that the world willingly lets die usually deserve their fate, especially if they are comedies. Do first-class comedies really get neglected? It is doubtful, and there are so few straight critical judgments in this book, so few instances when we can be certain that Mr. Brooks is bearing in mind the scale of achievement of world literature or even of later American literature. It is interesting that Keats's "Ode to Apollo" first appeared in Kentucky and it is interesting that Shelley's grandfather was born in Newark, New Jersey; but reflection imposes on us the comment that America in that age produced no Keats, no Shelley and gave a Saturday's child way of life to the one indubitable genius that she did produce.

That much of the English criticism of America at that time was unfair, politically biased, and uncritically hostile may be admitted; what Washington Irving wrote on that theme was just and temperate. But there was then, in America, no adequate audience for the free play of the mind; it was hard on Poe, on Cooper, on Irving himself. Conditions of publishing, the intolerance of public opinion, above all the long (then beginning and only recently won) battle against "colonialism" made the life of the true poet or critic hard, too hard. Mr. Van Wyck Brooks once asked how Shakespeare could have flourished in America; the answer is not very encouraging if we raise the question of his survival chances in the world of Washington Irving. Poe at Stoke Newington was in a happier environment than in Richmond or West Point and the long self-imposed exiles of Cooper and Irving tell us much. Yet both did their best work when they took American themes; Cooper was too tough-minded to hanker after the Alhambra or castles on the Rhine, but even the urban and gentle Irving achieved more when he wrote *Astoria* for his patron, John Jacob Astor, than when he imitated Addison or sentimentalized about English rural life in the age of Cobbett and Captain Swing.

Mr. Brooks aptly quotes Cooper's Mr. Steadfast Dodge, who rejoiced in the progress of American literature. "We have much of the best poets of the age, while eleven of our novelists surpass any of all other countries. Then to what a pass has the drama risen of late years! Genius is getting to be quite a drug in America." It was not quite like that and it was not an invention of the savage English critics that concealed from the conceited islanders the truths revealed to Mr. Dodge. He was on safer ground when he stressed the claims of pulpit and bar. For in political and economic discussion there was more life than in most forms of *belles lettres*. Mr. Van Wyck Brooks takes too broad and humane a view of what constitutes culture

to exclude the polemical writers like John Taylor, or the
political writings of Cooper, or the orators and debaters. But
he is, nevertheless, basically interested in men of letters or, at
any rate, in æsthetic effects. Mr. A. M. Schlesinger, junr., and
Professor Dorfman have recently shown how much living,
forcible controversy there was, what originality and prophetic
power were often displayed by these inquiring divines and
argumentative journalists and pamphleteers. But Mr. Brooks
hardly conceals the tepidity of his interest.

It is not, however, in the mind of the age of Washington
Irving, but in the world of Washington Irving that Mr. Brooks
is interested and interests his readers. And that world is first
of all the geographical setting. If this book has a hero it is
"America the Beautiful." It was the age of the great naturalist
travellers; there was Bartram, there was Alexander Wilson,
there was Audubon; in a slightly different field there was
George Catlin. These careful narrators and artists fed more
imaginations than those of their American readers whose local
pride and curiosity were natural enough. It was Bartram who
inspired, with his account of the "Isle of Palms," "blessed
unviolated spot of earth," that magical translation of Purchas
into the

> . . . gardens bright with sinuous rills
> Where blossomed many an incense-bearing tree;
> And here were forests ancient as the hills,
> Enfolding sunny spots of greenery.

"Every detail in the four lines," wrote John Livingston Lowes,
"which recollections of Purchas leave wanting or incomplete,
reminiscences of Bartram have supplied." And as Mr. Brooks
remembers, Bartram and his fellows inspired many more
readers than Coleridge or Wordsworth. Mr. Brooks has gone
to the life of Philip Henry Gosse for evidence of the effect of
the forest and the savannah, and of this rich tradition of the
American naturalists. He might have drawn a further example
from *Father and Son* where Edmund Gosse tells how the
memory of that enchanted past, for a moment, freed his father
from the prison-house of his dread religion. He recited from
the pocket Virgil that he had carried through Alabama:

> . . . *tu, Tityre, lentus in umbra*
> *Formosam resonare doces Amaryllida silvas*

and unwittingly opened a door through which the dedicated child escaped. But it is amusing to learn that from a Napoleonic officer, Colonel Landi, who had settled in Louisville, Mayne Reid drew for *The Boy Hunters* and from Mayne Reid, William James learned his boyish faith that "a closet-naturalist" must be "the vilest kind of wretch."

But the American land meant more than the vast laboratory of the ornithologists. Irving himself was almost as citified as Lamb. But little old New York was then really little and it was only a few years before Irving's birth that General Sullivan's war had made settlement safe up-state. The frontier was still not very far away in space or time from Manhattan, and even less from Cooperstown, where the young son of what it was becoming obsolete to call the patroon, found his theme in the lands that had been the battle-ground of the Five Nations. Wolves were a danger to cattle not far from the growing little metropolis where Lorenzo da Ponte was ending his days, all dreams of being the Cæsarian poet put away and his lively old age not even shadowed by the elegant melancholy of the Countess Almaviva's

Dove sono i bei momenti
Di dolcezza e di piacer?

Over the mountains, into the great valley, the settlers poured, and with them the pastors, poets, teachers, orators. Each new state had its modern Athens; each new city its local leaders of the march of intellect. There were older centres of a genuine if not very original literary culture. There was the opulent and beautiful and stagnating city of Charleston. There was the new capital of Virginia, Richmond, where the boy Poe was to see the niche which, combined with his London memory of the Elgin marbles, evoked "the glory that was Greece." There were centres of culture that were seen with a suspicious eye, like New Haven, then earning—or getting— the title of a "seat of science and of sin." And into this new world poured all kinds of travellers: the exiled son of Philip Egalité, who was to reign in the Tuileries and die in Twicken- ham, Talleyrand, Cobbett, Joseph Bonaparte, and his nephew, Charles Lucien, the naturalist colleague of Wilson and

Audubon. There was Priestley and there might have been Coleridge. Mr. Brooks successfully shows how false is the picture of an America cut off from the great winds of doctrine and passion that were sweeping the world. He shows, too, and successfully shares his excitement with his readers, the growth in material equipment and the genuine gourd-like progress of the country. It was the American emphasis on the future and the European reluctance to leave the present or the past that were the most fruitful causes of embittered controversy. Not only the new capital but the new nation was a thing of "magnificent distances" at the end of which the American could see the new city, the new commonwealth, while the visitor could see only the raw present, the pigs on Broadway, the swamp on Pennsylvania Avenue, the barbarity of the inns, the savagery of some of the people.

The reaction of the European to some of the characteristics of the new American society was not always unreasonable. American resentment of foreign criticism had its counterpart in resentment of American criticism. Tocqueville and Dickens were both alarmed by the intolerance of American public opinion—not merely the intolerance of the city mobs or the frontiersmen, but of the richer classes. Mr. Schlesinger has pointed out that Cooper's protest against imposed intellectual and political conformity was directed against his own class, the rich Federalists who had become Whigs or rather anti-Jacksonians. The spirit that led to the mobbing of the Mormons in other regions and sections of the population, led to social pressure being directed against the nonconformist whatever his mark of difference might be, Catholicism in Massachusetts, Abolitionism in Illinois. There was a marked falling off in the level of political discussion and of intellectual freedom in Virginia. Jefferson's foundation of the University of Virginia seems, in retrospect, less like the coping-stone of the new enlightened society he had planned than a last rearguard action of the cool, enlightened, sceptical Virginian gentry against the triumphant hosts of evangelical religion and passion-ridden politics. It was in part this feeling of unease in social intercourse, this pressure to conform, that irritated many European visitors and drove them into unjust and sometimes slanderous criticism. They were told so often that America was the only "free" country, so often patronized as being subjects, even serfs, of "effete monarchies," that they were tempted to retort by dragging the slavery skeleton out of the cupboard or by dragging the red rag of dangerous thoughts before the bulls of good American society.

The certain condescension in foreigners did not stop with that generation. Nor did that reflex action, the boosting and boasting and the drowning of the critical spirit in a flood of patriotic emotion. It was such emotion that led Americans in the past—and Mr. Brooks in the present—to take seriously such doggerel as "Maryland, my Maryland." It was this spirit that led to innocent disregard of statistical probability. So Mr. Brooks writes of Lippard living in "a vast old abandoned Revolutionary mansion . . . a dwelling with five-score empty rooms." Five score is a hundred, and there are very few private houses in New York to-day which have a hundred rooms. Nor is it easy to believe that the Philadelphia of 1800 had thousands of French families. One may be a little surprised, too, that Mr. Brooks has not identified the Frenchman whom Cooper met and who had "written a witty work on a journey round his own bedchamber" as Xavier de Maistre. It is easier to understand the slip that has turned Sault-Saint-Marie into Sioux-Saint-Marie. The *Encyclopédie* that Dupont de Nemours procured for his American friends was presumably Panckoucke's edition, not Diderot's, and Westminster, not Eton or Harrow, was the favoured public school of the wealthy American of colonial days. But Mr. Brooks has succeeded, by his mosaic reconstruction of the American scene, in making it living, interesting, full of promise and of real if limited achievement. If he cannot make it more than that, the fault lies not in him but in the world and the age of Washington Irving.

XXXIV

"THE LAND OF STEADY HABITS"

(1946)

Let observation with extensive view
Survey mankind from China to Peru.

THIS, or something like it, was the commission given to a committee of the United Nations entrusted with choosing a place to be the local habitation of the new world organisation.

It appears that (unless the Assembly revolts) it is Stamford that is to be the centre of the new federal district of the embryo Parliament of Man. Stamford, not Philadelphia, nor Boston, nor the high mountain plateau of Colorado, nor the remote and empty hills of the Dakotas. A few weeks ago London was full of boosters "selling" Chicago and other American metropolises to delegates who in their heart of hearts still yearned after San Francisco. And the prize has (so far) gone to a state and a region whose consciousness of merit requires little advertising, which regards its noisier great neighbours, New York and Massachusetts, with suspicion. Now the moderation, sobriety and complacency of the state are rewarded—a gift horse now being looked in the mouth.

Connecticut is the most southerly of the New England states. Its boundary with New York is highly artificial, representing seventeenth-century deals and conflicts between Dutch and English settlers. The new U.N.O. reservation crosses the state line, but it is on the Connecticut side that the centre of gravity lies. It is with Connecticut law and custom that U.N.O. will have to deal. And Connecticut law and custom are still marked by a good deal of Yankee conservatism and stubbornness. First of all the state is an embodiment of the "dissidence of dissent." It is not merely that the early settlers were, like all the New Englanders, enemies of Right-wing orthodoxy; that, in a way, was easy enough. But they were enemies of Left-wing orthodoxy too, and removed themselves from Massachusetts and defied the party-line to settle in the wilderness. Once settled there, the dissenters were not much more tolerant than English Anglicans or New English Puritans, but there is that streak of double nonconformity to be allowed for. Yet if in more modern times Yankees and Irish and French-Canadians and Italians and Poles have got along without totally destroying the original character of the state—well, that is a lesson for troublesome Europe and Eurasia. What the "nutmeg state" could do the rest of the world can do.

The "nutmeg state?" Yes, and some assert it is so called because the shrewd Connecticut Yankee, travelling abroad, was not above selling wooden nutmegs to the natives. But nobody ever sold wooden nutmegs to the Yankees. Was not the greatest of all Yankee salesmen, Barnum, a resident of Bridgeport, just on the edge of the new reservation? Did he not announce the great truth that "there is another sucker born every minute?" But few of them are born in Connecticut— which truth delegates and visiting newspapermen should remember.

The United Nations are moving into a crowded little community, but into one that has a great deal of natural beauty for its size. There are the marshes and beaches of Long Island Sound and the stony fields and pastures and woodlands of the coastal plain and the great rocks that rise above the Gothic towers of Yale on each side of New Haven, all making a landscape that recalls, almost as much as the shore north of Boston, some of the astringent character of the poetry of Mr. T. S. Eliot. Inland there are hills and woods as lovely as any England knows, and then, in the broad Connecticut Valley, a noble river scene indeed. There is the state capital, Hartford, capital of American insurance and actuarial prudence. Just across the Massachusetts line is Springfield. And each city is the home of one of those great local American newspapers. The delegates will have little excuse if they neglect the *Hartford Courant* and the *Springfield Republican*. Along the valley the Poles grow tobacco and the Italians have their little vineyards.

On the hills above Hartford lies the Broadway, or Chipping Camden, of America, the lovely village of Farmington, where Mr. Wilmarth Lewis houses his immense collection of documents to illustrate the life and letters of Horace Walpole. At New Haven is Yale University and at New London the stretch of river where Yale rows against Harvard. There are the plants that make the Yale locks and the Waterbury watches and the Meriden silver plate and aeroplanes and submarines and all kinds of highly skilled crafts. No area in the United States, or, perhaps, in the world, has such a level of high technical skill, just as no area in the world can compete with Greenwich (Connecticut) for the number of indignant millionaires per rod, pole, or perch. For its size the state can offer plenty of variety, plenty of character, and plenty of good advice and good example.

It would be an interesting experiment to plant this international body, with its special privileges and special problems, in this area. Of course, it may be that the delegates and alternates and experts will all ignore the natives and live in the spiritual equivalent of a concession. It is to be hoped not, and it will not be easy, for the Connecticut Yankee has an inquiring turn of mind. He will have no hesitation in asking (if he is not told) "What's cooking?" So the delegates might as well get used to it, get used to discussing the modern equivalent of the price of bullocks at Stamford Fair. Some will be well advised to do that; others will be as well in the Stork Club in New York (48 minutes away; 100 trains a day). Others can get their sense of proportion restored by going to see the solar and other greater systems in the New York Planetarium. Others will be reminded of the variety of human nature by discovering that, even in sober Stamford, there is a district that got, if it did not wholly earn, the name of Sodom (the township was founded by an English immigrant a century ago).

But there is more the delegates can learn than that. They are moving into a state that has been a free republic since it got a charter from Charles II. in 1662 empowering it to make its own laws and elect its own Governor. It was the leaders of the infant settlement who in 1639 laid down in their "Fundamental Orders" that "where a people are gathered together

16

the word of God requires that to mayntayne the Peace and Union of such a people there should be an Orderly and decent Government established." What Connecticut knew it needed—and what it provided—three hundred years ago the world needs now. May there be an omen in the location of the United Nations in the "land of steady habits!" What better aim than a world of steady habits?

XXXV

THE ENIGMA OF ABRAHAM LINCOLN

(1947)

THE latest addition to the admirable series of *American Political Leaders*, edited by Professor Allan Nevins, is, from its theme, the most important of all.[1] For Lincoln is not only the greatest of American political leaders, he is in many ways the least intelligible. He was secretive in the sense that he kept his inner thoughts from his closest friends; he was difficult to understand; and he did not always take pains to make his motion of mind intelligible. He was indifferent, too, to the chronicling of his external life. His early years he dismissed as "the short and simple annals of the poor" and, until he became a national figure (which was not earlier than 1858, seven years before his death), there was no particular reason why his life should have been closely watched, even by his friends. After all, Johnson was an old man before Boswell set himself to investigation and attention, and Lincoln's nearest equivalent to Boswell, his friend and partner, Herndon, had far less care for the canons of evidence than had Boswell. Herndon suffered, too, as Professor Randall points out, from his conviction that he had a kind of historical inner light. He was, he thought and said, a "psychologist." (Professor Randall over-stresses this claim by making Herndon present himself as a practitioner of psycho-analysis, which is not the same thing.) Then, in spite of the masses of available Lincoln papers of all degrees of value and credibility, the central corpus of documents left by his son to the Library of Congress is sealed until the present year.

But the greatest difficulty facing the Lincoln biographer

---

[1] *Lincoln The President.* Springfield to Gettysburg. By J. G. Randall. In 2 vols. Eyre & Spottiswoode. 32s. the two volumes.

does not arise from the methodological errors of Herndon or the secretiveness of Robert Lincoln, or of his father. It arises from the phenomenon described by Mr. Lloyd Lewis under the title *Myths After Lincoln*. Almost at once, the murdered President was made to endure apotheosis and turned over to the hagiographers. As the Lincoln cult grew, so grew the legend. And it was not a mere accretion of legend of a type familiar to sacred and profane history. There was deliberate manufacture of an orthodox version of the life and acts of the martyr of the Republican Party. The custodians of the Republican shrine had the same interest in profitable popular devotion as had the monks of Canterbury or Compostella. And no Bollandist revisions were encouraged by the politicians who found Lincoln dead more valuable and manageable than he had been when alive. An orthodox historiography, with its "good" and "bad" things, its "good" and "bad" men, was created. Its basic text was the vast *Life*, by Nicolay and Hay, and a very good and very readable version of it has been given to the British public by the late Lord Charnwood.

For long that legend has been under fire. It has been attacked with self-defeating violence by amateurs like Edgar Lee Masters. It was undermined by the industrious and critical Beveridge, the more effectively that he was as loyal a Republican as John Hay. All the resources of the acute scholarship of the modern American professional historian have been turned on to this central problem. And in the opinion of his colleagues, chief "master of them that know" has been Professor Randall of the University of Illinois. The first volumes of this great study are now available in this country. They will delight the lover of historical detective work and will tell the common reader more about the kind of problem faced and solved by the most famous and enigmatic of modern democratic leaders than could any gilded version of the old kind.

There will be many points on which dispute will still rage. Sometimes it may be held that Professor Randall "leans over backwards." Thus Professor Wiley's revision of the old story of the loyalty of southern Negroes to their masters and their masters' cause goes further than is admitted here. The professional reader gets from the narrative, and from the notes, something like the pleasure Hazlitt got from seeing the great Irish handball player, or that Lincoln would have got, for that was his favourite game. But this is a book for amateur as well as professional, for it is a study of dilemmas still with us and of types of problems and personalities that recur in each generation in a free society.

Professor Randall is perplexed and angered and almost mystified by the disproportion between the formal causes of the Civil War and its gigantic and revolutionary character and results. There were so many problems facing the extravagantly growing American society in the decade before the Civil War diverted American interests and profoundly distorted the character of American federal institutions. Slavery, and the narrower problem of the relations of the federal government to it, were only spasmodically dominant in the American public mind. The statesmen who planned and executed compromises, like the mass of the people in all states, even in New England and the Deep South, wanted peace in their time. And those who blew on the low fire did not, save in a very few cases, want to burn down the house to roast their own panacea at the flames. Even the extreme Abolitionists of the Garrison School were mainly concerned to clean their hands and consciences of their share in the federal sin. The fire-eaters of the South were far more frightened than hurt and far more frightened than combative. There was no plan for the forcible destruction of the "peculiar institution" in the South; there was no Machiavellian conspiracy of an "aggressive slaveocracy" planning the creation of a vast slave-holding "Lebensraum." Explanations after the event, even that most brilliant economic theory of the necessity of southern aggression, Cairnes's *Slave Power*, were far too symmetrical. What was crystal clear when seen from Galway after the die had been cast was not clear at all in Douglas's Washington or Lincoln's Springfield, even in Rhett's Charleston.

As Professor Randall makes plain, over and over again, the dramatic contrasts of orthodox Republican historiography make the real character of the slow slide into war and revolution impossible to discern. The famous debates between

Lincoln and Douglas in the Illinois senatorial campaign of
1858 deserve their fame as a decisive episode in the rise of
Lincoln as a national figure. But not only are they not very
impressive reading to-day, either as dialectical exercises or as
contributions to American oratory, they show, if coolly considered, how narrow was the difference between Lincoln and
Douglas, how much the two old rivals and friends had in
common, how comparatively accidental was the fate that made
them appear to be leaders on opposite sides of the abyss.
Douglas knew and insisted on this point, for it paid him to
dwell on the notorious and revealing fact that the Buchanan
administration, in Washington and Illinois, was more concerned to defeat and discredit him than to defeat the leader of
the "Black Republicans."

This rule or ruin policy was pursued to the very end, to
the murder of the national Democratic party by the southern
extremists in the presidential campaign of 1860. At Charleston
and at Baltimore the Democratic enemies of Douglas, in North
and South, combined to create a situation that made the
election of Lincoln inevitable. Nor is it without significance
that such prominent agents in this policy as Stanton and Ben
Butler, once the war had begun, jumped on the radical band-
wagon, became bitter enemies of the South, disloyal servants
of Lincoln, pursuing, on the other side, a policy morally and
politically identical with that which had led to the disruption
of the Democratic party and so of the Union. Rightly reacting
against traditional and excessive denunciations of President
Buchanan's administration in its last troubled months,
Professor Randall is surely too tolerant of a policy that had
so bedevilled politics for the three years before the crisis. To
break Douglas was the aim of the drabbest politicians in all
camps. And looking at those enemies, it is hard not to say of
Douglas what General Bragg said of Cleveland: "We love him
for the enemies he has made."

It is now a commonplace of American historiography that
the Republican party that emerged from the war, the party of
Grant, the fourteenth amendment, Conkling and Blaine, was
not the "party of moral ideas" that was formed, more or less
spontaneously, to fight the Kansas-Nebraska Bill and in 1856

went to the polls under the banner of "Free Land, Free Men and Frémont." But, as is here shown, that party fought only one presidential election. Lincoln was a far better spokesman for such a party than Frémont had been, but it was not such a party that chose him in 1860. The serio-comic history of the reference to the Declaration of Independence in the Chicago Convention, the disillusionment of genuine zealots like Joshua Giddings, as well as the even more significant rallying to the new party of Simon Cameron, founder of that apostolic (or diabolic) succession of Pennsylvania bosses that has ended (if it has ended) only in this generation, showed the change. It was so complete a change that Douglas was perfectly justified in pointing out that Republican policy towards the fugitive slave law and to the allegedly fundamental question of slavery in the territories had, when they came into power, become simply his policy. The victorious Republicans stole Douglas's clothes without any time-wasting explanations in the manner of Peel.

From any point of view that the question is looked at, even extreme northern or extreme southern, the cause of the war in 1861 is almost invisible. The southern zealots for secession at any price would have been justified in leading their states out of the Union had Douglas been elected. For the Republican practice was simply that of the "Freeport doctrine," an insistence that slavery in the northern territories was a question for political metaphysicians, not for practical men to dispute over, much less fight over. As for areas in which slavery might possibly find a foothold (New Mexico, for instance), a Republican Congress imitated Douglas in not caring whether slavery was voted up or voted down.

So evident was the approximation in practice of the two contending parties on the eve of war that the compromisers had reason to hope for success and the zealots reason to fear that success. Even after South Carolina and her southern neighbours had seceded, there was a reluctance to admit that the secession was intended to be permanent. A Georgian, like Alexander Stephens, who knew Lincoln and had guaranteed his integrity, did not suddenly become transformed overnight by the secession of his state. Prudence was not at a discount except possibly in South Carolina. And it was a misfortune that it was in South Carolina that the materials for a crisis were provided.

Because the war began with the firing on Fort Sumter, it has been easy to argue that it must so have begun and, another stage in the argument, that it must so have been planned to begin. The history of the relations of the federal government with its tiny garrison in Charleston harbour is astonishingly tangled. To a naturally complicated situation, Lincoln's new Secretary of State, Seward, contributed his quota of independent action. The leaders of South Carolina and of all the Deep South had a plausible ground for suspicion of double dealing; they had, too, a motive (not much dwelt on here) for provoking federal action that would undo the effects of that great and possibly fatal blow to the newborn Confederacy, the refusal of Virginia to secede. But since the decision to send supplies to Fort Sumter was made, and since Lincoln made it, there has been, ever since the end of the war, an attempt to pin on him not only a charge of breach of faith but a charge of deliberate provocation. "The bleating of the kid excites the tiger." The federal garrison was exposed so that its fate should rouse the North to a war of conquest. It is a charge that illustrates the rigours of American controversy and recalls the venom of the current investigations of Pearl Harbour, with President Roosevelt in the role of Lincoln and the Pacific Fleet in the role of Major Anderson's little garrison. Professor Randall shows on what flimsy foundations the charge is based; could obsessions of this kind be uprooted as well as confuted, the case would be closed.

More complicated is the charge (or view) that Lincoln, by discouraging compromise in the months before he took office, prevented peace from being maintained. The whole question has recently been gone over with great acuteness and learning by Professor Potter. If Lincoln, by accepting and forcing on his party any of the compromises advocated, could have satisfied the extremists of the South, he, by his refusal, made the great decision. But not only is it not certain that the extremists would have been satisfied, that they would have been content in 1861 to see the Union saved as it had been in 1850—and the relative strength of the South grow weaker with every census—there is this to be said for Lincoln. He thought his election meant, and ought to mean, *something*. He thought it was no menace to any legitimate and constitutional right of the slave states.

That Lincoln took such a responsible view of his constitutional duty he made manifest under great stress, over and over again, as President. He held, in his heart and conscience, that slavery was wrong, but he also held that he had a political duty not identical with, and in some cases opposed to, his private ethical preferences. He had taken an oath "to . . . preserve, protect and defend the Constitution of the United States." He would keep that oath even when it meant supporting and enforcing so deeply distasteful a law as the fugitive slave law of 1850. But it seemed to him that concessions to morbid fears of northern aggression against the slave states must have an end.

Perhaps Lincoln's own sceptical sagacity, his own resignation to the ineluctable facts of human life, his own humanity and toleration, made him under-estimate the power of human passion and human folly. He did not appreciate how much comparatively reasonable southern leaders, Davis and Stephens, were driven on by hag-ridden fanatics and demagogues like Rhett and Yancey. As Professor Randall insists, the new Confederacy had no use for people like Yancey and Rhett in authority; they had not even much use for Toombs. But they played their disastrous part all the same. And Lincoln's election was (if it had any meaning at all) in part a northern reflection of the southern extremists' action. It seems to be Professor Randall's opinion that only one man, Stephen Douglas, could, had he been elected in 1860, have preserved the Union without fighting. But it was the Yanceys and the Rhetts who made his election impossible. What they would not accept from him as a candidate they would have refused to accept from him as a President. As Pugh, at Charleston, had been forced to say to his rabid party colleagues, "Gentlemen of the South, you mistake us—you mistake us—we will not do it," so was Lincoln by his voluntary silence forced to say that he would not do it.

But there remains the question of how things had come to this pass. And here it is difficult not to feel that Professor

Randall has done a most admirable and necessary work of destruction, but has not himself produced a solution of the problem.

The North was not eaten up with anti-slavery zeal; the more rational part of the South was not convinced by the new defences of slavery provided by the ideologues, or by the pathological fears of the too vigilant watchers on the threshold. Garrison was not in himself important; neither was Weld; neither were the authors of the *Pro-Slavery Argument*, or the friends and enemies of *The Impending Crisis of the South*. If northern fears of the extension of slavery into Kansas were nonsensical, so was the southern insistence on the intrusion into the North, under the fugitive slave law, of the ugliest features of the southern police system. As Professor Randall points out, the number of slaves who escaped north was trifling and secession was, in any case, less than no remedy, since it would bring the Canadian border to the Ohio River. Yet the South insisted on the most rigorous administration of the law. *Uncle Tom's Cabin* was not a model novel or a model tract, but it was a great event and one of its two themes is the infamy of the fugitive slave law. The whole world, outside the South, was with Eliza crossing the ice. The South insisted on an ostentatious identification with the bloodhounds. It is difficult to feel any sympathy with the alleged moral zeal of Republican politicians like Ben Wade or Zach Chandler, but behind them, and in innocent support of them, even in their most vindictive and malignant activities, were millions of honest Americans who agreed with Abraham Lincoln that if slavery was not wrong nothing was wrong. And the South was more and more noisily insisting that slavery was right and that President Lincoln should do the dirtiest of its dirty work.

For we must not lose sight of the increasing tension created in American society by the continued existence of slavery. The hard-boiled Republican politicians who wanted no nonsense about the Declaration of Independence, the spokesman of the "Cotton Whigs" who denounced its "glittering generalities," the southern clergy who took comfort in quoting "Cursed be Canaan" and the southern politicians who, more or less politely, banned Jeffersonian doctrine, were all registering the indubitable fact that slavery was an anomaly of a most profound kind. Professor Dumond has recently argued, with great power, for the plausibility of the view that the existence of slave states in the Union was a threat to the progress of democracy; the danger was in the nature of the institution, not in the wickedness of the slave-holders. And Mr. Schlesinger has argued, again with great force, that it was the necessities of the political alliance with the slave states that sterilized Jacksonian democracy.

It is surely significant that two statesmen so cautious, so conservative, so little censorious in their later years as were Lincoln and Seward, each found himself, once in his life, forced to utter revolutionary doctrine, to ask if a "house divided" could stand, to talk of an "irrepressible conflict." And how soon, we may ask, did Lincoln form the view set out in the Second Inaugural that slavery was a national sin duly punished by God, a reiteration of that terror which had come over Jefferson when he thought of American slavery and remembered that God was just? The Civil War might have been avoided and, in many ways, was a most disastrous solution, yet the problem was urgent.

Lincoln's own original plan for gradual emancipation would not have had full effect till 1900. Can we see slavery co-existing with the new integrated, industrial America, with the influx of millions of immigrants from Europe, with the rise of international socialism and capitalism? Can we see a United States Government forced to pacify the South by gentle treatment of the formally illegal slave trade, forced to appear in the world as lagging behind Tsarist Russia, an anomaly in the mixed but moving world of Gladstone and Bismarck, of a new Japan and a partitioned Africa? Just because the immediate issues were unimportant, because the war was not wanted, the fact that it came, that all the luck was with the forces making for extremism, is significant. It seems almost as if the American people were moved by some mass passion to end, one way or the other, their divided state. They had been forced to say

Zwei Seelen wohnen, ach!, in meiner Brust,

for long enough.

It is this internal tension (which might be explained on
Dr. Myrdal's theory of the "American Dilemma," the
dangerous strain set up by the contrast between the egalitarian
theory and the inegalitarian fact) that, in part at least, accounts
for the success of the Radicals. They had Lincoln against
them; they had Seward against them (and yet his alleged
Radicalism had been his chief handicap in 1860). The elections
of 1862 showed how narrow was the basis of their strength in
the North. (Professor Randall does not discuss the theory that
even the narrow Republican margin in that election was due
to coercion in the border states.) Yet they won battle after
battle and might have won, with difficulty, the last battle
against Lincoln that they won with ease against his far more
vulnerable successor. Professor Randall illustrates their success
in many fields and he deplores it. But he does not wholly
explain it. Some of their success was due to rigorous party
discipline. Professor Randall has few, if any, good words to
say for the American party system, and it certainly was not a
very creditable or serviceable instrument of government in the
war years or after. There was a conservative majority in Congress *if* the Republican minority acted with the Democrats and
"Unionists." But to do so was to defy Thaddeus Stephens and
the party. Few dared do that and few survived any efforts at
rebellion.

Had Douglas lived, his alliance with Lincoln might have
gone farther. It would have made a great difference if he and
not Stanton had entered the Cabinet in 1862, or if he had
been outside it, a rallying point for the "war Democrats." The
term would not have been as ambiguous as it became, had it
meant the followers of the "Little Giant." Horatio Seymour
and the rest were very inadequate substitutes. (Since Professor
Randall gives Lincoln best in his controversy with Seymour
over the draft riots, he might have given a reference to the
defence of the Governor of New York by Mr. Stewart
Mitchell.) But the Radicals had another advantage beside
their discipline, passion, unscrupulousness and greed. They
knew that a war on the scale of the Civil War could not be a
war merely for "the Union as it was and Constitution as it is."
It was bound to have a revolutionary result, which was one

basic reason why wise southerners should have avoided war at all costs, for even a southern victory would have involved profound changes in southern society. The Radicals were not forced by their doctrine to shut their eyes to this fact.

But their passions, prejudices and selfish party interest blinded them to other equally important facts, above all to the fact that war is fought, not argued. In a fascinating and, from its sobriety and controlled passion, a most moving section, Professor Randall examines the great test case of General McClellan. The degree of malignancy with which McClellan has been pursued by orthodox Republican historians suggests a bad conscience or the consciousness of a bad case. The treatment of McClellan by Nicolay and Hay comes near the historical equivalent of subornation of perjury. The facts tell so much one way that it took great ingenuity and energy to cover them up. McClellan made the Army of the Potomac from a mob into an admirable fighting force in nine months. The plan he formed and, as far as he was permitted, carried out was the plan belatedly adopted by Grant in 1864 after the failure of his bull-rushes on Lee's positions. When McClellan was stopped in the middle of his campaign, disaster after disaster fell on the Union armies in and around Washington. Against the violent protests of the Radicals and their allies in his cabinet, Lincoln restored McClellan to his command; the dissolving army rallied; Washington was saved; Antietam stopped Lee.

Then came a delay that gave ground to all kinds of charges, from the customary civilian impatience at military slowness to malignant accusations of treason and plot. McClellan was again removed, this time for ever, and when, weeks later, the offensive was undertaken by Burnside it ended in the bloody and pointless disaster of Fredericksburg, the most demoralizing defeat ever suffered by the Army of the Potomac with the possible exception of Cold Harbour in 1864. Under McClellan neither disaster would have occurred. His removal may well have prolonged the war by years and cost hundreds of thousands of lives. It is the most disastrous mistake made by Lincoln and it was made, and here is its lesson, under pressure from an eternal type of civilian warrior, indifferent to the problems of war in peace, and in war confident that sound political ideas, a taste for demagogic rhetoric and a suspicion of hide-bound professionals (so often fighting from a mere sense of duty and patriotism) are adequate equipment for the would-be Carnot or Churchill. A great deal of the nonsense talked in Washington in 1862 was being talked, *mutatis mutandis*, in 1942, and it is to be hoped that the grim lesson, so admirably brought out by Professor Randall, is pondered there and here and that the fact that "political warfare" is simply an adjunct to, not a substitute for warfare is appreciated. When it is not, we have campaigns planned by editors and congressmen and carried out by windbags like Pope. For (admirable example of his methods) Professor Randall makes his most effective point by naming the generals who, had the Radicals had their way, would have led the armies of the United States, in all probability, to more Bull Runs and Chancellorsvilles and then to final failure.

Professor Randall ends this part of his work with Lincoln at length master in his Cabinet and with Vicksburg and Gettysburg at last ending that long nightmare of military defeat and futility. It was with full consciousness of what the battle had meant to the Union cause and what the war meant in more than legal and constitutional terms, that Lincoln journeyed to the dedication of the cemetery at Gettysburg. It was, again, with his supreme sense of the fitness of things, that he let Edward Everett draw on his eloquence and learning, his memories of Thucydides and his constitutional lore, to praise the dead and argue the true meaning of the constitutional phrase, "We, the People of the United States." The President of the United States had something different and better to do. To do it, he had pondered and revised, for weeks before, the very brief speech of dedication he had planned. It was no happy improvisation. So the famous speech was delivered and—one of the happiest of Professor Randall's revisions—it was not, as legend has it, ignored or treated as inadequate. It was accepted as admirable, as worthy of the occasion. A few saw more in it than that. And if the audience and the newspaper readers did not at once realize that they were hearing or reading one of the masterpieces of the English tongue, the only document of

American history that has competed with the Declaration of Independence, they are hardly to be blamed. But they did realize that something of great moment had been said and that the man who had said it had risen, slowly and in anguish, to a height above the battle and above the issues and passions of the hour. From that height he did not, for the year and a half left to him, descend.

XXXVI

THE UNFINISHED CITY

(1947)

I N 1801 Mrs. John Adams, wife of the second President and the first mistress of what was not yet known as the White House, hung up her washing in the great East Room of the "Executive Mansion." The new federal capital was unfinished; it still is, 146 years later, when the village—no, that is too flattering, the hamlet—has grown to a city of over a million and is the capital of the most powerful nation on the earth. For Washington is an example of the limitations of planning. Its site was chosen by a most able estimator of land values, General Washington. Its plan was made by an ingenious engineer, Major L'Enfant. In the last generation at least, money has been lavished on its development, and most of its natural disadvantages have been overcome by the resources of modern technology. Yet Washington is always about to be in a state of being complete. Only it never is.

When I first stayed in it, twenty-one years ago, the Plaza between the Union Station and the Capitol was filled with temporary shacks that had housed the flocks of typists brought in to win World War I. That open space has not been covered over in World War II., but even more temporary shacks have been erected (it is on the way to the airport that you see them now) and the most incongruous hutments lie in the shadow of the vast imperial Roman offices built in the dark days of President Hoover. Despite the erection of new buildings on the scale of Versailles, despite the spilling over across the Potomac into Virginia of such gigantosauruses of buildings as the Pentagon that houses the War Department, central Washington has its shacks. They house the Navy; some of them date from the days when Franklin D. Roosevelt was Wilson's

Assistant-Secretary of the Navy. They house, or housed, part of the State Department; a friend of mine was lodged for a while in a hut bearing a name that suggested a musical-comedy theme-song, "Temporary U." But it seems as unlikely now as at any time in the history of the capital that the main, almost the sole, business of Washington, the government of the United States, will be housed entirely in buildings designed for the purpose and worthy of the dignity of the institutions served. No, there will still be huts; there will still be plates on incongruous edifices bearing the names of bureaux and independent offices that can find no room in the marble palaces of Pennsylvania Avenue.

The unfinished character of Washington is an old story. It used to be a joke at the expense of the "city of magnificent distances" when only a mud path lined by a few shacks joined the Capitol to the White House a mile away. Supercilious British visitors like Tom Moore could laugh at American braggadoccio. This scattered collection of huts and unfinished public buildings would never be a city! Two generations later, it looked as if Moore was right. When Lincoln came to Washington to be inaugurated it was markedly unfinished. A contemporary witness testified gloomily to frustrated hopes. "The President's house, the little dingy State Department, set squat on the ground now occupied by the north wing of the Treasury, the War and Navy on Seventeenth Street, the Post Office Department, and the Interior, were the only completed public offices of the capital. The Washington Monument, the Capitol, and the Treasury building were melancholy specimens of arrested development." To the exiled foreign diplomats, Washington was something like Addis Ababa as depicted in *Black Mischief*. It was a small and shabby capital for what was already a great nation. It was, so suspicious Northerners thought, proof of Southern perfidy that Washington was still unfinished. Lincoln was right in insisting that, war or no war, the new dome should be put on the Capitol, even though the rebel armies lay just across the river. But it was no accident, no conspiracy; it was in the nature of Washington to be for ever growing out of its clothes. It still is. And as children often do, it insists on growing in awkward directions. The

17

Capitol, the Supreme Court and the Library of Congress are still on the edge of the city. True, there are now miles of little houses, rather like Colindale, that stretch into Maryland behind the group of monumental buildings on Capitol Hill, but "nobody who is anybody" lives there; an invisible frontier cuts all that region off from the capital of the United States. You might as well live in Baltimore and be done with it—far better, as the Baltimoreans will rightly insist.

But Washington is not only buildings that recall Diocletian flanked by constructions that recall a mining camp. It is people; and the great mark of Washington is that so many of its inhabitants have elsewhere their abiding city. True (as Mr. Jonathan Daniels points out in his acute and entertaining book *Frontier on the Potomac*[1]) it is hard, once you have tasted of the splendours and miseries of Washington life, to "go back to Pocatello." It is not only ex-Senators who hang around Capitol lobbies and the capital's bars. Quite minor officials, newspapermen, lobbyists, cannot tear themselves away from the sacred area that lies between the Potomac, the Capitol and, say, Dupont Circle. If the victims of Washington are socially minded, the area must be extended at least up to the British Embassy and out to the better parts of Georgetown. Washington doesn't need a fountain of Trevi; they nearly all come back or refuse to leave.

Yet Washington is not, in many cases, the legal residence of its most important inhabitants, for all politicians must keep up a legal residence elsewhere. And many important officials come to Washington only for brief spells of service, or so they plan. Yet they tend to stay longer than they had decided to, and they tend, after a return to the outside world, to come back. It is not only the southern charm to which even so confirmed a Yankee as Henry Adams testified. It is the fascination of seeing, or thinking you see, the wheels go round. Henry James called Washington "the city of conversation." It may have been that, but it is certainly now the city of gossip, high, low and middle. It is not only the city of gossip, but the city of court gossip. More than once I have advised British officials going out to Washington not to waste time on Bryce or other

[1] (Macmillan. 12s. 6d.)

authorities but to read Saint-Simon or Proust. For they are
going out to a court, the court of the White House and the
other rival lesser courts; there is Chantilly, the Palais Royal as
well as Versailles. There is Congress; there is the Supreme
Court. But, above all, there is the White House, which got its
name and colour when it was painted to cover up the scars left
by its burning at British hands in 1814.

In one of the most effective passages of his book Mr.
Daniels, at the time an important White House official,
describes the day in which the terrible news came from
Georgia and Vice-President Truman was sent for. He was
with his colleague, the Speaker of the House of Representatives, relaxing after a day spent in presiding over the Senate
of which he had been so recently a member. And in a moment
all was changed; he was no longer "Harry"; he was "Mr.
President." In his hands lay power far beyond that in the
hands of any other man in the world, perhaps in the hands of
any man in the world's history, for the first great secret told
President Truman was one most carefully kept from Senator
Truman and Vice-President Truman, the secret of the atomic
bomb. And it was for him to decide when and if it was to be
used.

This is the fascination of Washington; this is its reason for
being unfinished. There is a steady and irreversible concentra-
tion of power in the capital; since 1933 Washington has cast
its shoe over New York and what is said and done there
shadows the world. The little man walking briskly in the early
morning followed by his secret service guards is the President
of the United States, the man from Missouri "who has to be
shown." The White House (perhaps the only really satisfactory
building in Washington) is the power-house. And so the
American people feel who come on pilgrimage to this artificial
Mecca. It is easy to laugh at the tourists moving from Capitol
to White House, from the shrine in the Library of Congress,
which holds the Declaration of Independence and the Constitution, to the Japanese cherry-trees round the Jefferson
Memorial. Fathers and mothers, daughters and sons (more
daughters than sons, I guess), they are typical of all kinds of
Americans for whom Washington is the centre of "the last,

best hope of earth." Our bright young people know better than that. Yet as a few weeks ago I stood with the rest of the audience as the nine Justices of the Supreme Court filed in, I looked at the serious, impressed, attentive faces of the parents and the children. I watched them as the crier made his pro-clamation and the justices relaxed to listen to the opinions being read, with an ease that did not destroy dignity. The final words of the court crier rang in my ears: "God save the United States and this honourable Court." The audience thought, if it did not say, "Amen." They felt that this was one of the most important places and most important ceremonials in the world; here they were united to one of the great symbols of their country. *Senatus populusque Romanus*. It was a living, growing relation. And maybe that is why Washington is still unfinished; it is because the United States is unfinished too and is not to be penned up and delimited in accordance with even the most advanced and ingenious blue-print.

XXXVII

THE AMERICAN ACADEME[1]

(1947)

IT is nearly a century since Taine, in all the self-satisfied pride of a *Normalien*, illustrated the unmetaphysical character of English thought by pointing out that the English called a barometer a "philosophical instrument." Professor Schneider, it may be surmised, has some fears of corresponding criticism from his professional colleagues who may raise their eyes from the latest logic to ask what Mulford (even though he was translated into Japanese) is doing in a serious *History of American Philosophy*. But the author of this learned, acute and entertaining work has no real doubts that the men and themes he is discussing are the men and themes that ought to be discussed. If they are not the kind of men and topics that are discussed in philosophy "departments" and trade papers to-day, well, the fault may be with the professional philosophers. For what Professor Schneider writes of the "founding fathers" (to borrow a phrase from Warren Gamaliel Harding) is true of a good many other men and schools dealt with here.

It is somewhat embarrassing to the historian of philosophy to point to John Adams, Benjamin Franklin, Thomas Jefferson and James Madison as cosmopolitan and distinguished expressions of the philosophy of the Enlightenment and then be compelled to admit that their writings are full of commonplaces and their minds full of confusions. They had no systems of thought, and they consciously borrowed most of the scattered ideas which they put into action. They are poor material for the classroom, but they are, nevertheless, still living forces as well as classic symbols in American philosophy.

The wisdom which makes Professor Schneider defy the purism of the trade is made manifest in the amount of time,

---

[1] *A History of American Philosophy.* By Herbert W. Schneider. Columbia University Press. London: Cumberlege. 25s. 6d.

space, learning and reflection he has devoted to a very important class of American writers and teachers with doubtful
claims to be "philosophers," the divines who (largely because
of the failure of the Jeffersonian enlightenment to strike deep
root) prodded the average American till he at least stirred
uneasily in his dogmatic slumber. Some of the prodders are
only interesting as martyrs like James Woodrow (Woodrow
Wilson's uncle); others, like Bowne of Boston University,
have some interest in themselves and others were men who,
with varying degrees of success, *did* grapple with the great
philosophical issues of the age, with Hegel as well as with
Herbert Spencer. To confine a history of American philosophy
to the kind of man and book recognized in Europe as "philosophical" would be to be forced to jump from Edwards to
Peirce, James and Royce, then to plunge into the schools and
controversies of the "Cornell group" and the "Chicago group"
(not the current neo-scholastic Chicago school but the pioneers
whose greatest name is John Dewey). Professor Schneider has
chosen the better part and one for which his previous labours
have admirably fitted him. For it is not only that the author of
The Puritan Mind is equipped to deal with Ramus and Ames
and Edwards and their *epigoni*, but the author of *A Prophet
and a Pilgrim* is equally adept among the eccentrics, from the
elder Henry James to the real lunatic fringe. He can assess
the influence of the Sandemanians as well as of *Aids to Reflection*.

It must not be thought that Professor Schneider is a
charitable historian of the type that finds "interest" in almost
all written matter, because it shows the "climate of opinion."
There is no attempt here to elucidate the non-existent, the
political theory of Henry Clay, the theistic apologetics of
Henry Ward Beecher, or the economic doctrine of Mark
Hanna. Professor Schneider likes them acute, consistent,
resolute; he is not a student of Calvinism for nothing. So if he
calls our attention to the philosophical ideas of Terence
Powderley, it is not because of the "light" they cast on the
ideology of the trade union movement two generations ago.
There is no study here of the ideological content of the mind
of Samuel Gompers. It is true that (happily for the reader) one
cannot acquit Professor Schneider of a taste, like King Auberon

Quin's, for "rich badness." George N. Sanders, one of the "Democratic philosophers" of the fifties, wrote articles, we learn, "so ridiculously extravagant that it would be an insult to philosophy to discuss them here." But we are given, to our profit and pleasure, a specimen of the philosopher's poetry:

> Age don't measure manhood's stamen: only labour's young and bold,
>   And inaction, loathsome hecatomb of God's abortions old.
> Thought is labour, and the progress or the death of mind marks time,
>   "Life is labour," "labour's progress!—is vitality a crime?"

But those Jacksonians who had something to say are treated sympathetically, and Professor Schneider brings to the study of the philosophical efforts, or even flounderings, of the middle nineteenth century sympathy as well as critical study. Thus he rehabilitates Mark Hopkins, once known as a famous teacher whose log seat was the American equivalent of Academe, though to-day he is remembered, if at all (and wrongly at that), as the eponymous hero of one of the most famous American bars.

One group of philosophers, it may be suggested, is rather harshly treated, the imported Scotch defenders of Calvinism or of "common sense." Professor Schneider knows (who better?) the vagueness of the term "Calvinism." With Professor Perry Miller he has broken down the old picture of a uniform, unchanging doctrine that lasted into the age of the elder Oliver Wendell Holmes. The "One-Hoss Shay" had had more of a strange eventful history than Holmes thought. Indeed, it is easy to detect in this book a marked sympathy with the conservative Calvinists who thought that your Emersons and Channings were woolly minded dodgers of vital issues. Andrews Norton was not a mere obstinate reactionary; he knew what New England religion had been about if young Emerson did not. But the freeing of American higher education from the death grip of a narrow philosophy is one of the great themes of this book, and the men who fought the rearguard action in Princeton and Columbia were Scottish importations. If the thought were not impious, one might suspect Professor Schneider of having no great liking either for Scottish philosophy or philosophers. He seems to have about as poor an opinion of the disciples of Thomas Reid as of the later defenders of Calvinism. Indeed, his severity to what he styles the "Edinburgh" school is so great that the city, if not the university, might protest that it can only claim Hume who is not vulnerable to the kind of criticism that Professor Schneider brings against the Scottish professors, and that the most nefarious of them, Hutcheson, Adam Smith and Thomas Reid, all held Glasgow chairs.

Some of this severity comes from imputing to Scotland the sins of people like McCosh and Nairne. But it is to give a false idea of the state of Scottish philosophy in the nineteenth century to treat either as representative. If, for example, Charles Carroll Everett had gone to Glasgow instead of Berlin in the sixties, would he have learned less or worse German philosophy from Edward Caird than he did from Gabler? If the typical Scottish philosophical exports to Princeton in the twentieth century were Kemp Smith and Bowman, it was less because of any change in Edinburgh or Glasgow than because Princeton was now the university of the two Wilsons (Woodrow and Edmund), of John Grier Hibben and of F. Scott Fitzgerald. It is, perhaps the same bias that results in such startling strains on space and time as a phrase such as this:—"Like Ferguson, Carlyle and Erasmus Darwin in Scotland."

This defect is probably a minor flaw caused by Professor Schneider's intent watch on the American ball. He would presumably share Lord Russell's surprise at Dr. Dewey's resentment of the imputation to his American experience of some of the most characteristic aspects of his doctrine. Professor Schneider is too learned in the history of American thought not to notice the national flavour it acquired, almost at once. In the eighteenth century orthodoxy had already to fight against the conviction that "a man who has been born in Boston has no need to be born again" although the joke is later than the state of mind it describes. Calvinists and Transcendentalists alike had to fight Longfellow's

> solid man of Boston.
> A comfortable man, with dividends,
> And the first salmon, and the first green peas.

Whatever they did, cheerfulness kept breaking in and it was in the true spirit of Charles Eliot's Harvard that the young

Santayana was refused permission to write his thesis on Schopenhauer and had to produce something on Lotze instead. But Santayana himself, so Professor Schneider contends, is as much a product of the mental climate of Cambridge (Mass.) as was William James. Of his doctrine we are told that "it is, nevertheless, just to point out that there is so much of the 'ultimate Puritan' in its austerity and so much of naturalistic metaphysics in its doctrine that it eventually betrays its natural origin in America, whatever may be its eventual fortune under clearer skies and among people of more delicate taste." So much for Avila!

Professor Schneider reveals (possibly unconsciously) the influence of the totality of American culture and of its regional cultures when he illustrates a doctrine of the great Charles Peirce from his analysis of what we mean by saying "An apple pie is desired." The eloquence with which the great logician goes on—"An apple pie, then, is desired—a good apple pie, made of fresh apples, with a crust moderately light and somewhat short, neither too sweet or too sour, &c.," is (as all readers of Mr. Belloc's verses should agree) proof positive that Peirce was a New Englander.

It is, however, when he deals with Royce that Professor Schneider makes most use of "composition of place." For him Royce is above all a Californian, not merely as being a pupil of Joseph Le Conte at the University of California, but as a "native son" of a state where philosophical systems, like films and olives, are naturally "super-colossal." One of Royce's most characteristic works, given its due place here, is his history of California. (It was not, strictly speaking, an essay. It was commissioned as a volume in the "American States" series, a collection of rather drab narratives. What the sponsors got was much better than what they asked for, but Royce on the San Francisco lynchings and the presence and absence of a true spirit of community loyalty in the mining camps, is certainly not what they ordered.) It may be surmised again, that Professor Schneider is not an uncritical admirer of the exuberant spirit of the Golden State (does he not describe Mr. Aldous Huxley as "the Californian neo-orientalist"?) But being fond of philosophical wit, he quotes Royce's excellent joke, at the expense of James's pragmatism "so help me future experience." His own joke at the expense of Royce is even better. It was possibly a legitimate or at any rate a natural result of the mathematical bias given to Royce's thinking by Peirce that he ended up by arguing that

> the Hope of the Great Community in economic society rests chiefly on the extension of insurance. For insurance is an association on the triadic principle of interpretation; the insured, the insurer and the beneficiary . . . Insurance against insurance would make dialectically the most perfect community, though its time span would be no doubt brief.

If Professor Schneider rather deflates Royce, he restores to some of their original importance the St. Louis Hegelians. They are more than merely "interesting" and if they have in the past been underrated it was partly due to the automatic eastern superiority to which Henry Adams gave expression in his account of his visit to the Louisiana Purchase Exposition in *The Education*. But the St. Louis Hegelians were far more competent, philosophically, than was Henry Adams. The *Journal of Speculative Philosophy* was a creditable periodical and Harris and Snider were not mere amateurs. It was due to them that many of the controversies and movements for liberation that, in other regions, took place in a theological context were debated and promoted in more purely philosophical terms. Of course, St. Louis was a very Germanic city, but so was Milwaukee—without Hegel being a rival ground to beer of its national fame. And when the real German philosophical learning of the group is remembered, their irony at the meagre philosophical equipment of the leaders of the Boston and Concord Transcendentalists was very natural. Snider "explained that in the interests of freedom Emerson" negated "institutions, but realized his own objective or synthetic freedom in becoming an institution himself." The author of this criticism deserved a wider audience than the "Denton J. Snider Association for Universal Culture" provided.

But the "laic" atmosphere of St. Louis was not easy to reproduce. So elsewhere it was in controversies over religious faith that some of the most important discussions of philosophical themes arose. The leaders were subject to hostile criticism as well as heresy hunts. Garman of Amherst was covered by the college's finally making him a D.D., and his aim was to demonstrate the truth of Christianity, but there were observers (and trustees) who objected to the raising of doubt, even if it was only raised to be crushed. Garman, however, gave a philosophy to the permanently grateful Calvin Coolidge, an achievement that Professor Schneider does not mention, much less assess. But there is no visible sign in the life or oratory of William Jennings Bryan that he was affected at all by his exposure to the Platonism of the Jacksonville "Akademe," although he was not only a student at Illinois College but lived in the house of Dr. Hiram Jones.

It is a matter for reflection that to-day few professional philosophers in America (or elsewhere) seem to have the power of inspiring faith or doubt, fear or affectionate trust. It is, in part, due to the fact that the public cannot be expected to take an interest in "the highly syncopated pipings of Herr Wittgenstein's flute." but still more to a professionalization of philosophy that Professor Schneider obviously thinks is, at best, a mixed gain. *Mind* and its equivalents we still have, but not the old and eminently philosophical discussions of the *Popular Science Monthly* of sixty years ago.

It is because philosophy is so widely interpreted here that an impression of its general importance and worth is so convincingly given. It is because Professor Schneider finds philosophical reasons for dealing, critically but seriously, with Alexander Hamilton and Hawthorne, Edwin Arlington Robinson and Melville, that he deals so well with Peirce and James, and it is because John Dewey is so much in that tradition that he makes so inevitable a terminus. In his pursuit of philosophical thought and attitudes, Professor Schneider has accumulated a vast and most valuable bibliography and a great deal of odd information. The curious, for example, may ask themselves what is the connection between Rosmini and the Order of Charity at Domodossola and the Fabian Society; they will find the answer here. But they might understand Henry Adams better if they knew that his wife did not merely die but committed suicide; they might find the defeat of the American Enlightenment more comprehensible if they knew that even Mr. Jefferson could not impose the heretical Thomas Cooper on his new university of Virginia. The "climate of opinion" of America is surely illustrated by the Oneida Community having to dissolve not (as is suggested) purely for economic reasons, but because of hostility bred by the sexual communism of the Perfectionists; while a generation later Amana was forced to abandon its economic communism not merely because of the effects of "the world's slow stain" but because of the decline of its competitive position in the textile industry. Professor Schneider is tough-minded and (all critical rights reserved) open-minded enough to please William James. And this is a book that William James would have liked, for many good reasons, including its serious appreciation of the philosophical merits of his father.

XXXVIII

THE NEGRO DILEMMA[1]

(1947)

"THIS is an age of the world when nations are trembling and convulsed. A mighty influence is abroad, surging and heaving the world, as with an earthquake. And is America safe? Every nation that carries in its bosom great and unredressed injustice has in it the elements of this last convulsion." With this warning the author of the most famous and important book ever written on the American Negro question told her countrymen of the coming storm. But it was not merely a prudential warning of the signals of the tempest that Harriet Beecher Stowe addressed to the American people on the eve of the great civil war. It was an appeal, too, to the American conscience. "He shall appear as a swift witness against those that oppress the hireling in his wages, the widow and the fatherless, and that *turn aside the stranger in his right*: and He shall break in pieces the oppressor. Are not these dread words for a nation bearing in her bosom so mighty an injustice?"

Mrs. Stowe was but repeating the essence of the famous outbreak of Thomas Jefferson. "Indeed, I tremble for my

[1] *The Mind of the South*. By W. J. Cash. New York: Alfred Knopf. $3.
Black Metropolis. By Horace R. Clayton and St. Clair Drake. Cape. 18s.
The Making of a Southerner. By Katherine Du Pre Lumpkin. New York: Alfred Knopf. $3.
An American Dilemma: The Negro Problem and Modern Democracy. By Gunnar Myrdal, with the assistance of Richard Sterner and Arnold Rose. Harper. 42s.
New World A-Coming: Inside Black America. By R. Ottley. New York: World Publishing Company. $1.
Slave and Citizen: The Negro in the Americas. By Frank Tannenbaum. New York: Alfred Knopf. $2.
American Daughter. By Era Bell Thompson. Gollancz. 9s. 6d.
Up From Slavery. By Booker T. Washington. An Autobiography. With an Introduction by Jonathan Daniels. (World's Classics.) Oxford University Press. London: Cumberlege. 3s. 6d.

country when I reflect that God is just." She but anticipated what Lincoln was to say in the Second Inaugural when the "terrible swift sword" had, for four years, taught the lesson of the slow justice of the Lord. And, in spite of the formal victory of liberty, in spite of the putting down the mighty from their seat, the problem remains.

It is a strange enough reflection that the nearest rival to *Uncle Tom's Cabin* should be the work of an eminent Swedish economist and of his admirably chosen team of collaborators, black and white—that in this day the sociological study with all its apparatus of evidence and assessment, with its difficulties of methodology candidly set out, should do, at any rate for the intelligent public, what the great fictional tract did for the slavery question. "So you are the little woman that made this great war," said Lincoln to Mrs. Stowe. No such praise or blame can be imputed to Professor Myrdal. His object has been to enlighten, not to inflame; to force reflection, not to drive (however innocently) to violent action. The problem is seen and set out, as far as may be, in scientific terms, and the Carnegie Corporation have got what they asked for, the opinion of a very eminent European specialist on the greatest sore spot of American life.

"As far as may be," but that is only a short way. For Professor Myrdal knows better than anyone else how short a distance can be run by the mere scientific observer, neutral in moral judgment, compiler, computer, but never a judge or even a witness. The mere sociology of information that Professor Lynd has attacked is not the science or pseudo-science exemplified here. For the title of this great book has been admirably chosen. The Negro problem in the United States is a dilemma and it is an American dilemma, not merely the problem or the wrongs of the 10 per cent. of the American people who have the misfortune to own some share, great or small, of African blood. And because it is a problem, a dilemma for all Americans, this book is the most profound study of American society, by a European, since Tocqueville's master-piece of a century ago. The resemblance is not merely in merit and, to some extent, in method; it is a resemblance in theme, for if the real title of *De la Démocratie en Amérique* ought to have been "De l'Égalité en Amérique," the dilemma illustrated in the fifteen hundred pages of Professor Myrdal is the contrast between the formal equality of American life and this permanent challenge to the egalitarian thesis, the American caste system based on colour.

The dilemma is not a new one. When Jefferson wrote in the Declaration of Independence that "all men are created equal," he did not forget that he was a slave-holder, any more than he forgot, when the struggle over the Missouri Compromise awoke him "like a fire bell in the night," that he was the most honoured citizen of a commonwealth based on slavery. It was the dilemma on which Lincoln tried to impale Douglas; it is the dilemma which is presented all over the world to-day to the defenders of the American free way of life. Every lynching or sanctioned murder in a convict gang, every political career like that of Senator Bilbo or Governor Talmadge, is a renewal of intolerable scandals like those that threatened the authority of the Holy See. And nothing could be easier than to rest simply on charges of odious (and incompetent) hypocrisy, to see in the pretensions of American democracy not the claims of Jefferson's or Lincoln's doctrines, but the shameless impudence of Barnum, in the missionary zeal of the American churches a scandal greater than any given by a Borgia pope.

If Professor Myrdal were a mere computer and narrator, he might have been content with letting the facts tell that story. But he is wise as well as learned and the story he has to tell is one of greater interest, more human, more hopeful and yet more terrible. For the true conscious hypocrite is rare and American society is not hypocritical. It is faced with a dilemma and that dilemma is a result of its virtues as much as of its vices. It is because the Declaration of Independence is not, for the average American, what Rufus Choate and the "cotton Whigs" tried to make of it, a collection of "glittering generalities," without meaning or importance, that there is the dilemma. As Professor Myrdal points out, the American version of the caste system is so difficult a problem because it is so imperfect a system. If there was a true caste system, on Indian lines, American Negro misery might be greater but American white discomfort at the sight of that misery, and its social and political consequences, would be much less. The impact of western democracy on Indian life may produce, perhaps is producing, for the caste Hindus, a comparable dilemma, but the process is new. In the United States it is nearly two centuries old, since the converging testimony of the Enlightenment and the Christian revival, since Jefferson and John Woolman. If a society is based (as South African society is based) on a frank acceptance of the rights of one race over the other, with just as much "justice" allotted to the inferior as the superior thinks it can afford, at any rate an apparent stability is achieved. But in a society like the American, where the formal political religion of the nation is in flagrant contrast with much of its practice, a grave internal strain is imposed. For like Macbeth, the average American, faced with the egalitarian implications of his political religion, either admits that he cannot say "Amen" or, saying it, must, like the publican, pray for mercy on a sinner.

It is often said that the Negro was better off under slavery, a dictum usually based on a very imperfect knowledge of what slavery meant, even when the master was not a Legree nor the slave victim an Uncle Tom or a Cassie. It is nonsense unless it is interpreted as Professor Myrdal interprets it. *If* American society definitely kept the Negro in his place, that place might be more secure. *If* the Negro skilled worker could never compete effectually with the white skilled worker, he might have more chance of exercising his skill in his admittedly inferior caste position.

The optimism of Booker Washington, his conviction that the Negro mouse-trap maker would be allowed to attract the world to his door, that "any individual who learned to do something better than anybody else—learned to do a common thing in an uncommon manner—had solved his problem, regardless of the colour of his skin," was, perhaps unconsciously, based on the survival into the first generation after Emancipation of the old view that skilled and hard work was rightly left to the Negro, not only by the old masters but by those former gentlemen of leisure, the poor whites. That white and black might compete for the same job, that from some of the new jobs in mill and factory the Negro would be excluded, that the new political masters of the South, the poor white and their demagogic leaders, would find it not unprofitable to assert a monopoly of the new opportunities opened up by southern industrialization, these were truths that Booker Washington presumably did not see when he wrote *Up From Slavery* round 1900, though he had abundant chances to see them before his death. And, as Professor Myrdal points out, in the short run, in this generation, it may pay the white worker to monopolize jobs like engine driving. A truly class-conscious worker would not reason this way, but class-consciousness is a thing that exists or does not; it cannot be assumed to exist because it should.

It is even possible that the extension of trade unionism since the New Deal may, in some industries, have weakened the Negro position by giving new force to labour monopolies. In the old days the Negro might break into an industry as a "scab," if in no other way. Now he cannot even do that in many industries controlled by the American Federation of Labour. But against this must be set the great gain of the comparatively successful drive of the leaders of the great rival federation, the Congress of Industrial Organizations, against race discrimination, not merely by the masters but by the men. Again, the reflection is forced on the reader of *Up from Slavery* that Booker Washington, with his insistence on the importance of good relationships with the leaders of Southern society, with his open admiration for great business benefactors like Carnegie and Rockefeller, with his dislike of strikes, was not merely doing an "Uncle Tom" act, betraying, servilely, the dignity of "the Race," but showing his usual sagacity. He had worked in a West Virginia coal mine; he knew whence Tom Watson and the other leaders of the insurgent poor whites drew their strength. Perhaps, the black working men and the white working men ought to have been friends and allies against the common foe—but it was a fact that they were not and Booker Washington was confronted with a condition, not a theory.

It is true that, under the old slave régime, some whites, the masters, the overseers, the dealers, the craftsmen and the small manufacturers who owned or hired slaves, had reason to

18

know them fairly well. So, too, had the white men who had Negro mistresses and children; they might know them well if they accepted their family responsibilities not only to their children, but to their coloured kinsmen, as they sometimes still do in rural Georgia; they might know them little if they were totally irresponsible, as was the unknown white father of Booker Washington. With each generation since emancipation, that kind of knowledge has diminished and its place has been only very imperfectly supplied by knowledge and association at a higher level. The relationship of the "big house and the cabin," on which Senhor Freyre lays much stress in his study of Brazilian slavery, has in general disappeared without being replaced by anything so human. For the taboos of slavery have remained, so that a leading New Deal official, wishing to discuss common business with a Negro colleague, had to draw down the blinds in his office lest Southern civil servants should see him in conversation with a coloured man, and both sitting! It is one of the many merits of Miss Lumpkin's admirable book that she makes intelligible the process of educating a Southern woman, of a distinguished family, into regarding Negroes as real human beings; that the sight of the sad and silent Negroes working as a free labour force in the fields shook Miss Lumpkin's conviction of the rightness of the stereotype of the happy life on the old plantation. *The Making of a Southerner* is a new *Up from Slavery*, seen from the other side, moving and most enlightening.

Equally valuable is *The Mind of the South*. The late W. J. Cash was one of the most remarkable Southern journalists of his time; his premature death was a great loss, but his book is likely to be a classic. For it deals with those Southern problems that might have existed had there been no slavery; with the exhausting climate that makes thought in high summer really an ordeal, with the creation of that interesting class, the poor whites, who had been, under slavery, in the happy position of being poor and idle, connected with the ruling class by colour and by a curious client relationship that yet preserved their independence, a soldier caste which awaited its chance to show its mettle—and took it. Although they had forgotten it, many were doubtless descendants of the white temporary slaves of the old colonial system (some of the planters were, too). But by the time that the "Cotton Kingdom" was in its glory, slavery was totally a matter of colour and the slave was both black and mere property.

It is to this society that Mr. Tannenbaum brings his great knowledge of Latin America. Why is colour prejudice less violent, why was slave law and custom less rigorous? Mr. Tannenbaum's explanation is ingenious. It was because the Iberian peninsula was used to slavery; slavery of Christians by Muslims, of Muslims by Christians, that the slave was regarded as property, as unfortunate, yet as a man. Because the Common Law had no adequate experience of slavery, it could not provide adequate legal concepts for the slave society growing up in America. *Las Siete Partidas* was a better legal background for Spanish America than the Common Law was for English America, or than French or Dutch law was for New Netherland or Louisiana. For example, emancipation was a most important corporal work of mercy in Spanish America; it was encouraged by the law and the Church. It was made increasingly difficult in the United States and the position of a freedman was far less eligible than it was in Cuba or Brazil. It was not, it may be surmised, the simple religious difference, although that had some importance. The ugly dilemma, recalled by Miss Lumpkin, that drove sound evangelical Christians to sanction Negro bigamy could not have arisen in quite the same form in a Catholic society. But the record of the Catholic Church in the modern United States in the face of the colour problem has not been better, if even as good, as that of the Protestant Churches.

Yet whatever the causes, the ignorance of the two races in face of each other has increased terribly in the past generation. The Negroes naturally know more of the whites than the whites do of them; the still very important servant relationship ensures that. But as race pride has grown, the Negroes have more and more kept to themselves. So a book like Miss Bell's is valuable, although not of the first order of merit. It is not that she has a less interesting story to tell than had Mr. Richard Wright, for instance; she has less literary talent. But the Negro society she describes in small towns in the western

States is one that is too little known. She did not suffer the worst forms of discrimination; she was perhaps slightly worse off than her Jewish friend, but not much; and neither suffered the full rigours of discrimination as they exist in Atlanta, or in a smart New York suburb. Her family were members of a community, not totally received but members all the same. It is a very different world that we come to in the descriptions of the Negro ghettoes of New York and Chicago.

In the most famous of those ghettoes, Harlem, Mr. Ottley lives and works, and his fascinating book will serve as a counterweight to less objective accounts of that almost too famous city of refuge. Mr. Ottley does not deny the colour, the often fantastic character of Harlem. But the Negro quarter of New York is not mainly a home of night clubs and of swing musicians. It is the terribly overcrowded home of people who, both by colour and by economic position, are at the little end of the American horn. It has some of the worst slums in New York, as well as smart apartment houses for the small class of rich Negroes. For the depressed people of the south and of drab northern cities it is a place of magic. It provided a home for such extravagant prophets of the return to Africa as Marcus Garvey (how different from Mrs. Stowe's George who set out for Liberia in so much more sober a spirit!). Harlem is the headquarters of "Father Divine," God for so many thousands of whites as well as blacks. It is the subject of novels and poems. Its superficially extravagant character reinforces the white stereotypes of the Negro, the openly admitted ones which make them children of a larger growth, the less openly admitted ones that, as Dr. Sigmund Spaeth and Miss Margaret Halsey both have pointed out, make of the Negro, man as well as woman, a rival of incredible sexual potency and fervour. Mr. Ottley, with an admirable candour, has written an individual report and a good one.

Black Metropolis is the less renowned but possibly more important "black belt" of Chicago. In the praiseworthy study of Messrs. Clayton and Drake every aspect of this enclave is examined: religion, business, social life, politics. Into Chicago for more than a generation now, Negroes have poured and law and custom have confined them to the deperately overcrowded area that lies beyond the "Loop" and runs out behind the gothic towers of the University of Chicago. Housing, the compression of most Negroes into this area, is the most important influential factor. Not all Chicago's Negroes live here, any more than all of New York's live in Harlem. But this is the heart of Chicago's Negro society; here they are dominant, at home. This is their Tel-Aviv. As is their uniform fate, the Negroes in Chicago suffer from the general weaknesses of American society. Their terrible housing problems are no worse than those of the Negroes in Washington or Baltimore. but the numbers involved are greater and more articulate. Their colour accentuates but does not create the housing problem. Mr. Joseph Lasch has shown what are its institutional bases for all the Chicago poor. And "blasted areas" like Chicago's can be seen in Minneapolis, with no strong coloured element to account for or, as the superficial would say, create the problem.

Over-crowded but alive, in the Black Belt the Negroes are creating their own life. They have their own societies, their own churches and forms of religion no more but not much less extravagant than those of the serpent-handling poor whites of Tennessee and Virginia. They have their intellectuals and their local Press. They are beginning to have their capitalists. The great local industry is gambling, above all "the numbers racket," and the Negro capitalist is given the funds to launch a department store more through the folly of his fellows than through prudent and ill-rewarded industry of the type preached by Booker Washington. The phenomenon is not necessarily Negro or American. The profits of English football pools are beginning to fertilize quite remote fields of business; gambling may be the modern proletarian equivalent of compulsory saving. The Churches are baffled by a phenomenon so universal; they hedge, neither totally condemning nor approving, acting, again, like the Methodist ministers in face of the economic necessities of slavery or an Irish priest confronting or accepting the power of the local gombeen man.

Chicago Negroes are also in politics. For Chicago was, until very recently, the only city sending a Negro to Congress. Negro politics in Chicago are more purely racial than they are

in New York, where the existence of other racial castes, like
the Porto Ricans, and the activities of open and concealed
Communists confuse the racial issue. But a Negro politician
in Chicago has one duty only, to be a good "race man," to see
that the loaves and fishes are distributed, to make it politically
profitable for Mayor Kelly or Colonel Arvey to fight the introduction of "Jim Crow" schools, to earn the personal attention
and appeal of President Roosevelt on his last campaign.

It is easy to be scornful of Negro politics and politicians,
to demand of them a political integrity that it would be
fantastic to demand of the white poor—or the white rich for
that matter. And it is, as Dr. Myrdal insists, in the field of
politics that the best hope of the Negro lies. It is tragic that
the Negro vote in Memphis, Tennessee, should be venal,
should support Boss Crump. But it is paid for in more than
dollars; it is paid for in parks and schools and crumbs from
the table of the American rich man—the white. If the Negro
can maintain his recently won political gains in the South, he
will be materially as well as psychologically better off, especially
as, in the South, politics are even more important as a substitute for law and regular administration than they are in the
North. At the heart of the dilemma, as Dr. Myrdal insists
again and again, is the refusal of the Southern white man, even
the negrophobe white man, to disown openly and completely
the dogmas of the American democratic system. Because he
gives lip service, he finds himself coerced by his own dignity
and conscience into giving some meaning to his words. The
bad conscience of the South is a notable phenomenon, even
when it is displayed in bad temper, in resentment of all
criticism, in authorized murder and mendacious history. Seen
against the claims of the American credo, the position of the
American Negro is an outrageous defiance of public doctrine.

That the American Negro whose position is least contested
should be Joe Louis is possibly a reflection on American
society. But the position of heavyweight champion of the
world is, in the real world, a position of importance. It was a
source of pride to the Irish Americans that its holder was
John L. Sullivan and the American Negro who contrasts, with
gratification, the admitted supremacy of Joe Louis with the

career of Jack Johnson is a good sociologist, as is the American Negro who rejoices that at last a Negro, not disguised as an Indian, is playing in big league baseball. This form of progress, like the increasing political importance of the Negro vote and the Negro politician, owes a great deal to the agonizing contrast between the American affirmation and the American reality. "Remember," said that great and wise man, Elie Halévy, "that the homage that vice pays to virtue is a real homage. Many a man gets good habits from the practice of hypocrisy." And so the very contrast between words and deeds that still embitters the American Negro is, perhaps, the best ground of hope that the pursuit of happiness will some day be open to a tenth of the American people on less extravagantly crippling terms.

XXXIX

FRANKLIN DELANO ROOSEVELT

(*April* 13, 1945)

Franklin Delano Roosevelt was elected President of the United States four times, a record which, before it was achieved, would have seemed totally fantastic. He served as President rather longer than Napoleon was Emperor of the French; and only this catastrophe of his sudden death has prevented his easily beating the record of the Fuehrer of that Third Reich which was to last a thousand years and which is collapsing at this moment. All over the world military, naval and industrial power of the United States has been used under the direction of the dead Commander-in-Chief to crush the last elements of malignant life out of the Nazi snake, to shatter the complacency of the Mikado in the sacred home waters of Japan. All oceans, all continents have seen and felt the power of the great free nation whose freedom-loving Chief is dead.

But although no single man in the history of the world has wielded so much and so varied armed power and few have wielded it as successfully, it is not as a war leader exclusively or mainly that we and the American people think of the dead Chief. When he was elected for the fourth time last November, victory was already in sight; it was a President for peace who was being chosen; a man who long before this war had shown the vision and courage of a real leader of men, and with that vision and courage a compassion and warmth of sympathy that is rarely found in great leaders and dominant political personalities.

Franklin Delano Roosevelt was born to opulence, to security, to sheltering from the hard and insecure life that is the lot of the majority even in the United States. Son of a great

Dutch-American family, kinsman and nephew by marriage of a President, product of Groton and Harvard, Franklin Roosevelt was, if not over-privileged, at least privileged, and he showed in his life that privilege of this kind need not cripple understanding or sympathy. From his remarkable mother, Sarah Delano, he inherited his good looks, his buoyant and resolute temperament. From another woman, his distant kinswoman Eleanor Roosevelt, whom he married while her uncle was President, he learned much of the social needs and social urgencies of the age.

Franklin Roosevelt's political career was in its beginning orthodox enough. His branch of the Roosevelt family were Democrats, which meant something but not much. He fought both the Republicans and the Democratic bosses in the New York legislature, but it was his eight years as Assistant Secretary of the Navy under Woodrow Wilson that introduced him to national politics, to the duties and opportunities and dangers of leadership in war time, and made him a fairly prominent figure. He ran for Vice-President in 1920 in the forlorn hope of saving American participation in the League of Nations; and then fate struck at him, malignantly; and for a less courageous man it would certainly have been finally. The vigorous, athletic, handsome young politician was stricken with infantile paralysis. He spent a year, he once said, learning to wiggle his toes. He learned patience, he learned understanding, but he remained a cripple for the rest of his arduous life.

Slowly he remade that life. In 1924 he made the famous speech for his friend, Al Smith, whom he called "the happy warrior"—a Wordsworthian phrase most suited to himself. In 1928 he became Governor of New York and he served two terms in that great office, becoming more and more a national figure. But to be frank, few who fought for his nomination and election as President in the dark year, 1932, when the springs of American business life were drying up, had any adequate conception of the great natural and political force they were elevating to the highest American office. When he took office in March 1933, a few weeks after Hitler became Chancellor, the prospects for the new tenant of the White

House were the blackest any President had known since Lincoln first entered it.

Then came the New Deal. How new it was, how efficacious it was, is a matter of controversy. What is hardly a matter for doubt is the sudden electric shocks of renewed hope and confidence that the American people got from a new chief who was ready to try anything once, was contemptuous of precedent and doubt, who brought to his terrible task a courage and gaiety and combative spirit that recalled the frontiersmen, recalled the making of America by what might have seemed fantastic optimism. No man was less prepared to "sell America short." It was no matter of pure economic re-organization. All the distressed and fearful American people, black and white, men and women, had to have faith in Americanism restored. They had to feel, to believe, that the President, the Union, cared for them, that they were not statistical units to be computed and, if necessary, put for good on the wrong side of the national ledger.

This renewal of faith in the good heart of the American Government, this practical demonstration that the Government of the United States, like Lincoln's God, loved the plain people of whom there were so many distressed and despairing millions —that was the first and greatest achievement of the New Deal, an achievement noted in more countries than the United States, above all in that Europe over which there was rising the black cloud of the Third Reich to whom the humanity, the sentiment, the freedom, the friendliness of the American way were as much foolishness as, so St. Paul says, was the Gospel to the Greeks. When Mr. Roosevelt ran for the second time and carried forty-six of the forty-eight States, the general bias, the general character of the New Deal was ratified by "We the People of the United States." That, as much as great works of social organization like the Tennessee Valley Authority, or the great engineering triumphs that covered the United States from New York to San Francisco, was the permanent legacy of President Roosevelt as the leader and spokesman of the under-privileged.

But, from the second term on, the President's gaze was turned more and more outwards. He saw the meaning of

Hitlerism; he saw the foundations of the Berlin-Toyko axis when they were barely above ground. That war was possible he saw very early; that war might be prevented if the free nations saw their danger soon enough he saw very early. At Chicago, in 1937, he proposed a quarantine of the aggressor nations—a step too bold for the American people and for other peoples. He tried in vain to secure from Mussolini, from Hitler, effective guarantees of at least quiescence. But the truth was too grim, the future too dark, for millions of Americans and non-Americans too, to see it in its true light. President Roosevelt was forced to see the decline, then the collapse, of all hope of stopping Hitler, short of war. And when war finally came in 1939 and the Neutrality Act was repealed and the great industrial resources of the United States made available to Britain and France, it was too late to prevent war, and it might well have seemed, when the flood gates of Nazi power were thrown open in the early summer of 1940, that it was too late to save freedom in Europe.

Many Americans thought so. So did triumphant Nazis. But the President of the United States did not think so. He decided—a bold decision that may well have been decisive—to throw what resources were then at his command—guns, ships, economic resources—into the scale of Britain, alone in face of the triumphant Third Reich. That policy was ratified at the unprecedented election of 1940 when, for the first time in the history of the Republic, a President was elected for a third term. Then came Lease-Lend and, in August 1941, the first of those war-time meetings with the Prime Minister that have been the bench marks of the slowly rising tide of victory. By the autumn of 1941, both Russia and Britain were beginning to feel in their veins and arteries the great transfusions from the incomparable industrial strength of the United States. Then came Pearl Harbour, a felon blow that was yet terribly effective. American defeats came to test the temper of men's souls and the powers of leadership of the President. He was as buoyant as ever, as confident that the war not only must but *could* be won. By the late autumn the turn of the tide was visible even to those of little faith, and they were many. It was visible, too, in Berlin. North Africa was liberated, then Sicily, then Italy. On the other side of the globe, the unavailing heroism of Wake Island was now redeemed by the desperate and dearly-bought victories at Tarawa and in the Solomons. Freedom was on its way back in Europe, in Asia.

And all this time, the boldest and greatest amphibious operation in history was being planned. The two great western leaders met, in Washington, at Casablanca, then with their eastern colleague at Teheran. The pattern of victory was beginning to appear and from D-Day, despite some disappointments and heavy cost in life, the death stroke was delivered. Before the President was elected for the fourth time, the American flag flew again in the Philippines and inside the bastion of the Third Reich where the great conspiracy against liberty and humanity had been so cunningly planned. If that plan did not succeed it was due in great part to the foresight and political courage of Franklin Roosevelt.

He lived long enough to see the assurance of victory made doubly sure, to see the chance saved of rebuilding the shattered world on something better and more enduring than mere force; and to see great force and power in the hands of nations chastened by their experience and forced to collaborate by mutual need. Inside the United States, the fourth term was taken as a commission to save the peace and happiness of the United States after victory, and as a proof that the American people, like other peoples, had learned that we are members one of another.

As one looks at the twelve years of constructive effort that an ironical spirit has set against the twelve years of Hitler, there is a deep consistency, a consistency of purpose and courage, the provision for all of the conditions of life in which life and liberty are rights really available to all, and the pursuit of happiness not a private sport of the class to which Franklin Roosevelt was born, but what it seemed in the early simple days of the Republic, the common right of the common man. A great leader has died with his work not finished but his fame secure, fame won in peace as much as in victorious war.